JOHN 15:13
GreaTeR LOVE HAS NO ONE
THAN THIS, THAT HE LAY DOWN
HIS LIFE FOR HIS FRIENDS.

STAY CLOSE TO JESUS

ALL MY LOVE
Olivia

....

PRESENTED TO

....

FROM

....

DATE

GOD
is FAITHFUL
 DEVOTIONAL

COUNTRYMAN®

A Division of Thomas Nelson Publishers

THOMAS NELSON®
Since 1798

God Is Faithful: MyDaily® Devotional
© 2014 by Thomas Nelson

Published in Nashville, Tennessee, by Thomas Nelson. Thomas Nelson is a trademark of HarperCollins Christian Publishing.

Thomas Nelson titles may be purchased in bulk for educational, business, fund-raising, or sales promotional use. For information, please email SpecialMarkets@ThomasNelson.com.

ISBN: 978-0-7180-4281-3

Printed in China

17 18 19 20 21 DSC 7 6 5 4 3

www.thomasnelson.com

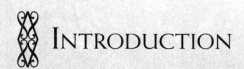

INTRODUCTION

The Bible says that God is always faithful. He never changes and you can count on Him in every circumstance. This devotional has been created by fifty devoted men of God as a reminder of the faithfulness of our Lord every day.

In your daily walk with the Lord, you can turn to Him and He will invite you to be faithful as He is faithful. Each day is filled with devotions that cover the emotions of everyday life and encourage you to spend time in God's Word.

It is our prayer that each devotion will be a blessing and touch your heart as you draw closer to the One who loves you unconditionally. For He has promised to never leave you nor forsake you.

Dr. Johnny M. Hunt
Senior Pastor
First Baptist Woodstock
Woodstock, Georgia

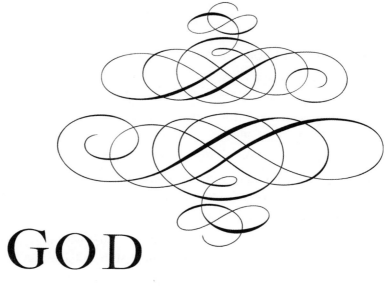

GOD
is FAITHFUL
MyDaily DEVOTIONAL

CONTENTS

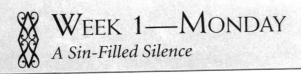
When I kept silent, my bones grew old through my groaning all the day long.

PSALM 32:3

Which do you want first—the good news or the bad? Many of us choose the bad news. Maybe we want to save the better for last. Or maybe the bad sweetens the good for us. The bad news of Psalm 32:3 can definitely make the good news sweeter.

And the bad news is the price of keeping silent about sin. When David "kept silent," he reported, "my bones grew old through my groaning." The implication is to confess your sin and experience God's forgiveness.

Confession is the only means of receiving God's forgiveness. Those who hope to receive righteousness in return for their good works misunderstand the law. God gave us the law so we could recognize our sin (Romans 3:20); God gave us His Son so we could be forgiven of that sin. And this is the process of forgiveness:

Conviction: "For day and night Your hand was heavy upon me; my vitality was turned into the drought of summer" (Psalm 32:4).

Confession: "I acknowledged my sin to You, and my iniquity I have not hidden. I said, 'I will confess my transgressions to the LORD,' and You forgave the iniquity of my sin" (Psalm 32:5).

Confidence: "You are my hiding place; You shall preserve me from trouble; You shall surround me with songs of deliverance" (Psalm 32:7).

....

Holy God, help me be aware when You are convicting me, ready to confess from those sins, and freed to live confidently in Your presence. I am grateful that You called me to be Your child.

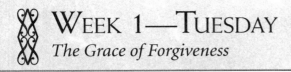

Blessed is he whose transgression is forgiven, whose sin is covered. Blessed is the man to whom the LORD does not impute iniquity, and in whose spirit there is no deceit.

PSALM 32:1–2

I t's a startling description of a man after God's own heart.

According to John Phillips in *Exploring Psalms, Volume One: An Expository Commentary*, David was one of the greats in all of Scripture—a great *saint*, a great *sage*, and a great *sovereign*. But he was also one of the greatest *sinners* of the Bible. Phillips writes, "He sinned with a high-handed rebellion and with a depth of cunning and duplicity which would astonish us did we not know the wickedness of our own hearts."[1]

David was a haunted man after his adulterous affair with Bathsheba and the murder of Uriah, but for an entire year after his sin, David put up a bold front. When God finally sent Nathan to confront David, the broken man recognized his sin, cried tears of repentance, and accepted God's offer of forgiveness.

David then promised in Psalm 51:13 to teach transgressors God's ways. David did so by writing Psalm 32, a *Maschil* or teaching psalm from the Hebrew hymnbook. Promise kept!

And what a blessing for subsequent God-followers! As St. Augustine wisely said more than fifteen hundred years ago, "The beginning of knowledge is to know thyself to be a sinner." He kept a copy of Psalm 32 over his bed as a daily reminder of his need for God's grace.

....

Spirit, thank You for helping me recognize my sin. Jesus, thank You for taking on the punishment for my sin. And thank You, God, for this grace-filled process of forgiveness.

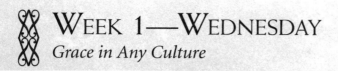

Blessed is he whose transgression is forgiven, whose sin is covered.

PSALM 32:1

In our postmodern culture, you'd think *sin* were a four-letter word. Rarely in mainstream media is sin a topic of discussion. Problems in people's lives are caused by a variety of things (parenting, socioeconomics, physiology) other than sin. In Psalm 32, though, David used four different words for sin.

Transgression is rebellion, a revolt against a lawful authority. David had disobeyed God's commandment: "You shall not commit adultery" (Exodus 20:14).

Sin is missing the mark or falling short of the target, the ideal, or God's established standards. As the apostle Paul noted, "All have sinned and fall short of the glory of God" (Romans 3:23).

Iniquity refers to being twisted, crooked, or bent, and human nature is definitely warped like that instead of being straight, perfect, and true. This condition is what we call "original sin," that is, the corruption of God's "very good" man and woman.

Deceit refers to the insincerity and duplicity of human nature. David chose deceit and guile over truth, seeking to hide his sins, and, when that failed, pretended nothing was wrong. We too can pretend that we have done, said, or thought nothing wrong; we can pretend righteousness.

In order to help us recognize our transgression, sin, iniquity, and deceit, God chastens us, lets us deal with consequences, allows us to hit rock bottom—so that we may know His forgiveness and cleansing. And that is grace in any culture.

....

Thank You, Almighty God, for the Scripture that helps me recognize my sin, for the Holy Spirit who convicts me of that sin, and for Your forgiveness that awaits my confession.

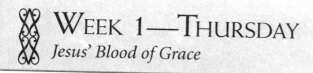

WEEK 1—THURSDAY
Jesus' Blood of Grace

Blessed is the man to whom the LORD does not impute iniquity, and in whose spirit there is no deceit.

PSALM 32:2

Sometimes a verse is a favorite because it is misunderstood. Romans 5:20, for instance, says, "Where sin abounded, grace abounded much more." But Paul countered those who think this is carte blanche to sin (more of a showcase for God's grace, right?) when he said, "Shall we continue in sin that grace may abound? Certainly not!" (Romans 6:1–2). Were we to continue in our sin, knowing it was sin, we would be cheapening God's grace toward us.

In *The Cost of Discipleship*, Dietrich Bonhoeffer introduced the concept of cheap grace.[2] Choosing to sin because we know we'll be forgiven is one among many examples. However, in light of the cost of God's grace—Jesus' death on the cross—we are not to be so casual about the forgiveness He extends us. Furthermore, the assurance of God's forgiveness is promised to the person "in whose spirit is no deceit." In other words, God promises to forgive only those who sincerely confess their sins.

When God forgives us, He washes away the stain of our sin (1 John 1:9) and lifts from us the great weight of our guilt. God removes the guilt we rightfully feel after we have chosen to sin. (The scapegoat of Leviticus 16:21–22 illustrates sin being removed from the sinners.) And when God forgives us, He regards our sin as a matter in the past, so He does not bring it up anymore as a ground for His displeasure.

When we cease to hide our sins (when we confess our sins), God will hide it under His blood (He will forgive us).

. . . .

Holy God, may I never hesitate to confess to You my sin.

GOD IS FAITHFUL

5

WEEK 1—FRIDAY
The Father's Gracious Chastening

When I kept silent, my bones grew old through my groaning all the day long. For day and night Your hand was heavy upon me; my vitality was turned into the drought of summer.

PSALM 32:3–4

Jesus Christ paid with His life for the forgiveness of our sins. Read that sentence again to hear it afresh—after costing Jesus everything, God's forgiveness is free to us.

But as David's experience—and perhaps yours—illustrates, we may not personally pay to be forgiven by God for our sins, but we can pay dearly when we choose unforgiveness, when we cling to our sins rather than confessing them and moving into the light of God's forgiveness.

As Charles Spurgeon noted, "God does not permit His children to sin successfully."[3] The chastening (disciplining) that we sinners experience isn't a judge's punishment of a criminal; it's a loving Father's dealings with His disobedient children to bring them to the place of surrender. The Lord's discipline is a biblical reminder of His love and desire that we "be partakers of His holiness" (Hebrews 12:10). We are therefore wise to confess our sin, trusting that God will "forgive their iniquity, and their sin I will remember no more" (Jeremiah 31:34).

The gratification of earthly desire that often prompts sin is elusive, a shadow, a fiction; but the blessedness of the justified, of the person to whom God imparted righteousness, is substantial, true, and eternal.

....

Lord God, clinging to sin takes my eyes off of You and robs me of my vitality. Remind me of Your fatherly love. Help me choose forgiveness and keep me from taking that first step toward sin!

DR. JOHNNY HUNT, FIRST BAPTIST WOODSTOCK, WOODSTOCK, GA

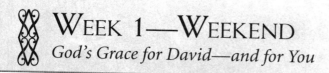

Week 1—Weekend
God's Grace for David—and for You

I acknowledged my sin to You, and my iniquity I have not hidden. I said, "I will confess my transgressions to the LORD," and You forgave the iniquity of my sin.

PSALM 32:5

In *Repentance: The First Word of the Gospel*, Richard Owen Roberts observed our requests for forgiveness come from pressure from three directions: *upwardly*, one's recognition of being "poor in spirit" (Matthew 5:3); *inwardly*, mourning over one's sin (v. 4); and *outwardly*, as "a hunger and thirst for righteousness" (v. 6).[4]

Apparently David experienced this work of the Holy Spirit before he wrote Psalm 32:5. In this verse, David came clean before God: "I acknowledged my sin to You." He confessed his sinful nature and brought it into the light: "And my iniquity I have not hidden." David had experienced both the pain that results from not confessing his sin and the truth of Proverbs 28:13—"He who covers his sins will not prosper, but whoever confesses and forsakes them will have mercy."

Ready to admit his sin and very aware of his iniquity, David was ready to confess to God: "I will confess my transgressions to the LORD." To confess is to be in agreement with God about one's sin.

In his sin, David was falling. In his iniquity, David was rebelling. In his transgression, David was straying. When he admitted his sin, became aware of his iniquity, and agreed with God about his transgressions, David confessed to God—and God forgave David's sin, iniquity, and transgression. And He will do the same for you.

. . . .

I join with David in praising You who "are good, and ready to forgive, and abundant in mercy to all those who call upon You" (Psalm 86:5).

GOD IS FAITHFUL

WEEK 2—MONDAY
Carried by God

Who shall separate us from the love of Christ? Shall tribulation, or distress, or persecution, or famine, or nakedness, or peril, or sword? . . . Yet in all these things we are more than conquerors through Him who loved us.

ROMANS 8:35, 37

In life we experience highs and lows, good times and bad—and we must understand that God is God in the valley *and* God on the mountaintop.

You may know the story of the poem "Footprints in the Sand." The speaker wonders why, during the most difficult times of life, there was only one set of footprints in the sand. Why had God left her alone in those trials and times of trouble? The Lord replied, "The times when you have seen only one set of footprints, is when I carried you."[5]

We experience hard times as individuals and collectively (we'll never forget 9/11, for example), and many times people want to blame God. The truth is, the evil one puts such ideas into the hearts of men, but God is always there to help us get through the aftermath. Such times of tragedy provide a tremendous opportunity for Christians to show the love of God through words and deeds.

Satan tries to use hard times to separate us from God, but hard times can actually push us believers closer to God. The hardest challenges and deepest valleys force us to rely on God. During those struggles we realize He is always there and all we need. We learn in a new way that God's grace is more than sufficient, that "we are more than conquerors through Him who loved us."

....

Lord Jesus, thank You for Your faithfulness and love in valleys and on mountaintops. Use me to bless those I know who are in a valley.

REV. BRIAN FOSSETT, FOSSETT EVANGELISTIC MINISTRIES, DALTON, GA

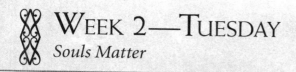

WEEK 2—TUESDAY
Souls Matter

The fruit of the righteous is a tree of life, and he who wins souls is wise.

PROVERBS 11:30

Lost souls are all around us. My eleven-year-old son, Jake, has a dear friend who plays baseball with him. Our entire family has been concerned about this boy's salvation and has prayed for him often.

Several months ago my son and his buddy came into the living room, and I shared in detail the gospel (Jesus' death, burial, and resurrection). He said he knew he was not saved, but wasn't ready. This only increased the weight of the burden we felt for him.

Recently, Jake's friend went to church with us. Afterwards, the boys wanted to go to the ball field to hit. I was exhausted, but I went anyway. From the bleachers I called to the boys to gather at home plate to pray before they started hitting. Jake said, "Okay, Dad, you can lead us."

As I walked onto that field, I felt nudged by the Spirit of God to share the gospel again with this young man, but this time I took a different approach. I said, "At the cross, the Lord got hit by the pitch intended for you, and you got the free base. You know, the Lord Jesus came and died for the sin of the world, but He rose again on the third day victorious over death, hell, and the grave. Then I asked, "What's keeping you from asking Jesus into your heart today? Anything?" He said no, and I had the awesome privilege of leading him to Jesus—at home plate. Now that is a home run! We need to make altars out of our end zones and baseball diamonds, our car pools and neighborhoods—because souls matter!

. . . .

Lord Jesus, help me to recognize the soul-winning opportunities all around me. Give me the words to speak boldly and in love.

GOD IS FAITHFUL

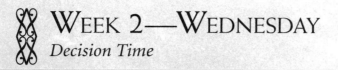

WEEK 2—WEDNESDAY
Decision Time

Whoever confesses Me before men, him I will also confess before My Father who is in heaven. But whoever denies Me before men, him I will also deny before My Father who is in heaven.

MATTHEW 10:32–33

Everyone must make a decision about Jesus.

James 4:14 reminds us that life is just a vapor. We must accept Jesus as our Savior and Lord in this life before it is too late.

Late one night last summer, I was watching TV when my usually calm wife came racing into the room. "Come in here! Now!"

I followed her into the bedroom and saw our thirteen-year-old daughter sitting on the edge of her bed crying projectile tears. God had convicted her that she was lost and needed to be saved. When she was younger, she had asked Jesus to be her Savior and been baptized, but suddenly she knew she was not truly saved. I hugged her tightly, proud of her for listening to the Spirit of God. She prayed and asked Jesus into her heart that very night. She confessed Him before men, and one day He will present her in heaven.

As an evangelist, I preach every year to thousands of people who are counterfeit Christians. They are church members, but not kingdom members. They have compartmentalized their relationship with God: He's number one on Sunday but basically irrelevant the rest of the week. How about you? Have you accepted Jesus as your 24/7 Lord? You are a free(will) agent; the decision is yours.

....

Lord Jesus, I know You alone offer forgiveness. I also know I need You to be my Savior. So I thank You, Jesus, for Your bloody cross and Your empty tomb. Thank You for salvation. Amen.

REV. BRIAN FOSSETT, FOSSETT EVANGELISTIC MINISTRIES, DALTON, GA

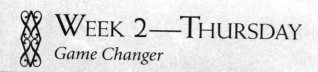

WEEK 2—THURSDAY
Game Changer

He who turns a sinner from the error of his way will save a soul from death and cover a multitude of sins.

JAMES 5:20

Many times people have said to me at the altar, "God feels a million miles away." To which I respond, "Who moved?"

God is the same yesterday, today, and forever. Feeling like He is a million miles away has nothing to do with Him. But the devil—who attempts to kill, steal, and destroy God's followers—wants to do everything to prevent you from being saved or, if you're already a follower of Christ, to keep you from being confident about that saving relationship. The enemy will make you fearful or prideful; he wants to ruin your fellowship with God and others, and he will distract you with vocation, leisure, or hobbies. Whatever his choice, we get back into fellowship with God the same way we entered into our relationship with Him: we repent.

God often uses fellow believers to come alongside us to rebuke us and move us toward repentance. Those people are game changers in God's kingdom. They know that when we wander from truth, we wander from Jesus, who is the way, the truth, and the life (John 14:6).

But God may want you to be that kind of game changer. If so, go to your wounded or wayward brother or sister in Christ with the right motives and attitudes. Ask God to use you to help the person return to Jesus.

....

Lord Jesus, use me this day to be a game changer. Give me wisdom, understanding, boldness, mercy, and compassion, so You can use me to help those You put in my path to return to fellowship with You.

GOD IS FAITHFUL

11

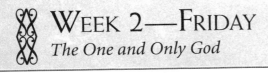

Week 2—Friday
The One and Only God

"You are My witnesses," says the Lord, *"and My servant whom I have chosen, that you may know and believe Me, and understand that I am He. Before Me there was no God formed, nor shall there be after Me."*

Isaiah 43:10

One of the most important things to learn about living the Christian life is this: God is God and you are not.

And one of the Big Ten is "You shall have no other gods before Me."

We in the twenty-first century aren't carving idols to worship, but we have plenty of other gods. We have, for instance, made gods out of money, degrees, vocations, possessions, family—and even self. In order for us to have a right relationship with God, these blessings must be in their proper place—which is less important than our relationship with God.

If we were asked, "What are your priorities?" most of us would respond "God, family, our job or ministry." But when we inventory our time, talents, and treasure, our calendar and our checkbook register don't reflect those priorities. We must continually assess our lives and listen for God's Spirit to help us truly live with Jesus as Lord.

One more thing. We don't *have* to go to church, read our Bible, pray, serve, give, or praise. We *get* to do these things. If you're approaching any of these activities as a burden, ask the Spirit to change your heart so that these ways of connecting with your heavenly Father are a joy that you desire.

....

Jesus, help me each day to live with You on the throne of my life as my Lord and King. Restore too, I pray, my passion and joy, my delight in being Your child. I love You, Jesus. Amen.

REV. BRIAN FOSSETT, FOSSETT EVANGELISTIC MINISTRIES, DALTON, GA

WEEK 2—WEEKEND
Do You Know That You Know?

Behold, I stand at the door and knock. If anyone hears My voice and opens the door, I will come in to him and dine with him, and he with Me.

REVELATION 3:20

T hat invitation is for you . . .

Of course the Lord—our Creator God who longs to forgive our sins and be in relationship with us—wants us to respond to His voice, but it is our choice. Since I'm an evangelist, people often ask me, "How do I know I'm saved?" You know because there is a change in your life. No change means no Christ.

When we teach our members how to share the gospel, we often have people write about the moment they were saved. Some were saved at a revival, vacation Bible school, Sunday school, or home. Sadly, some people just stare at a blank sheet of paper. They may have been going to church their whole lives, but they can't point to the time they started their personal relationship with Jesus. These people are church members, not kingdom members.

Only a right relationship with Jesus makes you a kingdom member. Being a good person or being from a good family will not get you into heaven.

I believe many people hear Jesus knock on the door of their heart, but refuse to let Him in. What about you? If you were writing about when you were saved, would your paper be blank? Do you know that you are saved? If not, pray this prayer.

. . . .

Lord Jesus, I know You died on the cross for my sins. I know You are a living God. So today I am answering Your knock on the door of my heart, turning from my sin, and asking You to be my Savior and Lord. Thank You for saving me.

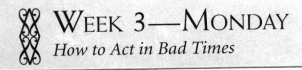

Week 3—Monday
How to Act in Bad Times

Servants, be submissive to your masters with all fear, not only to the good and gentle, but also to the harsh. For this is commendable, if because of conscience toward God one endures grief, suffering wrongfully.

1 Peter 2:18–19

Being faithful to the commands of Jesus Christ has never been easy—and it certainly wasn't for those believers who were slaves when the apostle Peter penned these words. While the writer did not defend the practice of slavery, he did define the patience of those saints who were slaves.

Peter clearly instructed these servants on how to respond to those "good and gentle" masters, but more importantly, he told them how to react to those who were "harsh." As someone wisely said, "The true test of genuine Christians is not how they react to suffering, which they deserve, but rather how they respond to suffering that they don't deserve."

Peter made that same point two thousand years ago: "For this is thankworthy, if a man for conscience toward God endure grief, suffering wrongly. For what glory is it, if, when ye be buffeted for your faults, ye shall take it patiently? but if, when ye do well, and suffer for it, ye take it patiently, this is acceptable with God" (vv. 19–20 KJV).

Seventeenth-century French playwright Molière expanded on that truth when he said, "The best reply to unseemly behavior is patience and moderation." Not responding to others in the same manner as they treat us not only honors God's biblical commands—but it also proves that Christianity is real!

....

Lord, give me patience especially in the face of insults, harshness, and unseemly behavior. In Jesus' name, amen.

EVANGELIST JUNIOR HILL, HARTSELLE, AL

We desire that each one of you show the same diligence to the full assurance of hope until the end, that you do not become sluggish, but imitate those who through faith and patience inherit the promises.

HEBREWS 6:11–12

F ew things are as offensive to God as slothfulness, and the Bible repeatedly warns against it. The writer of Proverbs wrote, "A slothful man hideth his hand in his bosom, and will not so much as bring it to his mouth again" (Proverbs 19:24 KJV). W. C. Fields once quipped, "The laziest man I ever met put popcorn in his pancakes so they would turn over by themselves."

While those two caricatures of lazy men may evoke a few smiles, God never finds laziness a laughing matter! That's why the writer of Hebrews issued the solemn warning "not [to] become sluggish." I like the way the NIV renders those words: "We do not want you to become lazy."

But perhaps the Living Bible's paraphrase offers the clearest and most helpful rendering of today's two verses: "We are anxious that you keep right on loving others as long as life lasts, so that you will get your full reward. Then, knowing what lies ahead for you, you won't become bored with being a Christian nor become spiritually dull and indifferent, but you will be anxious to follow the example of those who receive all that God has promised them because of their strong faith and patience." And with a promise like that, who could possibly have enough time to be lazy?

Lord, help me not be lazy when it comes to loving others and to investing in my relationship with You. Thank You for those people in my life who are examples of patience and faith in You. In Jesus' name, amen.

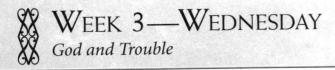

WEEK 3—WEDNESDAY
God and Trouble

In the day of prosperity be joyful, but in the day of adversity consider: surely God has appointed the one as well as the other, so that man can find out nothing that will come after him.

ECCLESIASTES 7:14

One of the biggest lies perpetrated upon uninformed believers is that "good things happen to good people, and bad things happen to bad people." Not only is that an untruth—it is a cruel untruth! It clearly violates the plain teachings of the Scriptures, heaping needless blame and unkind judgment upon the shoulders of those already in trouble.

Recently a woman told me of one of her friends who had been involved in a tragic automobile accident: "If that had happened to me, I would be checking up to see what was wrong in my life." Her assumption was painfully clear and, sadly, unkind—a troubled life meant an angry God was dealing with a sinning person. But to the contrary! Repeatedly the Bible declares, "Many are the afflictions of the righteous" (Psalm 34:19) and "All that will live godly in Christ Jesus shall suffer persecution" (2 Timothy 3:12 KJV).

Today's Scripture verse explicitly states, "In the day of prosperity be joyful, but in the day of adversity consider: *surely God has appointed the one as well as the other*" (emphasis added).

God often uses trials to bring us to a blessed place of usefulness. Just as gold cannot be refined without fire, so faith is rarely strengthened without heartache and sorrow. So, if you find yourself in much affliction, remember: God values your faith as gold and will refine it to make it purer and more precious.

....

Lord, help me bear my burdens with joy. And refine my faith so I am useful in Your kingdom. In Jesus' name, amen.

EVANGELIST JUNIOR HILL, HARTSELLE, AL

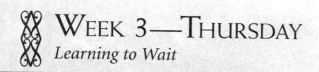

WEEK 3—THURSDAY
Learning to Wait

I will look to the LORD; I will wait for the God of my salvation; my God will hear me.

MICAH 7:7

For most of us, waiting is no easy task! It goes against our nature. Since we live in a day dominated by the fast, the quick, and the instant, waiting annoys and irritates us. The psalmist said, "My times are *in Your hand*" (Psalm 31:15, emphasis added), but most of us find our time more convenient when it's in our own hands or on our wrist! In a society extraordinarily obsessed with cell phones, watches, calendars, and schedules, waiting is considered an obscene waste of time.

But waiting is not always wasted—especially when you are waiting on the One whom Micah described as "the God of my salvation." Waiting may sometimes be unpleasant, but it is seldom unprofitable—and a delay is always better than a disaster! Rousseau summarized it well when he said, "Patience is bitter, but its fruits are sweet." St. Augustine added, "Patience is the companion of wisdom." And seventeenth-century writer Gracián said, "Hurry is the weakness of fools."

Learning to hear God's voice is one thing that simply cannot be done in a hurry. Many of us have met those special saints who have learned to wait on God. They possess a sweet confidence and a solid assurance of God's goodness—the sweet aroma of dignity that exudes confidence and assurance. They may be measured in their actions because they know that far more is often accomplished by waiting than by working. Oh, may we learn how to wait on God!

....

Lord, help me not to be in a constant hurry. Thank You for those special saints who have learned to wait on You. Help me learn from their example. In Jesus' name, amen.

Week 3—Friday
Looking Unto Jesus

Looking unto Jesus, the author and finisher of our faith, who for the joy that was set before Him endured the cross, despising the shame, and has sat down at the right hand of the throne of God.

Hebrews 12:2

*L*ooking unto someone implies far more than focusing our eyes on a person. The phrase infers a deep love, respect, and desire to emulate that person. It is akin to a grateful son saying, "When I think of the father I'd like to be, I look to my dad." And that is what the writer is exhorting us to do: we are to look to Jesus.

First, we should look to the salvation Jesus designed. Hebrews reminds us that Jesus not only authored our salvation, but also finished and completed it. Before the earth was formed, He planned our salvation, paid for it at the cross, and assured it with His resurrection. Oh, what a Savior!

Second, we are to look to the suffering He endured. Yes, Jesus endured the agony of His physical suffering, but He also endured the spiritual shame of bearing the whole of the world's sins. Thankfully, He despised that shame, paying the debt for our sins that we could never pay. Oh, what a Savior!

Third, we are commanded to look to the seat He has taken. Having made that final and complete sacrifice for our sins, He "sat down at the right hand of the throne of God." And He is still there today—ever making intercession for His children. Oh, what a Savior!

....

Lord, keep my eyes on the salvation You designed, the suffering You endured, and the seat You have taken where You ever intercede on my behalf. Thank You. In Jesus' name, amen.

EVANGELIST JUNIOR HILL, HARTSELLE, AL

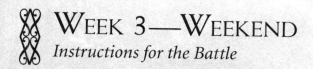

WEEK 3—WEEKEND
Instructions for the Battle

You, O man of God, flee these things and pursue righteousness, godliness, faith, love, patience, gentleness. Fight the good fight of faith, lay hold on eternal life, to which you were also called and have confessed the good confession in the presence of many witnesses.

1 TIMOTHY 6:11–12

While every word of the sacred Scriptures is helpful, when it comes to how the man of God is to live and conduct his ministry, Paul's letters to Timothy have become the gold standard. Some have even called these "God's Instruction Manuals" for preachers. Anyone called to the ministry who ignores these explicit guidelines is a ship without a rudder, drifting aimlessly with the shifting winds of the culture.

In today's verses, Paul gave Timothy two very explicit and pointed commands. First, he reminded Timothy of who he was. He was specifically called a "man of God." No preacher of the Word should ever forget that! It is a compliment laden with great honor, but it is also a command heavy with great warning. Those who forget who they are inevitably forget how they should live.

Second, Paul instructed Timothy about what he was to do. There were some things from which he was to flee. While Paul did not give a detailed list of "these things," a careful reading of the entire chapter clearly identifies them. There were other things that Timothy was to find—"righteousness, godliness, faith, love, patience, gentleness." Also, as a good soldier of Jesus Christ, Timothy was to fight for the faith. And, finally, he was to fasten himself ("lay hold on") to eternal life. Press on, man of God!

....

Lord, help me find righteousness, godliness, faith, love, patience, and gentleness so that I may serve You as a good soldier. In Jesus' name, amen.

GOD IS FAITHFUL

19

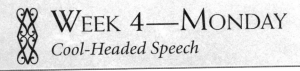

WEEK 4—MONDAY
Cool-Headed Speech

He who has knowledge spares his words, and a man of understanding is of a calm spirit.

PROVERBS 17:27

Those of us who follow Jesus often find ourselves in situations where we feel like we need to say something rather than remain quiet and perhaps be misunderstood. We do well, though, to consider a few things before we speak.

First, we may need to say nothing at all. This text informs us that knowledgeable people spare their words. The word *spare* means "to restrain or hold back." James 1:19 also exhorts Christians to be "slow to speak." That is more than just good advice; it is the instruction of God's Word.

Second, we need to be sure we have all the facts before we speak. A "man of understanding" is a person of reason and common sense who realizes that things are not always as they seem. There are at least two sides to every situation, and sometimes neither side is right. We need to take time to ascertain the facts and then reasonably discern them.

Third, we cannot let emotions control our tongue. The expression *calm spirit* is probably best understood today as a "cool head." It is just as important to know *how* to say something as it is to know *what* to say. We need to have our emotions in check before we speak.

Finally, when we don't know what to say, let's seek the Lord. He will give us wisdom and enable us to know what to say and how to say it. We shouldn't speak until we have a word—and we are sure that word comes from the Lord.

....

Father, give me wisdom today to know when to speak and when to be silent. May my words be helpful and my spirit honorable. Amen.

DR. BOB PITMAN, BOB PITMAN MINISTRIES, MUSCLE SHOALS, AL

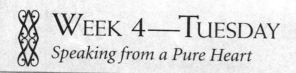

Week 4—Tuesday
Speaking from a Pure Heart

The words of a man's mouth are deep waters; the wellspring of wisdom is a flowing brook. . . . A fool's mouth is his destruction, and his lips are the snare of his soul.

PROVERBS 18:4, 7

Nothing reveals the true character of a person more than the words he or she speaks. Jesus taught that truth when He declared, "Those things which proceed out of the mouth come from the heart" (Matthew 15:18).

In our text for today, the writer of Proverbs provided a sharp contrast between the words of a wise person and the words of a fool. First, the words of the wise man are described by the phrases *deep waters, wellspring,* and *flowing brook.*

Deep waters are different from surface waters. Jude described coming apostates as "raging waves of the sea, foaming up their own shame" (v. 13). The raging waves are surface waters, often restless and foaming with filth. Deep waters are quiet, peaceful, and clean. A wellspring is a dug well that is filled with refreshing, life-sustaining water. A flowing brook is the outflow of the wellspring. It is not forced to flow; it flows naturally, quietly blessing those who experience it. The words of a wise person are peaceful, refreshing, life-sustaining words that minister grace to the hearers.

The words of a fool (Proverbs 18:7) are words of destruction and snares. The word *destruction* means "ruin." Unfortunately, the fellowship of many churches has been ruined by the destructive words of disgruntled members. The result (unintentional or not) often is that other members are ensnared into following them and thereby destroying church unity. Beware of becoming a follower of the fool!

. . . .

Father, may the words of my mouth speak life, not death; joy, not misery; harmony, not disruption; love, not hatred; peace, not strife. Amen.

WEEK 4—WEDNESDAY
Avoiding Contention

If a wise man contends with a foolish man, whether the fool rages or laughs, there is no peace. . . . A fool vents all his feelings, but a wise man holds them back.

PROVERBS 29:9, 11

Early twentieth-century American clergyman Vance Havner used to say, "A bulldog can whip a skunk, but it's not worth the fight." That is the sentiment of today's text. Only a foolish person is constantly argumentative and combative. A Christian is to live in peace with others. That does not mean we are to be passive in the face of unrighteousness and injustice, but it does mean that we do not go around looking for a fight. There are hills to die on, but not many. A story about Teddy Roosevelt goes that he had a dog that constantly fought with other dogs but always lost the fight. Someone remarked, "Mr. President, your dog is not much of a fighter." Roosevelt replied, "He's a good fighter, just a poor judge of dog." Choose your battles carefully.

At times in this world of irreverence and ungodliness, we believers must stand and declare, "Enough!" However, at other times it is best to keep silent. Contending with a fool is a no-win situation. He may become angry or he may laugh in your face, but either way he wins.

The word *feelings* (v. 11) means, literally, wind. It is no surprise that the foolish person is just a big bag of wind. It is a waste of time to become entangled in an argument with him. Do not be afraid to stand on biblical convictions, but avoid silly disputes that accomplish nothing. God in His faithfulness will give you discernment if you ask Him.

....

Father, enable me to be strong enough to speak up for You and wise enough to resist foolish arguing. Amen.

DR. BOB PITMAN, BOB PITMAN MINISTRIES, MUSCLE SHOALS, AL

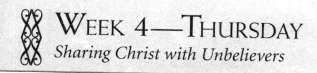

WEEK 4—THURSDAY
Sharing Christ with Unbelievers

Walk in wisdom toward those who are outside, redeeming the time. Let your speech always be with grace, seasoned with salt, that you may know how you ought to answer each one.

COLOSSIANS 4:5–6

Sometimes it seems difficult to know God's will, but it is certainly His will for believers to share Christ with unbelievers. In order to be an effective witness for Christ there are certain things that should be noted.

First, being an effective witness depends more on your walk than your talk. Paul admonished the Colossian believers to walk in wisdom. A person's walk is the way he conducts his life. To walk in wisdom is to walk in integrity and godliness.

Second, the effective witness must understand the spiritual condition of unbelievers, described in this text as "outside." They are outside any relationship with God, they are outside the family of the saved, and they are outside any hope for heaven.

Third, an effective witness must be aware of the urgency of sharing the gospel. We must "redeem the time." That means taking advantage of each opportunity to witness, realizing that time is a precious commodity.

Fourth, the effective witness must be able to explain in simple terms—not Christian lingo—the gospel to unbelievers. Our speech must be gracious, not mean-spirited, and it should be flavorful ("seasoned with salt"), not dull. We are to speak in a way that people will want to listen to us.

Because God desires to save the lost, He will be faithful to give us the words to speak when we are sharing Christ with unbelievers.

. . . .

Father, may my life and my lips be in harmony so that I may be an effective witness to those who do not know You. Amen.

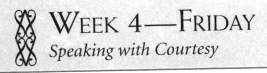

Week 4—Friday
Speaking with Courtesy

"I said, 'Age should speak, and multitude of years should teach wisdom.' But there is a spirit in man, and the breath of the Almighty gives him understanding."

Job 32:7–8

The book of Job presents a long debate between Job and his three friends, Bildad, Eliphaz, and Zophar. Standing alongside these men, listening to them present their arguments, was a man named Elihu. Job and his friends were men of age; Elihu was younger. He longed to be part of the conversation, but he had remained silent out of respect for his elders.

Such respect for one's elders is commendable. After all, some lessons cannot be learned in a classroom; they can only be learned by life experiences. Usually, people of age have acquired knowledge about living, and if they submit that knowledge to God, it becomes wisdom. Age should be both honored and given opportunity to speak.

There may be times, however, when customs involving respect and honor must give way to a clear word from God. The human spirit should always be listening to the Spirit of God, "the breath of the Almighty." When He speaks to us, we must speak that which He has declared.

Again, Elihu was not rude, nor did he insult his elders. He spoke courteously to them. He also made it obvious that he was not merely injecting his opinion into the discussion. He felt strongly that he had a word from God, a word that had to be spoken. God was faithful to Elihu in spite of his age and social customs of his time, and God will be faithful to you!

....

Father, speak to my heart in order that I may speak to others, always in a kind and courteous way. Amen.

DR. BOB PITMAN, BOB PITMAN MINISTRIES, MUSCLE SHOALS, AL

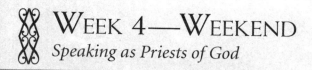

WEEK 4—WEEKEND
Speaking as Priests of God

Let my prayer be set before You as incense, the lifting up of my hands as the evening sacrifice. Set a guard, O LORD, over my mouth; keep watch over the door of my lips.

PSALM 141:2–3

Old Testament priests had two basic responsibilities: first, they talked to God on behalf of the people and, second, they talked to the people on behalf of God. In the New Testament, all Christians are priests. The apostle Peter declared that we are a "holy" and "royal" priesthood (1 Peter 2:5, 9).

As priests, we speak to God on behalf of people. That means we pray. The psalmist reminded us that our prayers to God are like incense and the evening sacrifice. Incense was offered every morning in the temple, and a burnt offering was offered every evening. Our prayer life is a form of worship, and our prayer life should be consistent. When in worship we lift up our hands, the act symbolizes both surrender and praise. And genuine, powerful prayer issues forth from a heart surrendered to God and overflowing with praise.

As priests we also talk to people on behalf of God. Speaking for God is a very serious responsibility and privilege that many have abused throughout history. In New Testament times, believers were warned to beware of false teachers, false prophets, and vain babblers—and, more important, not to become one of them.

Ask God to set a guard on your mouth and a watch on your lips. Speaking the truth in love is hard to do in your own strength. But God is faithful, and He will give you all you need—the words, the wisdom, confidence in Him—to speak on His behalf.

....

Father, may my prayers to You be acceptable worship and may I represent You well as I speak with clean lips and from a pure heart. Amen.

WEEK 5—MONDAY
God Is Faithful When You Face Sickness

Because you have made the LORD, who is my refuge, even the Most High, your dwelling place, no evil shall befall you, nor shall any plague come near your dwelling; for He shall give His angels charge over you, to keep you in all your ways.

PSALM 91:9–11

It is very appropriate that five of the six Scripture passages we will look at this week were written by David. If anyone was familiar with going through a crisis, it was David.

In contrast to this Old Testament passage, we *do* face plagues and sicknesses. Even so, God can be totally trusted.

When one of our daughters was fifteen, she began to complain of not feeling well. She was a basketball player and very active, but she got so weak she was barely able to run up and down the court. We would find her at home, looking tired and lying around, more than she ever had and more than a typical teenager does.

My wife, Jane, took her to a local physician. Later that week we got a call from the doctor informing us that she had type 1 diabetes, her blood sugar was over 800 (normal is around 120), and we needed to get her to the hospital. The following days in the hospital were traumatic for all of us—but God was faithful! He gave us sustaining grace and a sense of peace. Today, many years later, she lives a very disciplined lifestyle to control her diabetes. Not only has she experienced God's faithfulness, but she is one of the healthiest people I know and practically a poster child for how to be a healthy diabetic.

....

Lord, I am thankful that nothing can separate me from Your love. I can trust you in every crisis!

DENNIS NUNN, EVERY BELIEVER A WITNESS MINISTRIES, DALLAS, GA

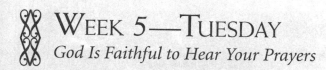

Week 5—Tuesday
God Is Faithful to Hear Your Prayers

As for me, I will call upon God, and the Lord shall save me. Evening and morning and at noon I will pray, and cry aloud, and He shall hear my voice.

Psalm 55:16–17

Although I grew up in church in North Carolina, I did not receive Jesus as my Savior until I was thirty-one. I came to know Christ in a very legalistic, rules-oriented church. Since that was all I knew at the time, I imposed strict rules on our three children. When they became teenagers, they began to rebel, and the most rebellious was our youngest daughter, Becky. After she quit school and ran away from home, we discovered the reason for her behavior: she was using drugs—and using them very heavily.

I was so angry that I was ready to wash my hands of her, but my dear wife is a godly mother and was totally unwilling to give up. Eventually I came around, and we found a long-term drug rehab center in Georgia. With the help of a deputy sheriff and a former cop, we took her forcibly, in handcuffs, and put her in that center.

As we returned home, our hearts were broken. It was the worst day of our lives. We began to pray as never before. Every evening, morning, and noon we prayed and cried out to God. We also asked everyone we knew to pray for her to repent. I am so thankful that God was faithful to hear our cries and bring Becky to repentance. She graduated from that program and has never relapsed. Today she is a godly mother herself. In fact, we co-teach the video series *Reclaiming Your Rebellious Teen*!

....

O Father, thank You for always hearing my prayers. May I never hesitate to call out to You for help.

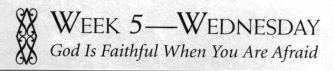

WEEK 5—WEDNESDAY
God Is Faithful When You Are Afraid

The LORD is my light and my salvation; whom shall I fear? The LORD is the strength of my life; of whom shall I be afraid? When the wicked came against me to eat up my flesh, my enemies and foes, they stumbled and fell.

PSALM 27:1–2

D avid knew what it was like to be afraid—which is why he repeatedly reminded himself that he need *not* be afraid.

When he wrote Psalm 27, he was being pursued by either Saul or Absalom. David asked the rhetorical question, "Whom shall I fear?" He then told himself again that God was his strength and his deliverer, and he remembered God's past faithfulness to him.

Several years ago my wife, Jane, went to the doctor for a routine examination—during which the doctor felt a mass in her abdomen. He immediately sent her to another office for an ultrasound. When the technician finished, she called the doctor and then told Jane that the doctor wanted her to go back to his office. Blood work strongly indicated cancer. We canceled our vacation, and she was scheduled for surgery.

I can still picture in my mind the night before the surgery. Jane and I sat on the sofa, held hands, and prayed. We remembered how God had been faithful to us so many times, as with Becky's addiction. We were both afraid of the uncertain future. I had the most fear. But as we prayed, God replaced our fear with a powerful sense of His presence and peace.

....

O God, You know my fears and worries. Help me remember Your faithfulness and not be afraid.

DENNIS NUNN, EVERY BELIEVER A WITNESS MINISTRIES, DALLAS, GA

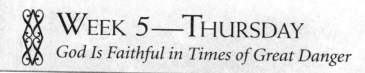

Week 5—Thursday
God Is Faithful in Times of Great Danger

I sought the Lord, and He heard me, and delivered me from all my fears. . . . The angel of the Lord encamps all around those who fear Him, and delivers them. Oh, taste and see that the Lord is good; blessed is the man who trusts in Him!

Psalm 34:4, 7–8

Maybe you've heard it said that fear lives right next door to faith. Again and again, David moved from fear to faith and, as a result, can assure us that God cares for those who trust Him.

In 2012, while away teaching a witnessing revival, I got a call that our son-in-law's niece, Olivia, had suffered a seizure at home. She had been taken by ambulance to a local hospital. An MRI showed a problem with her brain, and she was transferred to Scottish Rite Hospital for further tests. More tests revealed a mass of some kind in her brain. Surgery would be needed as soon as they completed some additional tests.

Surgery was scheduled for the coming Friday morning. I visited her on a Thursday evening at the hospital. I can still picture walking into her room. There in bed, lay fourteen-year-old Olivia, looking like an angel with an amazingly peaceful look. Before I left, we prayed. I was so touched as both her mom and dad prayed very similar prayers. They each told God that they loved their precious daughter enough to give their lives for her, and they asked for the surgery to be successful. Tears ran down my face as they told Him that although they wanted her to be well, they knew that He loved her more than they did, and they trusted Him with whatever happened.

Father, I am so thankful that whatever troubles and trials I face, You are with me, encircling me with Your love.

WEEK 5—FRIDAY
God Is Faithful When the Future Is Uncertain

Give ear, O LORD, to my prayer; and attend to the voice of my supplications. In the day of my trouble I will call upon You, for You will answer me.

PSALM 86:6–7

David asked the Lord to hear his supplications. Supplications are requests humbly made to someone who has the authority and power to grant them. David knew that whenever he prayed he was speaking to the LORD, who had authority and power to answer.

I was fifty-six years old when I was dismissed from my job. I had been a church pastor for nine years. The demographics of our community were changing rapidly, and I wanted to see our church change and thrive. As I tried to lead in that change, my heart and motivations were pure, but I made mistakes and unwise decisions. The church was in a lot of turmoil, so a vote was scheduled to determine if I would continue as pastor.

Just as David did, my wife and I prayed and made supplication to the Lord for His will to be done. We were both entirely confident that God was hearing our prayers and that His will would be done, and we were not the least bit afraid or even apprehensive. The day of the vote came, and by a margin of nine votes, I was unemployed. I was a minister without a ministry.

Many people were crying. Jane and I went around to each of them with hugs and assurances that it was all right, that God was in control.

Today, God has given us a ministry that has greater impact than anything we have experienced before. God *is* faithful in times of uncertainty.

....

Father, I am so glad that You hear and answer my prayers!

DENNIS NUNN, EVERY BELIEVER A WITNESS MINISTRIES, DALLAS, GA

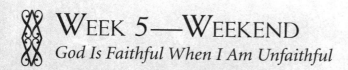

WEEK 5—WEEKEND
God Is Faithful When I Am Unfaithful

Seek the LORD while He may be found, call upon Him while He is near. Let the wicked forsake his way, and the unrighteous man his thoughts; let him return to the LORD, and He will have mercy on him; and to our God, for He will abundantly pardon.

ISAIAH 55:6–7

All week we have been looking at God's faithfulness during times of crisis. Sometimes those storms are part of life on this sin-soaked earth; sometimes they are Satan's attacks; sometimes we get caught in the fallout of someone else's sin; sometimes storms come to test our faith; and sometimes they come to bring glory to God.

Sometimes, perhaps more than I want to admit, I experience storms for another reason. Sometimes I experience storms that are the consequences of sin in my life. Isaiah was writing to the people of Judah who were experiencing God's judgment for their sin. If we do not respond to the conviction of the Holy Spirit when we willfully and continuously sin, we will experience hardships in our lives.

But God is faithful! As Isaiah said, if we forsake our wicked ways and thoughts and return to the Lord, He will have mercy on us and forgive us our sins.

When I am in a storm, the first thing I do is examine my life to see if unconfessed sin is bringing about God's chastening. I am so thankful that when I recognize my sins and forsake them, God is faithful to forgive me and cleanse me.

....

O God, I praise You for Your faithfulness! I praise You for forgiving me again and again and again!

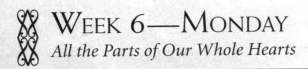

WEEK 6—MONDAY
All the Parts of Our Whole Hearts

Teach me, O LORD, the way of Your statutes, and I shall keep it to the end. Give me understanding, and I shall keep Your law; indeed, I shall observe it with my whole heart. Make me walk in the path of Your commandments, for I delight in it.

PSALM 119:33–35

One time I was talking with a friend about what it means to be whole-hearted. *Half-hearted* means "divided in our loyalties"; *double-minded* means "being loyal to two opposite causes, people, and so on." But what does it mean to be wholehearted?

Wholehearted means being fully committed to something or someone. But when we talk about loving God with our *whole heart*, we need to remember that our whole heart has good and not-so-good qualities. We all stumble sometimes, even on our best days. Loving God with our whole heart means that even on our worst days, we give all that we are—the good, the bad, the in-between—to God.

When we struggle to obey God's law, He still wants us to go to Him with our whole heart. He wants the hard parts of our heart as well as the soft parts, the rebellious parts of our hearts as well as the compliant parts, the doubtful as well as the hopeful, and the sad as well as the joyful. Our whole heart—that is what God wants. Always.

We don't have to clean up our hearts; we simply need to give God our whole heart. After all, only He can make our sinfulness clean and our brokenness truly whole.

....

God, show me how to give You my whole heart. And know how grateful I am that You receive me just as I am, how grateful I am for Your grace and compassion, Your acceptance and love.

DR. LARRY THOMPSON, FIRST FORT LAUDERDALE, FORT LAUDERDALE, FL

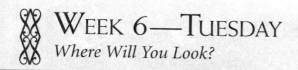

WEEK 6—TUESDAY
Where Will You Look?

I will lift up my eyes to the hills—from whence comes my help? My help comes from the LORD, who made heaven and earth. He will not allow your foot to be moved; He who keeps you will not slumber.

PSALM 121:1–3

According to some biblical scholars, when the psalmist said, "I will look up to the hills," he was making a play on words. He wasn't really saying that his help would come from the hills. Instead, he was ironically commenting on the different idols and temples built on the hills along the route to Jerusalem. The psalmist lifted his eyes to the hills and beyond, past the man-made idols, to the Lord, Creator of all.

This psalm is a song of ascent written by and for someone on a journey. Imagine a group of faithful Jews walking along the uphill path to the Holy City of Jerusalem. On the hills to both sides they see idols made of wood and stone, temples to competing deities, tragic substitutes for true worship.

This is a time for the travelers to evaluate where their help comes from. Those hills? No! Genuine help comes from God, the One who made the heavens and the earth. He's the One who keeps travelers safe on a rocky path.

What about you? Does your help come from man-made sources, whether money, relationships, power, prestige, or security? Real help comes from God, the One who will not sleep or slumber as He watches over us. The One who makes our way straight, our path clear. In Him we'll find help that matters.

. . . .

Show me, God, where I've been looking for help instead of looking to You—and enable me to put those things aside. I want to focus more fully on You.

Deal bountifully with Your servant, that I may live and keep Your word. Open my eyes, that I may see wondrous things from Your law. I am a stranger in the earth; do not hide Your commandments from me. My soul breaks with longing for Your judgments at all times.

PSALM 119:17–20

Have you ever felt out of place? Maybe it was a party, when your friends had already figured out preteen cool. Or your first board meeting, when you wondered what in the world you were doing there. Maybe it was the first time you spent a holiday with in-laws and couldn't believe all the family traditions you'd never experienced.

You get the feeling from the 176 verses in Psalm 119 that the writer had experienced some kind of version of all these scenarios. He begins the epic psalm talking about the different situations of the world, and how God is his strength in each one. However, in verse 19, he admits something: "I don't belong here. I'm a stranger. This isn't where I'm most at home."

For the psalmist, the answer to that not-quite-right feeling is to seek refuge in Scripture: "God, show me the wonder of Your Word. Let me find my identity in Your Word alone." And he does just that by celebrating God's Word throughout the entire psalm!

Haven't we all felt like our soul might break with longing for God? Our hope is in the same place as the psalmist's. We might be strangers in this land, but we're no stranger to the One whose Word is our beginning, our path, and our true destination.

....

Father, sometimes I don't know exactly where I fit in. Remind me through Your Word that I have a place with You where I can always be content.

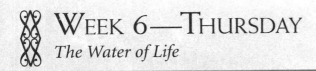

WEEK 6—THURSDAY
The Water of Life

O God, You are my God; early will I seek You; my soul thirsts for You; my flesh longs for You in a dry and thirsty land where there is no water. So I have looked for You in the sanctuary, to see Your power and Your glory.

PSALM 63:1–2

If you're reading this book, you probably live somewhere that has clean water flowing from faucets. And you have probably never experienced real thirst.

Our church, however, supports Nick and Jennifer, missionaries in water-starved Rwanda. These dear folks help remote villages reclaim rainwater, build reliable pumps, and differentiate between clean water and water with hidden microbes that might kill their children.

Halfway around the world from Africa, Tim is a missionary in Nicaragua who discovered a village where half the people had clean water and the other half didn't. He solved the mystery, devised a water-transport switch, and regulated the water supply at its source so all the villagers would have clean water.

These two places—one in East Africa and the other in Latin America—remind me that we Christ-followers have a responsibility to make sure Living Water as well as clean water is available to every person who thirsts. Like Nick and Jennifer, we may have to think of new ways to make it accessible. Like Tim, we may have to give up some of what we have so others can have what they need.

What will you and I do to make sure others have Living Water?

. . . .

Jesus, I pray Your blessed presence with those who don't have the basic essentials for living. Please show me my part in Your provision for them.

Week 6—Friday
Night Seasons

I will bless the LORD who has given me counsel; my heart also instructs me in the night seasons. I have set the LORD always before me; because He is at my right hand I shall not be moved. Therefore my heart is glad, and my glory rejoices; my flesh also will rest in hope.

PSALM 16:7–9

What keeps you up at night?

Some people have their most creative thoughts at night. They keep a notebook on their nightstand so they can jot down any night-bright idea that comes. My daughter, who has a young son and a newborn, says sleep is a nice idea but not always a reality. I know other people who can't sleep because of worry. Still others say their minds won't shut off.

David may have been in that last category.

The opening words of Psalm 16 suggest that he'd been thinking a lot. About the people around him. About his own loyalties. And about what it will take to follow God.

I like that David called these sleepless minutes "night seasons." They're not just fleeting moments soon overtaken by slumber, but holy seasons where he and God got honest with each other. And when David said his "heart" instructed him, the word he used means his inmost being, his deep soul. And that's what it takes to survive the night seasons. Notebooks are nice, and sheep are good for counting. But if you want to make it through the night season, open your deepest heart and be ready for God to minister to you.

God, sometimes I have desperate night seasons, and at other times those night seasons are the only times I truly hear You. Help me to be aware of Your voice all day and even at night.

DR. LARRY THOMPSON, FIRST FORT LAUDERDALE, FORT LAUDERDALE, FL

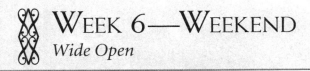

Week 6—Weekend
Wide Open

I will be glad and rejoice in Your mercy, for You have considered my trouble; You have known my soul in adversities, and have not shut me up into the hand of the enemy; You have set my feet in a wide place.

PSALM 31:7–8

We like to live big. Big houses. Big offices. Big cities. Even our little cars have big engines. Why do we like big so much? I think this psalm gives us a clue.

Throughout the psalm, David talked about his difficulties: competing tribes with worthless idols, enemies who are out to get him, and friends who act more like enemies.

David called out to God as his Rock, his Fortress, his Rescuer. And this is the psalm that Jesus Himself quoted when He spoke His very last words: "Into Your hands, I commit my spirit" (v. 5).

But then David surprised us. In the middle of this list of stifling circumstances, David got big. Life was hard, but David knew that God had rescued him and "set [his] feet in a wide place." *Merchab* in the Hebrew has been translated: *wide, spacious, safe, broad, large,* and even *wide open.* All these words speak of freedom, of plenty of space to move around and enjoy the pleasures God has for his people.

Are you asking God for a big place where you have room to discover all the goodness, grace, and love that He has for you? That's the kind of big I'd like. That's the kind of place I want to go with God.

....

Thank You, gracious God, for making it possible for me to be with You in wide, open spaces. When I'm there, let me truly savor Your goodness and breathe in Your love.

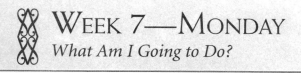

WEEK 7—MONDAY
What Am I Going to Do?

Rest in the LORD, and wait patiently for Him; do not fret because of him who prospers in his way, because of the man who brings wicked schemes to pass. Cease from anger, and forsake wrath; do not fret—it only causes harm. For evildoers shall be cut off; but those who wait on the LORD, they shall inherit the earth.

PSALM 37:7–9

I t's true. Every person you meet has just come through one of life's testing times, is currently going through one of life's testing times, or is about to enter one of life's testing times. No matter what you're facing, remember that unplanned (by you! God isn't surprised!) and undesirable (but probably not unfruitful) seasons are inevitable in life. Fortunately, God is not flustered, much less blindsided, by the events in your little corner of the world.

Psalm 37:7–9 offers comfort for the people in a testing time when their heart aches and God seems distant, uncaring, and uninvolved. What are those comforting words? *Rest, wait,* and *do not fret!*

When you don't know what to do in a given situation, are you willing to choose to trust God? Scripture teaches that we can depend on God even in the seemingly impossible situations of life. Sometimes living out our trust and dependence means simply resting and waiting. When we do wait on the Lord, He promises to renew our strength (see Isaiah 40:31).

When you find yourself facing the undesirable, unwanted, or unexpected, rest in your Sovereign Lord. God's promise of constant provision remains true even in your current pain, but sometimes you must wait.

....

Lord God, despite Your great faithfulness, Your wisdom, and Your good plans for me, I can find it hard to wait and hard to trust. Forgive me—and help my unbelief!

PAUL PURVIS, FIRST BAPTIST CHURCH OF TEMPLE TERRACE, TEMPLE TERRACE. FL

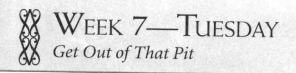
I waited patiently for the LORD; and He inclined to me, and heard my cry. He also brought me up out of a horrible pit, out of the miry clay, and set my feet upon a rock, and established my steps.

PSALM 40:1–2

All of us find ourselves in a pit from time to time.

Like Joseph, we may get thrown into a pit!

Like David, we may slip into the pit!

Like Elijah, we may find a pit and jump in.

Or, like Job, we may just realize that life is the pits!

The question is not "Will we face pits in life?" The question is "What will we do when we find ourselves in the pit?" David cried out to God from the pit, and God not only heard, but He helped. Just as He helped David, God will help you. He will plant your feet on solid ground and put a new song on your lips. He will move you from the mire to the choir, but you must receive His help.

Have you allowed the pit moments of life to define you? Avoid the temptation to become comfortable in the pit. Refuse to throw "pit-y" parties. Say good-bye to "pit-i-full" living. Remember, Jesus came out of the tomb so that you could come out of the pit! It's absolutely true: the same power that brought Jesus out of the grave can get you out of the pit. Cry out to Jesus, wait patiently today, and He will establish your steps.

....

Lord, the pit is a horrible place, but may Your comforting presence and all-sufficient grace transform this season with a bit of sweetness. Being in the pit may not be painless or quick. But with Your help, by Your grace, I know You will get me through.

GOD IS FAITHFUL

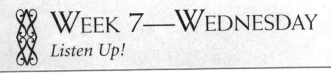

Give attention to my words; incline your ear to my sayings. Do not let them depart from your eyes; keep them in the midst of your heart; for they are life to those who find them, and health to all their flesh. Keep your heart with all diligence, for out of it spring the issues of life.

Proverbs 4:20–23

Listen up! Anytime my dad uttered those words, I knew I'd better give him my full attention. A former US Marine, he could sometimes be stern, and he always commanded respect. His words were usually significant.

As true as this was about my dad's words, it's truer still for the words of my heavenly Father. God's Word always deserves our full attention. Therefore, when Solomon, the wisest man aside from Jesus who ever walked the earth, says, "Listen up," you better listen up.

What's the important message here? Three simple words: "Keep your heart!" or "Guard your heart" (NIV). And when Solomon refers to heart, he means the wellspring of life, the very essence of our being.

So what is in your heart? Is your heart filled with things like bitterness, resentment, anger, jealousy, and regret? Or is your heart home to peace, love, joy, gentleness, and other fruit of the Spirit?

Your heart is a life-giving organ both physically and spiritually. Guard your heart! But when you fail—and we all do—and your heart becomes sick, God will help. This prayer can be ours: "Create in me a clean heart, O God!" (Psalm 51:10). God will honor that prayer, and when He does, then once again guard your heart!

....

Keep me, Lord, alert and aware—using the sword of Your Spirit, Your written Word—as I guard my heart that I might glorify You in my life.

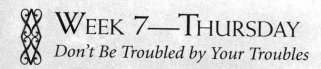

"Let not your heart be troubled; you believe in God, believe also in Me. In My Father's house are many mansions; if it were not so, I would have told you. I go to prepare a place for you. And if I go and prepare a place for you, I will come again and receive you to Myself; that where I am, there you may be also."

John 14:1–3

You may remember *The Music Man,* that fun story of a man who promises to keep the children of River City out of trouble by turning them into a fine marching band by his "think" method. To first convince these parents of the need, the Music Man pointed out—in a song—the trouble they had in River City: nothing good could come from *pool halls!*

How do you define trouble? Lost jobs? Broken relationships? Poor health?

God's Word teaches that in this world we will all have trouble, but our troubles need not trouble us. In John 14, Jesus gathered His disciples, fully aware of the troubles surrounding His coming death, troubles they were about to face, and in that context, He commanded them, "Let not your heart be troubled."

Jesus knew this could happen only if the disciples changed their focus, and He may want you to do the same today. Our troubles begin to shrink when we focus not on the day's problems but on God's provision that day. God's prescription for our problems is the promise of His presence then and now.

....

Lord Jesus, You taught very clearly that in this world, I will have trouble. Fortunately, Almighty God, You have overcome the world. And that being the case, may I know Your peace and not be troubled by my troubles.

WEEK 7—FRIDAY
More than Enough

The young lions lack and suffer hunger; but those who seek the LORD shall not lack any good thing.

PSALM 34:10

I t's interesting to hear David proclaim the total sufficiency of God. Here the same David, who fed his selfish desires in an illicit relationship with Bathsheba, boldly declared that seeking the Lord is the only answer to a person's greatest hungers and wants. David even encouraged us to join him in feasting on God's goodness when he said, "Taste and see that the LORD is good" (Psalm 34:8).

And that is hard-won and good advice! Anytime we seek to meet our needs outside of God's will, we end up wanting more. We find ourselves less than satisfied and usually even more unsettled. But every time we allow our heavenly Father to meet our needs according to His riches (Philippians 4:19), we always discover that He is more than enough. We see that He knows what we need even better than we do! No wonder David wanted us to discover this truth: "those who seek the LORD shall not lack any good thing."

Jesus spoke a similar message in Matthew 6:33: "Seek first the kingdom of God and His righteousness, and all these things shall be added to you." The secret to having everything you need is realizing He is all you need.

....

Lord God, You know how I am bombarded with "new" and "improved," with "buy this" and "dress like that," with bills to pay and an uncertain retirement and more. So I ask You to help me learn to be content. Teach me, I pray, to make the conscious and ongoing decision to trust Your supply. May I seek You with my whole heart and experience every good thing You have planned for me.

PAUL PURVIS, FIRST BAPTIST CHURCH OF TEMPLE TERRACE, TEMPLE TERRACE. FL

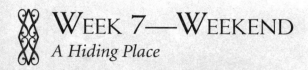
In the time of trouble He shall hide me in His pavilion; in the secret place of His tabernacle He shall hide me; He shall set me high upon a rock.

PSALM 27:5

Every child has one—that place to go to get away from the world. When your friends hurt you, your parents frustrated you, your dog bit you, or you simply stubbed your toe, you went—perhaps you even ran—to your hiding place, right?

As you got older, your problems got bigger, and your hiding place took on different forms. Instead of hiding under your bed, in your closet, or in the woods behind your house, you ran toward somebody or something that you thought might fill the void you felt in your soul, at least for a moment. Don't do that anymore! Instead go to the hiding place to which God invites you.

God's Word directs us to a hiding place that always makes things better. It is, as David says in Psalm 27:13, "the goodness of the LORD in the land of the living." If you are a follower of Jesus Christ, He is your hiding place. He is your light in dark times; He is your strength in seasons of weakness. You can hide in Him, but you must first seek Him, find Him, and then run to His hiding place.

As this week draws to a close, spend some time contemplating God's great faithfulness. Decide to rest in Him. Resolve to follow His Word and do His will no matter how difficult your life is. Remember, the Lord Jesus *is* your hiding place!

....

Lord, You are a rock, a fortress, a shield, a strong tower for Your people. I could have no better hiding place than You! Thank You!

Bless those who persecute you; bless and do not curse. Rejoice with those who rejoice, and weep with those who weep. Be of the same mind toward one another. Do not set your mind on high things, but associate with the humble. Do not be wise in your own opinion.

ROMANS 12:14–16

The more our heart becomes like Jesus' heart, the more we will feel the hurts and the joys of others.

During His lifetime, Jesus demonstrated the ability to identify with the emotions of those around Him. At the marriage feast in Cana, Jesus joined with those who were rejoicing. Later, He wept with Mary and Martha at the tomb of Lazarus. Unfortunately, many of us lack the ability to empathize because we are too consumed with our own feelings.

When writing to the Roman believers, Paul wanted them to see the connection between what they believed and what they did. If, for instance, we truly believe that the Christian life involves putting others first, then we will empathize with the people around us.

When people are hurting, we can show the love of Christ by sharing their pain. For many of us, however, the real challenge comes when we try to share people's joy in their successes. Can we express genuine joy when someone gets a better job, especially one we wanted? Are we truly happy when their child gets a scholarship and our child doesn't?

Examine your heart. Consider how you react to the emotions of others. Spiritual maturity means we can hurt when people hurt, but it also means we can be happy and rejoice when they are blessed.

....

Lord Jesus, help me to love people with Your love and to come alongside them in their joy as well as their sorrow.

PHIL WALDREP, PHIL WALDREP MINISTRIES, DECATUR, AL

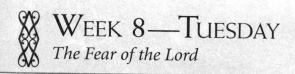

WEEK 8—TUESDAY
The Fear of the Lord

In the fear of the LORD there is strong confidence, and His children will have a place of refuge. The fear of the LORD is a fountain of life, to turn one away from the snares of death.

PROVERBS 14:26–27

The book of Proverbs is about making the right decisions. People often go the way that benefits them the most, refusing to think about the consequences of their decisions or worrying more about what other people think they should do. Solomon called these people "fools." By contrast, godly people fear God—and God alone.

But fearing God is not trying to please Him in order to avoid punishment; instead it is a respect and reverence rooted in love. A child who loves and respects her parents fears them in a healthy and appropriate way. This healthy fear motivates the child to please and honor her parents. As Solomon reminded us, that kind of fear of the Lord gives us confidence and security.

In the book of Daniel, King Nebuchadnezzar threatened to throw Shadrach, Meshach, and Abed-Nego into a fiery furnace if they refused to bow down to the golden statue of him. These young men's fear of the Lord was greater than their fear of King Nebuchadnezzar! Their properly placed fear gave them confidence to obey God (Daniel 3:16–18).

The fear of the Lord is the foundation of any life that honors God. If the fear of the Lord controls our hearts, we will obey God's Word, and then, walking in His way, we will find confidence to face any obstacle or conflict we encounter. Actually, fear of the Lord provides an endless supply of all we need for living a godly life to the fullest!

....

Teach me, Lord, to fear You and to honor You in all I do.

See that no one renders evil for evil to anyone, but always pursue what is good both for yourselves and for all. Rejoice always, pray without ceasing, in everything give thanks; for this is the will of God in Christ Jesus for you.

1 THESSALONIANS 5:15–18

Conflict is a part of life. Sadly, some of the worst conflicts we Christians have are with other Christians in the church!

Writing to the church at Thessalonica, Paul encouraged the believers to respond to hurting people. He also advised them how to respond when someone hurts them. Revenge should be avoided out of respect for Christ.

Paul didn't stop there. He understood that church conflict often occurs because people have the wrong outlook on life. They seek their own personal desires rather than the good of the church. So he gave three instructions:

Choose joy. Paul reminded the early church that persecution cannot rob our joy unless we allow it. Joy is a sign of a spiritually healthy Christian.

"Pray without ceasing." Prayer allows us to rejoice during a time of trial. When prayer is woven into our daily lives, we can more easily look at temporary problems from an eternal perspective.

Be thankful "in everything." We can't be thankful for some things, but we can be thankful in everything. One reason for thanksgiving is that God uses bad things for our spiritual good (Romans 8:28).

For Paul, key to avoiding conflict in the church are members who always choose to rejoice while they are praying with a grateful heart!

....

Enable me, I pray, to "rejoice always, pray without ceasing, [and] in everything give thanks."

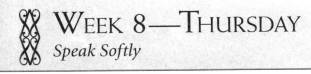

WEEK 8—THURSDAY
Speak Softly

A soft answer turns away wrath, but a harsh word stirs up anger. The tongue of the wise uses knowledge rightly, but the mouth of fools pours forth foolishness. The eyes of the LORD are in every place, keeping watch on the evil and the good.

PROVERBS 15:1–3

Maybe you've heard the expression "Talk is cheap." It means that what we say doesn't mean anything unless we back it with our actions. A wise and godly person, however, knows that words have power and that we should use them carefully. Godly people also know that the words we use and the way we use them can be constructive or destructive. When we have a conflict with another person, emotions will be involved and tensions can rise. Wisdom teaches us to control our emotions and guard our words.

Solomon wrote that we should respond to conflict with a "soft answer." We should speak—in New Testament terms—with a Christlike spirit in contrast to using "harsh words" that escalate tempers.

Every word we speak reflects our personal character. What we say reveals who we are (Matthew 12:35). Wise people choose their words after considering how they may be heard and the possible results of speaking them. A fool, on the other hand, "pours forth" foolishness—or, to use a Southern cliché, "constantly spouts off."

For the believer, the ability to control our tongue reveals self-control, a fruit of the Spirit. May we be filled with the Holy Spirit and empowered to say the right words, at the right time, in the right way!

....

Jesus, You who have words of life, teach me to choose my words carefully and to speak them wisely.

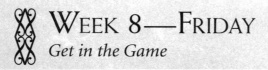

WEEK 8—FRIDAY
Get in the Game

If then you were raised with Christ, seek those things which are above, where Christ is, sitting at the right hand of God. Set your mind on things above, not on things on the earth.

COLOSSIANS 3:1–2

Sometimes athletes are just off. Everything they try fails. After a poor decision, the coach might ask the player, "What were you thinking? Get your head in the game!" Coaches know their player's thoughts are probably on something other than the game–and this happens to believers too. Our behavior reveals when our minds are not on heavenly things.

In Colossians, Paul spent the first two chapters telling Christians what to avoid. In particular, they were to avoid the false teachings of the pagans. One characteristic of the pagan religions is the lack of connection between belief and behavior. Pagan worshippers could sacrifice and give without their devotion to their gods affecting their daily lives.

Christians, on the other hand, are to be different. Because of our relationship with Jesus Christ, we are to "seek" and to "set" our desires on spiritual matters. Seeking means desiring after what God desires, and that desire implies that we are keeping our lives pure. When we set our minds, we think of our Christ as we make decisions and live our lives. We ask ourselves questions like "What would He want us to do?" and "What does the Bible teach about this action?" Setting our minds on things above means focusing our attention on God's eternal kingdom as we live our daily life in this fallen world. I want my head in the game!

....

Lord, You know how easily distracted I am. Help me set my mind and my heart on things above that my life will glorify You.

PHIL WALDREP, PHIL WALDREP MINISTRIES, DECATUR, AL

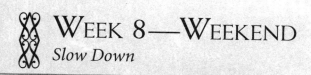

Week 8—Weekend
Slow Down

Let every man be swift to hear, slow to speak, slow to wrath; for the wrath of man does not produce the righteousness of God. Therefore lay aside all filthiness and overflow of wickedness, and receive with meekness the implanted word, which is able to save your souls. But be doers of the word, and not hearers only, deceiving yourselves.

JAMES 1:19–22

Conflict will come into our lives, and when it does, we have the opportunity to honor God by responding as His Word says we should.

James's words above reflect the views of the other writers we have read this week. He summarized what our response should be when conflicts come:

Listen. The text implies that we should listen to those who are teaching God's Word. When we do, we learn truth and can apply it. The text also implies that we should listen to others. If we fail to listen, we can't hear what others are saying or what God is trying to say to us.

Think before we speak. Conflicts bring emotions. When we are emotionally engaged, we often say the first things that come into our mind. James reminded us to be "slow to speak," to think about what we say before we say it.

Avoid anger. When we sense we are losing control of our emotions, we should stop, take a deep breath, and reflect on what is happening. Anger fails to "produce the righteousness of God."

We know what God's Word says about dealing with conflict. Now we need to obey.

....

Lord, I want to always be a doer of Your Word!

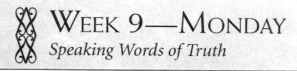

"A good man out of the good treasure of his heart brings forth good things, and an evil man out of the evil treasure brings forth evil things. But I say to you that for every idle word men may speak, they will give account of it in the day of judgment."

MATTHEW 12:35–36

The old saying is "Sticks and stones may break my bones, but words will never hurt me." Jesus took exception to this line of thinking. He taught that words are powerful in both a positive and a negative way. We must therefore set a watch over our hearts, for the mouth speaks forth that which fills the heart. Wicked men will speak words against you just as they did against your Lord.

In Matthew 12 the Pharisees condemned Jesus' disciples for picking grain to eat on the Sabbath. They brought accusations against Jesus and conspired to destroy Him. And they accused Jesus of being demon possessed.

Jesus did not quarrel, but He did speak truth.

When the enemies of truth come against you verbally, it is important to respond properly, and that means guarding your words. Your tongue must not be set on fire with the heat of hell. Rather, let your speech be tamed by the Holy Spirit. And remember that God lives in you! So die to yourself and ask His Spirit within you to help you speak forth the words of Jesus.

One more thing: you don't need to defend yourself. God is more than able to protect you.

....

I thank You, Lord, for Your life-giving words of truth! May I build my life on them!

DR. TED H. TRAYLOR, OLIVE BAPTIST CHURCH, PENSACOLA, FL

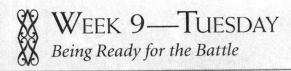

Week 9—Tuesday
Being Ready for the Battle

Be strong in the Lord and in the power of His might. Put on the whole armor of God, that you may be able to stand against the wiles of the devil.

EPHESIANS 6:10–11

The devil wants to bring you down, and one of his strategies is to use people to come against you. Attacks do not mean you are missing God's will. Paul constantly faced enemies and hard times. He was jailed, beaten, threatened with death, stoned, shipwrecked, almost drowned, cold, and hungry (2 Corinthians 11:23–30). Many lesser men would have given up on following Jesus.

Paul shows us how to battle. First, he says to be strong in the Lord. We will fight more effectively when we are confident that our faith in Jesus makes us safe in the Lord's care.

Second, we are to find our strength in the Lord and not in ourselves. Only the strength of God can win the war against Satan.

Third, Paul instructed us to put on the full armor of God:

The Belt of Truth: Do not believe Satan's lies.

The Breastplate of Righteousness: Christ's righteousness has been credited to your account, and God sees you as blameless.

The Shoes of Peace: Stand firm in your faith; trust in God's truth.

The Shield of Faith: Deflect the enemy's attack and stay strong.

The Helmet of Salvation: Protect your thoughts.

The Sword of the Spirit: Read God's Word regularly. Daily is ideal.

....

Thank You, Almighty God, for making Your strength available to me. Prompt me to call on You and rely on that strength especially whenever I face the enemy.

Week 9—Wednesday
Losing Our Lives for Christ

Jesus said to His disciples, "If anyone desires to come after Me, let him deny himself, and take up his cross, and follow Me. For whoever desires to save his life will lose it, but whoever loses his life for My sake will find it. For what profit is it to a man if he gains the whole world, and loses his own soul?"

Matthew 16:24–26

In today's passage Jesus asked a pointed question: "What will a man give in exchange for his soul?" (v. 26). A man might gain the whole world, yet lose his soul, and that is the worst possible exchange.

Jesus, however, spoke of an exchange that is absolutely worthwhile: lose your life for His sake and you find life. And we do that by going after Jesus. When we pursue Him, we find life! How is that done?

> **Deny ourselves.** It is one thing to deny ourselves things and quite another to deny our actual self. Self is strong and wants to be in control. Self will run to the front of the line to exalt itself. The key to following Jesus is not to follow self. So, as you begin this day, lay self to rest. Live for Another: live for the Lord Jesus.
>
> **Take up His cross.** Jesus died first to His will and then He died on the cross. We are to follow His steps and die to our will, to our self.
>
> **Follow Jesus.** Read about Him. Talk with Him. Ask Him for guidance. Watch for evidence of His presence with you.

So follow Jesus. Like any journey, it begins with a first step. Take it!

. . . .

Teach me to die to self; to choose Your will, not mine; to lose my life for Your sake.

DR. TED H. TRAYLOR, OLIVE BAPTIST CHURCH, PENSACOLA, FL

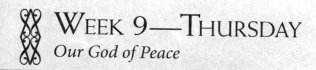

WEEK 9—THURSDAY
Our God of Peace

May the God of peace Himself sanctify you completely; and may your whole spirit, soul, and body be preserved blameless at the coming of our Lord Jesus Christ. He who calls you is faithful, who also will do it.

1 THESSALONIANS 5:23–24

In today's devotional passage, we learn something about the work of our God, the God of Peace. He calls us, He is faithful, and He sanctifies. What a God we serve!

The God of Peace works both vertically and horizontally. First, the vertical. We can know peace with God because He sent Jesus to die in our place as payment for our sins.

The God of Peace also enables us to have peace with one another, peace on the horizontal level. Jesus enables us to have the humility, transparency, and communication that relationships demand. As Jesus' followers, we must walk in peace with God and man.

God's work in us is called sanctification, and it happens in our spirit, soul, and body. The *spirit* is our inner being. It is here God brings the second birth and works in our soul to release His presence in and through us. The *soul* speaks of our mind, will, and emotion. It is here we must be broken and choose submission to Jesus. It is here God transforms us into the image of Christ. Then, sanctification of our *body* is displayed when our actions glorify the Lord.

We will all stand before the God of judgment, but He will find complete and blameless those of us who name Jesus as our Savior.

. . . .

Thank You, God of Peace, for enabling me to know peace with You through Jesus Christ and peace with others by the work of Your Spirit.

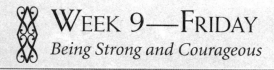

WEEK 9—FRIDAY
Being Strong and Courageous

As for me, I trust in You, O LORD; I say, "You are my God." My times are in Your hand; deliver me from the hand of my enemies.

PSALM 31:14–15

Psalm 31 is a lament. As David faced his enemies, he cried out to the Lord with tears of distress. Verses 9–12 reveal his extreme physical and emotional stress: David felt alone and forgotten. People had slandered him, and the terror of hate-filled enemies was at hand. What is one to do in this kind of stress?

This psalm tells us: Take courage. Trust in the Lord. Look to the goodness of the Lord. Run to the Rock of Ages as a shelter in the storm.

In the 1970s, Psalm 31:14–15 became reality in my life. I was a college freshman, and my draft notice came. Those were the days of the lottery, and I had a low number. It seemed as if I should pack my bags for Vietnam. A college dean approached me about joining the National Guard, saying I could trust him to take care of me. I asked for twenty-four hours to pray. I wound up reading Psalm 31 and sensed God asking me to place my time in His hands, not the dean's. So I thanked the man and then took my Army physical. A few days later, the president ended the draft. It was the first time I placed all of my hope in God alone.

Storms come sooner or later. When they do, be strong in the Lord and take courage. Place your days in God's hands.

. . . .

My relationship with You, Jesus, enables me to be strong and courageous. Thank You for the privilege of being in relationship with You!

DR. TED H. TRAYLOR, OLIVE BAPTIST CHURCH, PENSACOLA, FL

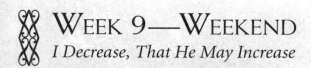

WEEK 9—WEEKEND
I Decrease, That He May Increase

I have been crucified with Christ; it is no longer I who live, but Christ lives in me; and the life which I now live in the flesh I live by faith in the Son of God, who loved me and gave Himself for me.

GALATIANS 2:20

Galatians 2:20 has been important to me for many years. One of the first verses I memorized as a young preacher, it has been a guiding light. Let me share some principles from that verse that God might use in your life:

Die to self. We are to let the self die daily. When the self—our will, our desires, our pride—has died, Jesus lives through us. When I came to understand that the world had seen enough of me and heard enough of me, I was poised to live fully for Christ, to decrease so He can increase, to be eclipsed so the Son of God can shine.

To live is Christ. Jesus is the Sufficient One. He is the Source of life. He is the Savior. His is the kingdom, the power, and the glory forever. When you are weak, Jesus is strong. Therefore we do not boast except in the person of Jesus.

Live by faith. Trust Jesus. Walk by faith in Him, not based on what you see.

Memorize this verse and then live it daily. Bow before the throne of God. Trust Christ alone for the needs of the hour. He is able! And give Him glory throughout the day.

....

Lord Jesus, You ask nothing of me that You Yourself haven't experienced. Enable me to die to my will. Teach me to live for Your glory. Grow my trust in You that I may walk with You every minute of every day.

Do not be afraid of sudden terror, nor of trouble from the wicked when it comes; for the LORD will be your confidence, and will keep your foot from being caught.

PROVERBS 3:25–26

A vacuum cleaner salesman knocked on the door of a remote farmhouse. When the woman of the house opened the door, he walked in and dumped a bag of dirt on the floor.

"Now," boasted the salesman, "I want to make a bargain with you. If this super-duper new vacuum cleaner doesn't pick up every bit of this dirt, I'll eat what's left."

"Here's a spoon," said the farmer's wife. "We don't have any electricity."[6]

This humorous story illustrates the danger of self-confidence. Americans are often taught the values of self-esteem, self-assurance, and self-confidence. There's just one problem: you don't find these "values" anywhere in the Bible. In fact, Paul told us in Philippians 3:3 that we should "have no confidence in the flesh."

Even though self-confidence is an American value, it's not a biblical one. This does not mean we should not have confidence. We can actually have confidence in Someone infinitely greater than ourselves. The Bible says "the Lord will be your confidence." The Hebrew word for *confidence* is intriguing. It can be translated either *confidence* or *stupidity*. The difference between true assurance and self-deceived foolishness is determined by the source of our confidence. When your assurance is based on Christ, it leads to certainty about the decisions you make on your faith journey.

....

Heavenly Father, keep me from foolishly placing confidence in myself. Help me to trust in Your strength to keep me from wickedness.

DR. JIM PERDUE, SECOND BAPTIST CHURCH, WARNER ROBINS, GA

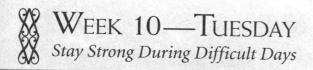

WEEK 10—TUESDAY
Stay Strong During Difficult Days

Do not cast away your confidence, which has great reward. For you have need of endurance, so that after you have done the will of God, you may receive the promise.

HEBREWS 10:35–36

Hebrews was written to Jewish Christians who were facing increasing persecution. The author, fearful his audience of Hebrew believers would turn away from their faith in Christ and revert to their former religion, challenges them with these words: "Do not cast away your confidence." These converted Jews were in danger of throwing away their trust in God. God warned them not to abandon their faith.

The author boldly challenged followers of Christ to stay strong during difficult days. Our faith in Christ "has great reward." Indeed, the Bible tells of a great "promise" which we will receive when we run the lifelong race of faith with patience and endurance. As believers, we are challenged to endure hard times and remain faithful to Jesus no matter the cost.

Hebrews 11 records many examples of those who went through great difficulty but still followed God in faith. Hebrews 12:2 challenges us to run the race God has given us with patience and confidence: "Looking unto Jesus, the author and finisher of our faith, who for the joy that was set before Him endured the cross, despising the shame, and has sat down at the right hand of the throne of God." We need "endurance" to face the challenges around us. God's Word promises "a better and an enduring possession . . . in heaven" for those who name Jesus as their Savior (Hebrews 10:34).

. . . .

Lord, please help me to stay strong in my faith whatever my circumstances in the midst of life's difficulties. When times are tough, help me to trust in You and not in my own strength. Remind me each day to keep my eyes on Jesus.

GOD IS FAITHFUL

Week 10—Wednesday
Confidence When You Pray

Now this is the confidence that we have in Him, that if we ask anything according to His will, He hears us. And if we know that He hears us, whatever we ask, we know that we have the petitions that we have asked of Him.

1 JOHN 5:14–15

First John is in your Bible for one main reason: to provide confidence to believers who are struggling with doubt. John wrote to encourage followers of Jesus and to remind them eternal life awaits them.

Here in this life, although we have not yet received our eternal inheritance, we have access to all of the resources of God through prayer. God promises "that if we ask anything according to His will, He hears us." And if we know God hears us, we also know God will grant us the "petitions that we have asked of Him." We can have "confidence" God hears and answers our prayers.

It may sound as if God has provided a blank check to the Christian, saying He will do anything as long as we ask for it. Though, there is one important qualification: our requests must be "according to His will." If you are truly following Jesus with your whole heart, your desires in prayer will only be in accordance with God's plan and purpose for your life.

Prayer, therefore, is not giving God directions or ensuring His plans line up with our desires. Prayer is ensuring our will lines up with God's purposes and then asking that His "will be done on earth as it is in heaven" (Matthew 6:10).

. . . .

Gracious God, thank You for hearing me when I pray. Teach me to pray according to Your will and for Your glory.

DR. JIM PERDUE, SECOND BAPTIST CHURCH, WARNER ROBINS, GA

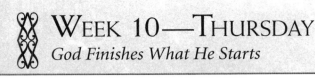

Week 10—Thursday
God Finishes What He Starts

I thank my God . . . for your fellowship in the gospel from the first day until now, being confident of this very thing, that He who has begun a good work in you will complete it until the day of Jesus Christ.

Philippians 1:3, 5–6

Have you ever started a project you didn't finish? You may have an unfinished task hanging over your head right now. Sometimes we start a project with the best intentions, but we do not finish the job. We have all had these types of tasks. It is a common problem for many, but it is not at all a problem for God.

The Bible tells us God finishes what He starts: "He who has begun a good work in you will complete it." God started His work of grace in your heart, and He always finishes what He starts. Remember, we are all a work in progress. God's work within us takes a lifetime, but He always finishes the projects He starts.

Salvation is a threefold work of God. First, there is justification: He declares us righteous in His sight. Then comes sanctification: we are ever growing in our relationship with God through the work of the Holy Spirit in us. Finally, there is glorification: when we get to heaven, we will be sinless people in a perfect place. God worked in your past through justification, He is at work in the present as He sanctifies you by the power of His Spirit, and in the future He will glorify you. He always finishes what He starts.

....

Faithful God, I know You are a God who leaves no project unfinished. Thank You for the work of grace You have begun in my life through salvation. Continue to work in me daily for my sanctification as I seek to serve and honor You.

"Most assuredly, I say to you, he who believes in Me, the works that I do he will do also; and greater works than these he will do, because I go to My Father. And whatever you ask in My name, that I will do, that the Father may be glorified in the Son. If you ask anything in My name, I will do it."

JOHN 14:12–14

Greater works! Can you imagine doing greater works than Jesus did? This is almost unthinkable, but that is exactly what Jesus said. Read the passage one more time. Although the apostles were given power to perform miracles, I do not necessarily believe these words mean we can heal the sick, feed a multitude, or raise the dead.

Jesus meant the work He had done was just the start of the spread of the gospel. He had also opened the door for God to work in amazing and powerful ways in people's lives. Think about it: Peter preached at Pentecost, and three thousand people were saved. Today, we can fly around the world in less time than it took Jesus to travel to a distant town. We have the power to reach more people than those in Jesus' time ever imagined.

It has been written "it is not the believer *himself* who does these 'greater things'; it is God working in and through the believer."[7] The only reason we can do greater works is because Jesus did the greatest work: His death and resurrection made a way for the Spirit of God to dwell in us. Through Christ, we can make a significant impact for eternity.

....

God, would You use me to see great things accomplished in this world to bring glory and honor to Your great name?

DR. JIM PERDUE, SECOND BAPTIST CHURCH, WARNER ROBINS, GA

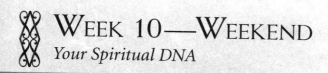

WEEK 10—WEEKEND
Your Spiritual DNA

My little children, let us not love in word or in tongue, but in deed and in truth. And by this we know that we are of the truth, and shall assure our hearts before Him. For if our heart condemns us, God is greater than our heart, and knows all things.

1 JOHN 3:18–20

John said we can "know" we are children of God by the way we love one another. Our love for other people reveals the reality of our relationship with Jesus. Even when "our heart condemns us," we know God is "greater than our heart." Faith gives us confidence in God's love for us even when we doubt, even when we do not understand.

The Message paraphrases verses 19 and 20 in a way that might be helpful: "This is the only way we'll know we're living truly, living in God's reality. It's also the way to shut down debilitating self-criticism, even when there is something to it. For God is greater than our worried hearts and knows more about us than we do ourselves."

I know I belong to my parents and I am their child. For one thing, there is a bit of a resemblance. I also have some of their personality traits and characteristics built into me. Even with these visible traits, if I ever doubt that I belong to them, there is an even more conclusive test to give me full assurance: DNA. Godly love is the spiritual DNA of a believer. If you know God, you will have love, and if you have love, it is proof you know God!

....

Gracious Father, thank You for giving me the confidence I am Your child even when doubts and fears assail my heart. Help me to faithfully exhibit the greatest proof of my relationship with You: a life of love.

GOD IS FAITHFUL

61

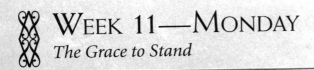

If You, LORD, should mark iniquities, O Lord, who could stand? But there is forgiveness with You, that You may be feared. I wait for the LORD, my soul waits, and in His word I do hope.

PSALM 130:3–5

God is holy, totally distinct, separate, and morally pure. The angels at His throne do not cease to cry out, "Holy, holy, holy" (Revelation 4:8). Man, on the other hand, is sinful. You and I have sinned repeatedly in thought, attitude, word, and deed. How could we possibly stand before this holy God? And how could we ever be made right with Him?

We can be in right relationship with God because, in addition to being holy, He is also unfathomably gracious and merciful. Jesus came into our world to save us from sin's hold on us and its consequences, not to condemn us. God wants to forgive all our sins so that we can stand in His presence "blameless with great joy" (Jude 1:24 NASB). No matter what you may be guilty of today, His wonderful forgiveness is available to you right now through the Lord Jesus Christ. The blood Jesus shed on the cross can wash the vilest offenders white as snow. All you have to do is turn to Him in genuine repentance and true confession. He is ready to forgive you. Are you ready to go to Him?

....

Dear God, I stand in awe of You. Thank You for Your mercy and grace. Thank You for the precious blood of Jesus Christ. Thank You that by Your grace, I can be totally and completely forgiven. I am guilty of _____, and I am so sorry. Forgive me, Lord. Wash me clean and make me pure before You. I claim this forgiveness because You have promised it to me. In Jesus' name, amen.

PASTOR JEFF SCHREVE, FIRST BAPTIST TEXARKANA, TEXARKANA, TX

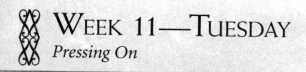

WEEK 11—TUESDAY
Pressing On

Not that I have already attained, or am already perfected; but I press on, that I may lay hold of that for which Christ Jesus has also laid hold of me. . . . I press toward the goal for the prize of the upward call of God in Christ Jesus.

PHILIPPIANS 3:12, 14

Do you feel stuck in life? Does it seem like you have fallen in a ditch, so to speak, unable to move forward because of failures—or successes—from the past? Mark it down: God takes no pleasure in a derailed, ditch-dwelling Christian. He wants you to get back on track and moving forward as a force for Jesus Christ.

God is the great *I Am*, not the great *I Was*. As such, He desires for us to live in the present, not the past. He calls every one of His followers to press on in obedience and the power of the Holy Spirit. Yesterday is gone, and tomorrow may never come. All we have is today. So God says to you today, "My child, walk with Me. Let Me shine like the sun through you as you yield yourself to Me. I have good works for you to do this day that will let people know that I am real and that I am alive in you."

....

Dear God, I don't want to live stuck in a ditch, feeling like my life has lost meaning and purpose. I want to press on with You. Thank You for the victories as well as the valleys of the past. Let me learn from them and move forward. Thank You that You have good plans for me. I choose to walk by faith, and I am excited about today. In Jesus' name, amen.

GOD IS FAITHFUL

63

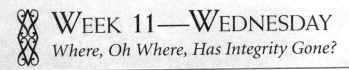

WEEK 11—WEDNESDAY
Where, Oh Where, Has Integrity Gone?

If I have walked with falsehood, or if my foot has hastened to deceit, let me be weighed on honest scales, that God may know my integrity.

JOB 31:5–6

Integrity. It seems to be an ignored, if not completely forgotten, virtue in our world today.

Modern culture believes that image is everything and that perception is reality. If you can fool the people with smoke and mirrors, so be it. But the problem is God sees past the façade; He sees through to all the falsehood and deceit.

Job was a man of integrity. He had moral soundness and uprightness of character. As a person of integrity, he had nothing to hide from God or people and therefore had nothing to fear. When he examined his heart to look for sin, he didn't find anything that he hadn't confessed and dealt with. This righteousness made it doubly hard for him to understand why his life was falling apart. Yet God wasn't punishing Job; the holy One was purifying him. Job was being tested, and he passed with flying colors. He remained a person of integrity through weeks of intense and painful trials and tribulations. What an example for us!

When you do a personal integrity exam, what do you find? Are you living a morally upright life, walking in righteousness and truth? Or are you hiding secret sins in the deep recesses of your heart? The time is now to step on God's moral scales and come clean.

....

Dear God, I want to be a person of integrity, a person who has nothing to hide. Forgive me for my hidden sins. Enable me to bring them to the light and put them under the blood of Jesus. Please help me to walk in the light, to live in truth and uprightness. Amen.

PASTOR JEFF SCHREVE, FIRST BAPTIST TEXARKANA, TEXARKANA, TX

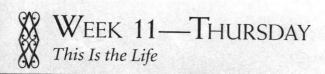

WEEK 11—THURSDAY
This Is the Life

If you live according to the flesh you will die; but if by the Spirit you put to death the deeds of the body, you will live. . . . You did not receive the spirit of bondage again to fear, but you received the Spirit of adoption by whom we cry out, "Abba, Father."

ROMANS 8:13, 15

Are you living the life the Lord wants you to live? Are you growing in your intimacy with Jesus? Is the Father becoming more precious to you each day? Are you seeing more and more victories over your sinful thoughts, deeds, and attitudes as you walk with Jesus in the power of the Holy Spirit? If not, let me encourage you: God wants all these wonderful things to be true for you.

The Christian life was never designed for any of us to live in our own strength. Whenever we try to conquer the flesh with the flesh, we fail miserably. But when we yield ourselves to the Holy Spirit's power, we experience victory over lust, greed, jealousy, bitterness, and the like. The Holy Spirit lives inside every true believer. He is present in us, and He desires to be preeminent in us, to be commander of our hearts. That is what the Bible calls Spirit-filled living. When we live that way, we truly live.

. . . .

Dear God, I am tired of fighting sin in my own strength. I need your strength. Holy Spirit, I want You to be in complete control of me. I make the choice to yield my will to Your will. Fill my life with Your peace, joy, and victory as I surrender to You. I am excited to truly live in Your power and love. In Jesus' name, amen.

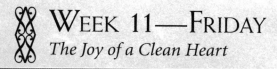

Week 11—Friday
The Joy of a Clean Heart

Create in me a clean heart, O God, and renew a steadfast spirit within me. Do not cast me away from Your presence, and do not take Your Holy Spirit from me. Restore to me the joy of Your salvation, and uphold me by Your generous Spirit.

Psalm 51:10–12

King David was a man after God's own heart, yet he sinned greatly. He committed adultery with Bathsheba, a married woman. When she realized she was pregnant from their one-night tryst, David then covered up his adultery by arranging for her husband, Uriah the Hittite, to be killed in battle. David's adultery was a passionate, hot-blooded sin, but the murder he oversaw was a calculated, cold-blooded sin. In short, David's heart was deeply stained with iniquity and desperately in need of cleansing.

Psalm 51 is David's prayer of repentance. In it, David asked God for forgiveness, restoration, and a change within. He asked God to keep His hand on him and to restore the joy of salvation to his heart. Praise God for answering David's sincere prayer of contrition.

Maybe you have sinned greatly just as David did. Maybe you need to make Psalm 51 *your* prayer of repentance. Let me challenge you to commit these verses to memory and to pray them back to God as necessary. When you do, you will know the grace of forgiveness and cleansing. God is indeed a forgiving God. He will wash you thoroughly and completely when you go to Him. It took David almost a year to get his heart right with God, and he was miserable that entire time. Don't waste any time.

....

Lord, help me experience the joy of a clean heart. (Pray Psalm 51.)

PASTOR JEFF SCHREVE, FIRST BAPTIST TEXARKANA, TEXARKANA, TX

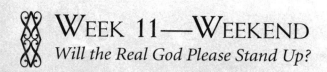

Be merciful to me, O Lord, for I cry to You all day long. Rejoice the soul of Your servant, for to You, O Lord, I lift up my soul. For You, Lord, are good, and ready to forgive, and abundant in mercy to all those who call upon You.

PSALM 86:3–5

When you close your eyes to picture God, what do you see? Is the God you envision good and gracious, merciful and compassionate? Or do you see a God who is angry and disgusted, who disapproves of you and your ever-erring, ever-straying ways?

The sad truth is that many people have in their mind a faulty picture of God. They don't see Him as good and ready to forgive even though that is how the Bible describes Him. These people see God as stern and ready to unleash His righteous wrath.

How different would your life be if you envisioned God the right way, as the father of the prodigal son? Do you remember what that father did with that wayward boy? He ran to embrace and forgive his repentant son. Although that boy reeked with the foul stench of the pig sty, the father kissed him repeatedly. He put a robe on his son's back, a ring on his finger, and shoes on his feet. Then he threw the party of all parties and invited the town to celebrate with him! The Lord indeed is "abundant in mercy to all those who call upon Him."

Dear God, I stand amazed at how good You are. I am overwhelmed by Your love for me. I don't want to live another second believing the lies of the devil. I want to live in the truth and experience Your goodness, forgiveness, and mercy. In Jesus' name, amen.

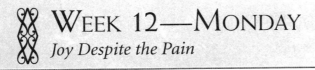

WEEK 12—MONDAY
Joy Despite the Pain

In this you greatly rejoice, though now for a little while, if need be, you have been grieved by various trials, that the genuineness of your faith . . . may be found to praise, honor, and glory at the revelation of Jesus Christ.

1 PETER 1:6–7

Have you ever experienced extreme anguish, deep sadness, or major disappointment? Of course you have. We all know what it is like to face feelings of despair, distress, and anguish.

Problems bring pain. Sometimes we bring those problems on ourselves. Sometimes they come from other people or life's circumstances. But the simple reality is, problems and pain come.

In our text, Peter spoke of having joy in the midst of trials and suffering. He used the phrase, "greatly rejoice." This phrase is an intense, expressive term that means to be joyful and abundantly happy.

With the contextual discussion focusing on salvation, Peter called us to remember our security in Christ whenever pain comes. Before we get caught up with all that is happening down here in our present lives, we need to get caught up with what is going on in heaven.

Peter told us what Jesus told us and what we know from experience: we are going to experience trials. It may be a battle with physical illness, a bad work situation, conflict in your family, or perhaps the relentless daily grind of life.

And, as Peter said, God will use these trials to see if our faith is real.

Does your faith hold up to the test? When life gets rough, do you throw in the towel, or do you grab your Bible?

....

Father, whenever pain enters my life, help me respond in a way that is pleasing to You. May everything I do bring You glory.

PASTOR STEVE FLOCKHART, NEW SEASON CHURCH, HIRAM, GA

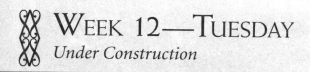

WEEK 12—TUESDAY
Under Construction

Being confident of this very thing, that He who has begun a good work in you will complete it until the day of Jesus Christ.

PHILIPPIANS 1:6

Wow, what a verse! What a promise! What a mighty God we serve!
The apostle Paul was absolutely confident that God never starts something that He doesn't finish. God never does anything halfway. God, who did a work *for* us through salvation and who is doing a work *in* us through sanctification, will complete this work.

Did you notice who initiated this work? God! It's His work! And what work is this work? The work of salvation and sanctification.

In Acts 16, we have three incredible stories. We read about Lydia, the wealthy woman from Thyatira who was saved and allowed Paul to start a church in her home. We read about the demon-possessed girl who was saved. Then we read about the Philippian jailer who was saved after the imprisoned Paul and Silas had a praise-and-worship service at midnight. Paul may have been thinking of these people when he wrote that God will complete that which He started.

When did you come to Christ? Were you a child, a teenager, or an adult? The work that God started in you at that point, He will complete! Isn't that an exciting thought? All of us are still under construction!

You no doubt have experienced trials, setbacks, and discouraging times. But remember that God started the work of grace in your heart and He promises that this work will be completed when Jesus comes back for His church.

....

Thank You, Lord Jesus, for the promises in Your Word!

WEEK 12—WEDNESDAY
"God, Please Make It Better"

The LORD is near to those who have a broken heart, and saves such as have a contrite spirit. Many are the afflictions of the righteous, but the LORD delivers him out of them all.

PSALM 34:18–19

When you least expect it, it comes out of nowhere. That phone call, e-mail, letter, or conversation.

Life is full of difficulties and disappointments. We walk through times that shake us to our very core and pain that seems unbearable.

Perhaps right now a storm is on the horizon. Maybe you're about to lose your home or your health is declining. Maybe you've lost a loved one and are trying to pick up the shattered pieces of your life.

We all must deal with pain and struggles. If you are heartbroken right now, if your spirit is crushed, know that your heavenly Father promises you that He will be ever so close to you during this painful time.

I've known some dark times in my own life, times of deep disappointment and sorrow. I often felt that God had abandoned me. My heart ached. I cried out to God in agonizing prayer, but I felt as if He wasn't listening. I prayed, "God, please make it better"—only to watch things get worse.

Those experiences are part of life. You will have that season in your life at some point. The key is to remember to cling to God's promises, this one in particular: "The LORD is near to those who have a broken heart."

....

Father, heal my broken heart as only You can. Help me stay focused. Keep me from becoming bitter.

PASTOR STEVE FLOCKHART, NEW SEASON CHURCH, HIRAM, GA

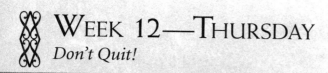

WEEK 12—THURSDAY
Don't Quit!

We are hard-pressed on every side, yet not crushed; we are perplexed, but not in despair; persecuted, but not forsaken; struck down, but not destroyed—always carrying about in the body the dying of the Lord Jesus, that the life of Jesus also may be manifested in our body.

2 CORINTHIANS 4:8–10

No matter who you are, you will have problems. You will experience deep pain and hurt. Pressures mount up, life seems to cave in, and you feel like giving up. Paul knew all too well what it was like to live this way. Criticism, conflict, violence, and death threats were a normal part of his life. Paul knew all too well what it was like to suffer trials and encounter difficulty. Even Paul surely went through seasons of doubt and discouragement. I am sure that he thought of quitting, but in order to finish his task, he relied on the presence and the promises of God.

The enemy is strong. He turns up the heat, and many times life can seem too much to bear. We feel like we are losing the battle. (Please tell me that I'm not alone in feeling this way!) Maybe you are there right now. If so, I have two words for you: Don't quit! Hang in there. Don't throw in the towel. Stay the course. You've come too far. Don't give up!

No matter what comes your way
No matter what trial you're facing
No matter how bad the odds against you are
No matter how discouraged you might be
No matter how dark the tunnel is . . .
Do not quit!

Lord Jesus, I will not quit! I will trust You and persevere.

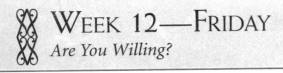

WEEK 12—FRIDAY
Are You Willing?

Blessed is the man You choose, and cause to approach You, that he may dwell in Your courts. We shall be satisfied with the goodness of Your house, of Your holy temple.

PSALM 65:4

David wrote Psalm 65 after God blessed him with a great military victory. King David was not only a warrior; he was also a worshipper.

David found great joy in worshipping God. His heart overflowed with love for God, and he was thrilled to be in the Lord's presence. David knew that he could not live without God's sustaining power. Once, when the ark of God came into Jerusalem, David started to dance. The Hebrew word for *dance* means "to hop and spin in circles." David was praising God with all that he was!

It is easy to praise God during the good times of life, but what about during the difficult times? Can we praise Him when life doesn't make sense? Can we worship Him when we despair?

I have some close friends who are missionaries in Peru. A few years ago, they lost their son in a tragic accident, yet I have watched this couple wholeheartedly worship their God many times since losing their son.

My brother lost his wife recently. It was sudden and unexpected; the circumstances were horrible and the aftermath, confusing. At her funeral, though, I watched him lift his hands to worship God.

Plagued by questions, yet worshipping.

Sobbing, yet worshipping.

Still shaking his head in disbelief, yet worshipping.

When life doesn't make sense, will you choose to praise God?

....

Father, help me worship You in the bad times as well as the good. No matter what comes my way, help me to know that You are God and You love me.

PASTOR STEVE FLOCKHART, NEW SEASON CHURCH, HIRAM, GA

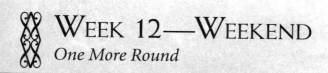
The Lord is faithful, who will establish you and guard you from the evil one. . . . Now
may the Lord direct your hearts into the love of God and into the patience of Christ.

2 Thessalonians 3:3, 5

Have you ever asked the question "Why do bad things happen to good people?" I'm sure a guy named Job living in the land of Uz asked that question a few times. In the story of Job, God permitted Satan to destroy Job's livestock and servants, his home, his health, and even his children.

At first Job responded with a statement of trust and total dependence on God. Then, like all of us, he asked the *why* questions of God.

Why are You allowing these things?
Don't You care about me?
What did I do to deserve this?
Why don't You intervene? You could do something!

Have you ever asked those questions? I have—and it's a terrible feeling to lose hope, feel discarded by God, and sense the enemy circling around you, magnifying all those negative feelings. When life knocks you down you can feel as if you're out for the count. Many times you feel that you can't muster the strength to go one more round or throw one more punch.

I remind you that God *is* faithful and He *will* see you through. He will battle the enemy for you—and, by the way, He has already won! So when you feel weakness setting in, when you don't have it in you to go one more round, hang on. Know that God will see you through!

. . . .

Lord Jesus, thank You that You understand my pain and identify with it. Today,
I choose to trust You. You are faithful!

GOD IS FAITHFUL

Week 13—Monday
Live Today Influenced by Tomorrow

You are all sons of light and sons of the day. We are not of the night nor of darkness. Therefore let us not sleep, as others do, but let us watch and be sober. . . . Let us who are of the day be sober, putting on the breastplate of faith and love, and as a helmet the hope of salvation.

1 Thessalonians 5:5–6, 8

The lives of believers should be noticeably different from the lives of those who are not yet followers of Jesus.

Paul drew pictures of those living in the light and those living in the darkness. Those who live in God's light see differently, act differently, and live differently from those still in the darkness because Christ-followers live in anticipation of His return. Paul called the believers in Thessalonica to intentionally live differently, specifically, to refuse to fall asleep. Sleep is indifference to, inactivity regarding, and ignorance about "the day of the Lord," when Jesus will return to this planet. Those who are in the light are not to lead that type of aimless life. Paul was making the case that our belief about the future should shape our present behavior.

Paul ended this passage with a three-pronged strategy for engaging those who are nonbelievers: faith, love, and hope. First, faith is *doing* something, not merely *feeling* something. The greatest expression of our faith—the greatest *doing* of our faith—is love. We are able to live with hope and confidence that Jesus is coming back.

....

So that people who don't know You might come to know You, Jesus, may I live in the light. May I live with faith in You, with love for You and for others, and with hope—with confidence—in Your return.

TREVOR BARTON, HAWK CREEK CHURCH, LONDON, KY

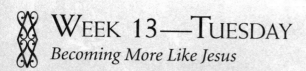

Week 13—Tuesday
Becoming More Like Jesus

"While you have the light, believe in the light, that you may become sons of light."
These things Jesus spoke, and departed, and was hidden from them.

JOHN 12:36

Speaking to His followers, Jesus invited them to believe in the light, to believe in Him. As they believed in the light, the qualities, characteristics, and nature of the light would become evident in their lives.

Followers of Jesus, however, occasionally complicate the concept of following Jesus. We love to splice theology and argue doctrine. When we do, we lose sight of the simple need to become more like Jesus. Said another way, it is easy to spend time discussing, debating, and writing about Christian beliefs, all the while neglecting Christian behavior.

Being a Christian is about *doing* something. Let me clarify: *salvation* is not about our doing anything; our salvation comes through God's grace alone, by faith alone, in Christ alone. We can do nothing to earn salvation. The *doing* that I'm talking about is living as "sons of light."

As we follow Jesus, we should become more like Him. Remember, nonbelievers found Jesus winsome and attractive. Sinners actually liked to be around Jesus! So if we are serious about reaching our unbelieving culture, becoming more like Jesus should be our primary goal. When we are more like our Savior, those who are far from Jesus will find themselves wanting to be near us. When they do draw near, we have the opportunity to shine God's light of truth and love into their dark world.

....

Lord, thank You for sending "sons of light" into my life so I might come to know
You. Now send me, I pray. Use me to bring others into Your eternal family.

Week 13—Wednesday
In the World to Influence the World

"Let your light so shine before men, that they may see your good works and glorify your Father in heaven."

Matthew 5:16

Think about what Jesus said in the Gospels. He frequently tied the *identity* of His disciples to their *responsibility* as disciples. Jesus said—paraphrased—You are sheep, therefore listen to the shepherd; you are the branch, so stay connected to the vine; and you are fishers of men, so reach out to people. Over and over again Jesus taught the disciples *who they were* (identity) in order to show them *what they were to do* (responsibility).

In the Sermon on the Mount, Jesus followed this pattern. First, He told His disciples they are the salt of the earth. As salt they were to flavor culture with morality and righteousness, and they were to act as a preservative against the culture's moral decay. Being salt requires wisdom because too much salt is destructive, and too little salt is ineffective.

Jesus also told His disciples they are light, and therefore, they were responsible for confronting darkness. Again, wisdom about being God's light is necessary because too much light is harmful and too little light isn't helpful.

Jesus called His disciples then—and us today—to live out their faith. Said another way, their *practice* of faith should support their *profession* of faith. The life of believers can either *attract* people and draw them closer to faith or *distract*, keeping them away from faith. We are in the world to influence the world for Jesus. Let's be someone's reason for faith, not their reason for unbelief.

....

Use me, Lord, as salt in this dying world and as light in its darkness. I want to be in the world to influence the world for You, Jesus.

TREVOR BARTON, HAWK CREEK CHURCH, LONDON, KY

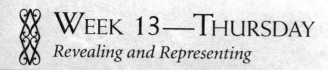

WEEK 13—THURSDAY
Revealing and Representing

"I am the light of the world. He who follows Me shall not walk in darkness, but have the light of life."

JOHN 8:12

J esus identified Himself as the Light of the World. He promised both light and life to those who follow Him, and the life Jesus offered was His own. After all, Jesus' death meant not only the forgiveness of our sin, but also the gift of Jesus' Spirit within us so that we can be His light.

Now that Jesus has returned to the Father, we who are His followers on earth are to represent Jesus and reveal Jesus to our culture just as Jesus represented and revealed the Father to the culture of His day. That's what Jesus meant when He taught that we believers are "the light of the world" (Matthew 5:14).

Paul described this purpose as being the "body of Christ." Paul also referred to Jesus' followers as "a letter being read by people" and "a fragrance that can attract or repel." The pictures are different, but the point remains the same. We are to allow Jesus to live through us as we live in this world. That means that we should—by God's power—live so that people see in us the grace, gentleness, mercy, forgiveness, love, truth, and kindness that we see in Jesus.

The greatest approach to influencing those people who are far from Jesus is to bring Jesus close to them.

....

Lord God, please help me be an accurate and effective advertisement for Jesus— for His goodness and His grace, His love and His truth.

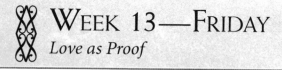
Sanctify the Lord God in your hearts, and always be ready to give a defense to everyone who asks you a reason for the hope that is in you, with meekness and fear.

1 PETER 3:15

Believers should always be ready to explain why they follow Jesus. We should not avoid faith-related conversations. Jesus and the New Testament writers invited us to faith built on information, not ignorance. They provided the information we need.

Not surprisingly, Peter said we should speak with gentleness and respect. The defense of our hope in Christ is always best communicated by love.

In *The Great Evangelical Disaster,* Francis Schaeffer said it well: "Let us be careful, indeed, to spend a lifetime studying to give honest answers. . . . So it is well to spend time learning to answer the questions of men who are about us. But after we have done our best to communicate to a lost world, still we must never forget that the final apologetic which Jesus gives is the observable love of true Christians for true Christians."[8]

Jesus said it better: "I pray also for those who will believe in me . . . that all of them may be one, Father, just as you are in me and I am in you. May they also be in us so that the world may believe that you have sent me" (John 17:20–21 NIV).

Jesus taught that the greatest proof of being His follower was for His disciples to love one another. When the early believers loved one another (Acts 4:32–35), the lost culture took notice. Just as love changed the world in the first century, love can change it again in the twenty-first.

....

Lord, make me a student of Your Word, empowered by the Spirit to share Your truth. Teach me to love with Your love.

TREVOR BARTON, HAWK CREEK CHURCH, LONDON, KY

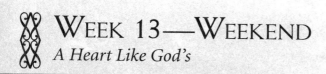

WEEK 13—WEEKEND
A Heart Like God's

The Lord is not slack concerning His promise, as some count slackness, but is longsuffering toward us, not willing that any should perish but that all should come to repentance.

2 PETER 3:9

God has a heart for those far from Him; so should we. God's love for the world, and His desire to see the lost come into relationship with Him, compels Him to be patient.

Jesus powerfully communicated that truth in the parable of the prodigal son. He introduced us to a younger son who did not want a relationship with his father and, in fact, wished his father dead so he could receive his inheritance. When the father gave the boy his inheritance, the son left home and lived on his own terms until he hit rock bottom.

However, Jesus informed us that while the young son lived out his rebellion, his father waited patiently for his return. When the son did return, the father did not lecture about mistakes or point out his errant ways. Instead he celebrated his lost son's return. He had a party in honor of his son who was lost but now was found (Luke 15:11–24).

Like the father in this parable, God deeply loves people who are lost. He is patient; He desires them to return and repent. When they do, He celebrates. We should treat unbelievers with the same love and patience as the God who desires to be in relationship with them. When we see them turn to the Father, may we celebrate wholeheartedly with Christlike joy.

. . . .

Father God, Your patience, Your love, Your forgiveness, Your rejoicing, Your celebration—Your grace, like the father's for his son who returned home—truly are amazing.

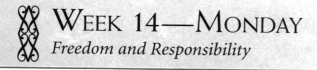

WEEK 14—MONDAY
Freedom and Responsibility

You, brethren, have been called to liberty; only do not use liberty as an opportunity for the flesh, but through love serve one another. For all the law is fulfilled in one word, even in this: "You shall love your neighbor as yourself."

GALATIANS 5:13–14

Freedom doesn't remove responsibility. Instead, it turns responsibilities into privileges.

The gospel frees us from having to pay the price for our sin and trying to earn our salvation, but we are not free to do just anything we *want* to do. Rather, we are free and enabled to do what God *needs* and *calls* us to do—to love Him and love others.

Before Jesus' death on the cross, sin kept us from loving, from doing what we needed to do. We were enslaved by the power of sin—until the gospel extinguished our passion to sin. Now we are liberated! Now we can soar, freed by Christ! But we are not to "use [our] liberty as an opportunity for the flesh." Instead, we are to honor and serve Jesus. Our life is no longer about us; instead we are to, acting in love, "serve one another." And when we serve others, we are really serving Jesus.

In ancient days, slaves had the *responsibility* of washing feet. Because of our freedom in Christ, we have the *privilege* of washing feet and serving others. Only people who know the freedom of God's grace and forgiveness will think and live this way. When the Lord liberates us from the prison of selfishness and sin, we who know God's forgiveness and love find ourselves in a wide-open space that brings opportunities for us to love and to serve in His name.

. . . .

Lord, thank You for freeing me to no longer serve my flesh, but to serve You, my risen Savior.

PASTOR JEFF CROOK, BLACKSHEAR PLACE BAPTIST CHURCH, FLOWERY BRANCH, GA

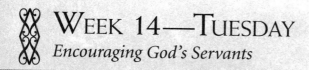

WEEK 14—TUESDAY
Encouraging God's Servants

Comfort each other and edify one another, just as you also are doing. And we urge you, brethren, to recognize those who labor among you, and are over you in the Lord and admonish you, and to esteem them very highly in love for their work's sake. Be at peace among yourselves.

1 THESSALONIANS 5:11–13

A godly older gentleman made the following remark to a few angry church members: "We just need to fire up our preacher!" His words were timely because some people were talking about asking the pastor to leave the church. It's always tragic to hear about a pastor being fired. It's also sad to hear about pastors who become so discouraged that they walk away from the ministry.

A well-known evangelical leader once estimated that nearly 1,500 pastors leave the ministry every month—and that probably wouldn't happen if God's church obeyed what His Word says concerning the relationship between the pastor and the people. The pastor is appointed by God to feed, intercede for, and lead the flock, and the flock is to esteem these leaders and submit to their leadership. After all, our leaders are a gift from the Lord. When we honor them, when we bless our leaders with our encouragement and support, God is pleased.

So fire up your pastor! Pray for him daily. Encourage him regularly. Follow his leadership as he follows Jesus, the Chief Shepherd. You will be a blessing to your pastor, and the Lord will bless you for obeying His Word.

Father, thank You for pastors who lead, pray for, and care for Your flock. Show me what I can do to encourage my pastor(s) today. In Jesus' name, amen.

WEEK 14—WEDNESDAY
Christianity: Christ in Us

The kingdom of God is not eating and drinking, but righteousness and peace and joy in the Holy Spirit. For he who serves Christ in these things is acceptable to God and approved by men. Therefore let us pursue the things which make for peace and the things by which one may edify another.

ROMANS 14:17–19

Has anyone ever said to you, "You look like a Christian"? What does a Christian look like?

Certainly Christianity transforms our life, but the change is more internal than external. The Spirit of God indwells our life the very moment we trust Jesus Christ as Lord and Savior. Our passage today reveals some of those inner realities that will be visible in authentic Christ-followers.

Righteousness—We have been made right with God through Christ. Our lifestyle reflects our obedience to Him.

Peace—An inner tranquility, an abiding peace—a product of the indwelling Holy Spirit—is evident in our relationship with God and others.

Joy—Jesus promised us full joy, and His Spirit produces a constant flow of joy whatever the circumstances of life. Nothing can extinguish our joy when we are fully yielded to the Spirit.

Finally, Christianity is not cosmetics, but Christ in us, manifesting His character in us. Don't forget what is absolutely essential—fully surrendering to God's rule and reign.

....

Lord, I praise and honor You who are my Sovereign King. I completely submit to You today. May others be drawn to you when they see that You reign in my heart. Amen.

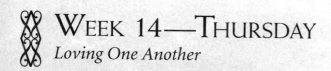

WEEK 14—THURSDAY
Loving One Another

Be kindly affectionate to one another with brotherly love, in honor giving preference to one another; not lagging in diligence, fervent in spirit, serving the Lord; rejoicing in hope, patient in tribulation, continuing steadfastly in prayer; distributing to the needs of the saints, given to hospitality.

ROMANS 12:10–13

Have you ever heard this funny little rhyme? "To dwell above with the saints we love—that will indeed be glory. To dwell below with the saints we know? Well, that's a different story."

Relationship fender-benders are impossible to avoid, even within the family of God. That truth is exactly why God gave us the following instructions for how we are to serve the Lord and others in His church.

- **"Be kindly affectionate to one another."** We are family, so tenderness and kindness should characterize our relationships.
- **Give honor.** Respect one another. Tell people how much you value them. Listen to them and place their preferences above your own.
- **Persevere.** Relationships are hard work, and so is prayer. Paul instructs, "continuing steadfastly in prayer." Praying for and with others is transformational.
- **Love Others.** Don't be stingy; be generous. You have received God's limitless love and grace, and you are to share love and grace with others.

....

Lord, thank You for the unconditional love You give me. Help me to love others the ways You love, to love sacrificially, to love not just with words, but with actions. Jesus, love others through me. Amen.

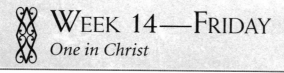

Week 14—Friday
One in Christ

I, therefore, the prisoner of the Lord, beseech you to walk worthy of the calling with which you were called, with all lowliness and gentleness, with longsuffering, bearing with one another in love, endeavoring to keep the unity of the Spirit in the bond of peace.

Ephesians 4:1–3

Unity is critical. When we believers are unified in the cause of Christ, we can do great things through His power. When we believers are not unified, we can't do very much; we find ourselves powerless.

Jesus Christ is the One who unifies us. We, His followers, are bound together by our commitment to one Lord, one faith, one baptism. It is our common belief that Jesus alone is Savior and Lord. We publicly profess this belief through believer's baptism.

Jesus prayed for His followers to be one (John 17:21). The closer we move to Jesus, the closer we will be to one another. A picture will clarify: think of your relationship with other believers as represented by the bottom points of a triangle. The point at the top of the triangle represents Jesus. The closer we believers move toward Jesus, the closer we get to each other. The closer we are to Christ, the more Christlike we will be. Our passage today mentions the Christlike traits of "lowliness and gentleness, with longsuffering." Our closeness will result in Jesus' character being displayed in our lives.

. . . .

Jesus, thank You for what You did in Your death and resurrection that unites me with You and other members of Your family. I want to move closer to You today—and stay close. I love You, Lord. Amen.

Week 14—Weekend
A Basic Human Need

That their hearts may be encouraged, being knit together in love, and attaining to all riches of the full assurance of understanding, to the knowledge of the mystery of God, both of the Father and of Christ.

COLOSSIANS 2:2

A Japanese proverb goes, "One encouraging word can warm up three winter months." Mr. Truett Cathy, the founder of Chick-fil-A restaurants, once said, "Do you know who needs encouragement? Anyone who is breathing!"

All of us need encouragement. Too many of our fellow human beings are starving and thirsting for encouragement. Maybe that one is you today? There is good news just like a discovered oasis in a parched desert, and this is it: God has provided the encouragement we need! He saved us through His Son and gave the Holy Spirit to come alongside us as the Encourager. He has placed us in His body, the church, where—our scripture today says—we are "being knit together in love." What a beautiful picture of the love and encouragement found in Christ. There is nothing like being in God's family.

God has brought us believers together, and He is the glue that holds us together. As He holds us, we share His love and submit to His Word—and the result is overflowing encouragement! And you may have realized that nothing encourages you more than when you are encouraging someone else. They are easy to find, for if they are breathing, they are a candidate for encouragement.

....

Lord, thank You for encouraging me! Help me see around me those people who need Your encouragement. Thank You for Your indwelling Spirit who encourages me and who enables me to encourage others. In Jesus' name, amen.

WEEK 15—MONDAY
God, Our Stronghold

The LORD is good, a stronghold in the day of trouble; and He knows those who trust in Him.

NAHUM 1:7

Are you sometimes frustrated that God seems to sit idly by while the wicked prosper, perhaps even at your expense? Questions about apparent unfairness plague all of us at times. Understanding, however, that God sees our faithfulness in those times is a real comfort.

Though the book of Nahum is largely unfamiliar, understanding it as a sequel to the Old Testament book of Jonah is helpful. After withholding His judgment due to Nineveh's repentance, God announced the city's destruction through Nahum because of the people's return to wickedness. This pronouncement of justice was a great encouragement to fearful Jews who trembled at the Assyrians' cruelty. In fact, it was the outcome Jonah had hoped for when he preached in Nineveh.

In this context, we see that people who are troubled, afraid, and oppressed find God a stronghold of protection. Though God often delays His judgment toward those who might hurt us (as He did in the book of Jonah), we should never interpret His delayed mercy as approval of injustice. God will avenge His children later rather than sooner (as we see in the words of Nahum). God knows that you are trusting Him and seeking to live according to His Word. The mystery that sometimes surrounds God's timing and decisions should never diminish our confidence in Him. God sees things as they really are, and we can trust Him fully to make things right at some point.

....

Lord, help me to trust You when others hurt me. Give me the wisdom to accept that Your timing never diminishes Your holiness or justice. Help me rejoice when my enemies repent and grieve when they do not. Amen.

DR. ADAM DOOLEY, SUNNYVALE FIRST BAPTIST CHURCH, MESQUITE, TX

Give us help from trouble, for the help of man is useless. Through God we will do valiantly, for it is He who shall tread down our enemies.

PSALM 60:11–12

Have you ever felt like God was your only way out of a bad situation? Maybe it was a relationship that only He could repair. Perhaps your reputation was unfairly maligned.

During a time of confusion and despair, King David realized that God was the only solution for the trial facing the nation of Israel. Interpreting a setback in battle as being forsaken by God, the Jews realized that—apart from divine intervention—they had no hope. Most of us can relate.

We might not verbalize that God abandoned us, but hardship and adversity can make us feel that way in our hearts, especially when people mistreat us. Sometimes what we see as evidence of God forsaking us, however, may actually be an opportunity to come to know Him better and trust Him more.

The notion that God is our last resort when life falls apart implies that we have other options when our circumstances are less difficult. This is false. Even on good days, we are no less dependent on God than our worst day requires. The only difference is that we are painfully more aware of our need in times of desperation. God does not change, even though our challenges and the people around us do.

....

Father, help me to see every hardship I face as an opportunity to know You better and trust You more. Teach me to trust You always—not only when it seems no one else can help me. Likewise, help me to depend on You when it seems as though I can handle everything on my own. Amen.

Week 15—Wednesday
Feeling Forsaken

Unless the LORD had been my help, my soul would soon have settled in silence. If I say, "My foot slips," Your mercy, O LORD, will hold me up. In the multitude of my anxieties within me, Your comforts delight my soul.

PSALM 94:17–19

God will never give you more than you can bear. I heard those words dozens of times after my son was diagnosed with leukemia. While the thought is good, the reality is exactly the opposite: God often gives us much more than we can bear so that we will turn to Him. Knowing God as our Burden Bearer is impossible unless we find ourselves with heavy burdens. These times are difficult, but God is more real to us when they come.

The psalmist experienced this reality when he reached the point of death. The word *silence* refers to a place for the dead, and God is the only One who prevents such tragedy. Knowing that the Lord will hold us up in times of trouble is the assurance we need to survive life's heartbreaking moments.

God will calm your anxieties and comfort your soul, but experiencing such mercy usually occurs against the backdrop of heartache. Our need to endure trials without receiving relief, however, does not mean God has forsaken us. To the contrary, it means He is investing in us. Each time God catches our slipping feet, we understand more of His mercy, and we feel His deep love for us.

....

Father, thank You for holding me up when burdens are heavy. Please release Your comfort in my life. Free me from my sinful desire to be in control and help me to rest in You. Enable me to see every trial as an opportunity to know You better. Amen.

DR. ADAM DOOLEY, SUNNYVALE FIRST BAPTIST CHURCH, MESQUITE, TX

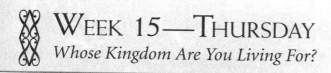

WEEK 15—THURSDAY
Whose Kingdom Are You Living For?

Seek first the kingdom of God and His righteousness, and all these things shall be added to you. Therefore do not worry about tomorrow, for tomorrow will worry about its own things. Sufficient for the day is its own trouble.

MATTHEW 6:33–34

What are your priorities? Before answering too quickly, consider the context of these popular words from Jesus. What are "these things" God promises to give each of us if we will seek His kingdom before anything else?

Matthew 6:25 reveals that we worry about food, health, and clothing because we don't trust God to provide these things. Furthermore, we often seek wealth to the detriment of our faith (v. 24), and that focus increases our anxiety over material things. And even though the future is not in our hands, building a life of ease or abundance becomes our ambition. In other words, we desire our kingdom more than we desire God's.

Despite our efforts to treat it as a lesser sin, worry is explicit evidence that we are not seeking God's agenda above all else. At its heart, anxiety is wrestling for control with the God who desires that we yield our spending habits, work ethic, goals for the future, thought patterns, and every other area of our lives to Him.

When we surrender to God's wisdom and plans, we choose to face the challenges of each day with confidence that He will meet every legitimate need that concerns us. Trust Him today. Focus on His will rather than your desires. Refuse to let worry steal the joy of walking with God.

Lord, I realize that my anxieties reveal my lack of trust in You. Forgive me— and increase my faith. Help me live each day for Your kingdom, not my own. Amen.

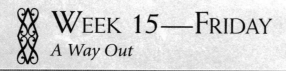

WEEK 15—FRIDAY
A Way Out

When you pass through the waters, I will be with you; and through the rivers, they shall not overflow you. When you walk through the fire, you shall not be burned, nor shall the flame scorch you. For I am the LORD your God, the Holy One of Israel, your Savior.

ISAIAH 43:2–3

Although God first spoke these words to the Israelites, this promise provides sure footing for all Christ-followers. Contextually, we have good reason to believe that many of Israel's troubles came in the form of God's discipline when His people turned away—and He can do the same today. The hope of this promise, however, applies to every trial or difficulty we encounter, whatever its cause.

Surely Isaiah's words evoked memories of God's mighty deliverance of Israel from the past. The "waters" and "rivers" are likely references to the Red Sea and Jordan River crossings. Walking "through the fire," knowing the flame will not "scorch you," brings to mind Shadrach, Meshach, and Abed-Nego. Regardless of how He provides, the point is that God always takes care of His people. He may not prevent or remove our troubles. God will, however, prove Himself faithful, not by taking our burdens away, but by walking every step of them with us. Even in the valley of the shadow of death, God promises to remain by our side (Psalm 23:4).

Real faith requires that we not only seek God for relief, but that we also rely on Him when we need endurance. Seeking a way out is fine. Seeking a way through with God's help is better. Only then do we really appreciate the permanency of His provision in our lives.

....

Father, forgive me for doubting Your love when bad things happen. Please grow my endurance when trials come. Thank You for never leaving me. Amen.

DR. ADAM DOOLEY, SUNNYVALE FIRST BAPTIST CHURCH, MESQUITE, TX

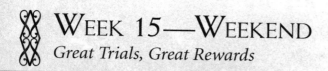

WEEK 15—WEEKEND
Great Trials, Great Rewards

Though I walk in the midst of trouble, You will revive me; You will stretch out Your hand against the wrath of my enemies, and Your right hand will save me. The LORD will perfect that which concerns me; Your mercy, O LORD, endures forever; do not forsake the works of Your hands.

PSALM 138:7–8

We can't be sure when or why David wrote this psalm, but his words still resonate with us, particularly when hard times come.

The notion that Christianity is a trouble-free faith could not be further from the truth. Our hope therefore is not the absence of trauma, but that we will be aware of God's presence when trouble comes. He promises to revive us, protect us, and, at times, save us from hardship.

Furthermore, God will "perfect" what concerns us: He will fulfill His purpose for the suffering we face by working it for good (Romans 8:28). That's why the greatest rewards in our walk with God often come during what we perceive to be the worst circumstances of our lives. He does not "forsake the works of [His] hands," and He works to bring beauty out of your pain. The question is not "Will He succeed?" but rather "Will you trust Him until He finishes?"

David reminded us that God is all we need regardless of how much our heart aches. Even when injustice continues or heartbreak lingers, you can trust that God will one day restore what is lost. Present pain cannot rob you of eternal reward.

....

Father, I am weak and often afraid. When I don't understand what You allow in my life, help me to trust why You put it there. Use every burden I face to accomplish the eternal purpose You have for me. Amen.

WEEK 16—MONDAY
God Always Knows Best

"For My thoughts are not your thoughts, nor are your ways My ways," says the LORD.
"For as the heavens are higher than the earth, so are My ways higher than your ways,
and My thoughts than your thoughts."

ISAIAH 55:8–9

The prophet Isaiah referred to Jesus Christ as the Suffering Servant, and that title definitely fits. Jesus paid the highest price possible for the sins of the world when He died on the cross as the perfect sacrifice for your sins and mine. What God did through His Son on Calvary that day is the greatest picture of how God's ways are so different from and so much higher than our ways. Our Sovereign God truly is incomprehensible. He went to amazingly great lengths to enable us to know Him and be in fellowship with Him.

We often don't understand what is happening in our lives. After all, we can only look at circumstances with our very limited vision, So when, in your pursuit of God and as you seek to do His will, you don't understand what He is doing in your life or why, what should you do? Choose to believe that God is always working His good plan in your life in His good timing. Choose to trust God: He is forever faithful to do what is best for you, even when you don't know what is best for yourself.

....

You, O Lord, are truly incomprehensible. You alone know life from beginning
to end, and You know what is best for me. I am choosing to trust You. Amen.

DR. RONNIE FLOYD, CROSS CHURCH, NORTHWEST ARKANSAS

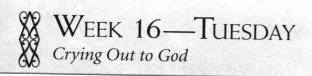

WEEK 16—TUESDAY
Crying Out to God

Attend to me, and hear me; I am restless in my complaint, and moan noisily.

PSALM 55:2

In this psalm, David poured out to the Lord his feelings about all he was going through at the time. As he shared his heart with God, he pleaded with God to listen to him. David was desperate, perhaps even feeling a deep sense of personal betrayal. He needed God to hear him, be compassionate, and answer him. So David told God openly and unashamedly of his agony, of "the terrors of death . . . fearfulness . . . and horror" that had overwhelmed him (vv. 4–5). David was begging God to hear him and bring down the treacherous enemies who want to kill him.

Although the circumstances will be different, from time to time in life, all of us feel as desperate as David. We sense the enemy, Satan, knocking on the door. We fear that destruction lurks just around the corner. We even doubt God, His goodness, His power, His love. When this happens, call out to God nevertheless. When He hears his children desperately call out to Him, He responds as any parent would. He will hear you, and He will do something about your situation. Therefore, do not be bashful, but call out as He desires. Admit your weakness. Affirm His greatness. There, at your point of desperation, your Almighty God, your heavenly Father, will meet you.

. . . .

Lord, I cry out to You today as I never have before. Hear me! I need You. I want You. Much is upon me. Help me, Jesus, now! Amen.

WEEK 16—WEDNESDAY
Returning to God

Come, and let us return to the LORD; for He has torn, but He will heal us; He has stricken, but He will bind us up. After two days He will revive us; on the third day He will raise us up, that we may live in His sight.

HOSEA 6:1–2

God is always calling His people back to Him. At times God's sovereign plan involves us walking through times of great difficulty and pain, and we may wonder if that season will ever end. When we don't sense God's presence with us—when He seems distant—we may find ourselves wandering away from His path, desperate for relief or escape. We need to remember that His invitation to return to Him is always there. He welcomes us back, ready to help us live in His will.

Wherever you may be in your walk with God today, however far you have strayed from His path, He is calling you to return to Him. He always wants you to come back to Him. So many Christ-followers miss out on joy because of the burdens they carry from past sins and damaged relationships. Remember, all that was nailed to the cross. Everything was settled there on Calvary once and for all. There He heals you and puts you back together. Be encouraged today: He is able to give you life again.

....

Gracious God, thank You for always being there, waiting for me. I commit myself to being all You want me to be. I want to know the abundant life available only in You! Amen.

DR. RONNIE FLOYD, CROSS CHURCH, NORTHWEST ARKANSAS

WEEK 16—THURSDAY
Trusting God at All Times

As for God, His way is perfect; the word of the LORD is proven; He is a shield to all who trust in Him. For who is God, except the LORD? And who is a rock, except our God? It is God who arms me with strength, and makes my way perfect.

PSALM 18:30–32

We have reminded ourselves this week that God's ways are much higher than our ways. Today's passage adds that God's way is complete. When we place our faith Him, He acts as our shield, our defense, and our rock. No one can compare! He strengthens us and makes our way complete. Since He is all of this and more, the Lord Almighty is a sure foundation for all of life.

We can trust the Lord completely and at all times, and an aspect of that trust is believing that He has a way for us. God rises up and protects us. No person and not the enemy himself can enter our lives unless our Sovereign Lord permits that entrance.

So trust God always. Let Him strengthen you as you walk in His way. Let Him shape you into the more Christlike person He wants you to be. There is no one like our God, and you can trust Him.

....

O Lord, I trust You right now with everything. Where else can I turn? Why would I even want to turn away from You? I know You love me. I know You are always working for good in my life. Amen.

Week 16—Friday
No Need to Be Afraid

Fear not, for I am with you; be not dismayed, for I am your God. I will strengthen you, yes, I will help you, I will uphold you with My righteous right hand.

Isaiah 41:10

Isaiah 41:10 is one of the most encouraging verses in Scripture. Read it again and marvel at the truth that, with God on your side, there is no reason for you to ever walk in fear. There is also no reason to look elsewhere for protection, help, or strength. Look to God! Gaze on Him! He is with you at all times. He strengthens His people when we look to Him. He will always be our Helper. He promises to hold on to us and do whatever is right for us.

So let go of whatever reason for discouragement or fear you have held on to. There is no need for you to be discouraged. Fear no longer needs to plague your life. Why? Because God is with you at all times. He will strengthen you when you are tired and weary. He will always be there to help you. In those moments when you may want to quit and run the other way, remember that He has you in His hands and will never let go of you.

Do not be afraid. God is with you

....

In the name of Jesus, I come to You, Father, praying, believing, confident that You are with me and that I can know Your strength as well as Your peace. Amen.

DR. RONNIE FLOYD, CROSS CHURCH, NORTHWEST ARKANSAS

WEEK 16—WEEKEND
"Now No Condemnation"

There is therefore now no condemnation to those who are in Christ Jesus, who do not walk according to the flesh, but according to the Spirit. For the law of the Spirit of life in Christ Jesus has made me free from the law of sin and death.

ROMANS 8:1–2

Romans 1–7 overflows with wonderful gospel truths about Jesus Christ, our Savior and Lord. The truths we find there launch us forward in life without any condemnation at all. Because of Jesus' death and resurrection, we are no longer guilty of our sin: we have been forgiven. Jesus has given us this new life free of condemnation for our sins. We now walk led by the Holy Spirit. The gospel of Jesus Christ has set us free.

Are you living as if you believe these truths? You can. Choose to believe what God says about removing your sin "as far as the east is from the west" (Psalm 103:12). Firmly refuse to carry any guilt or condemnation. Whatever its source, reject it. The Lord Jesus and His gospel have set you free from sin and its consequences, free from any guilt or condemnation. From this point on, fully believe this fact. Look to the Holy Spirit who is in you, who now guides you to live like God wants you to live. And God wants you to live free of all condemnation!

....

Dear Lord, keep me mindful that I am free of guilt and condemnation for the sins I committed, for the sins You've forgiven. Enable me to refuse false condemnation. Enable me to live empowered and led by Your Holy Spirit. Amen.

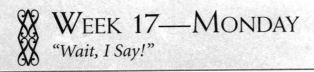
Wait on the LORD; be of good courage, and He shall strengthen your heart; wait, I say, on the LORD!

PSALM 27:14

Judging by the way most of us go through our days about our daily assignments, I think we all need to slow down! It does seem as though each day passes by at Mach speed as you and I travel in the fast lane! In our world of "instant everything," we seem to believe that God is actually in the same hurry we find ourselves in. No, my friend, He certainly is not. Besides, He knows the end from the beginning, and He has His perfectly-timed plan for us firmly in the grasp of His loving care.

A glass of water taken from a flowing river will be cloudy and murky. If you let it sit long enough, the sediment will settle to the bottom, and you can clearly see through the water. Sitting before the Lord and waiting on Him will allow the cloudiness of a hurried life to settle. Then you will more clearly see what God wants you to do. It takes courage to wait, but God tells us that He will strengthen us in every way as we wait on Him.

....

Most gracious heavenly Father, I bow before You in humble submission to all You have planned for me. Please help me to slow down and wait on You. In Jesus' name I pray, amen.

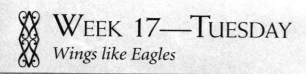
But those who wait on the LORD shall renew their strength; they shall mount up with wings like eagles, they shall run and not be weary, they shall walk and not faint.

ISAIAH 40:31

Consider the children of Israel for a minute. They were certainly experiencing all that life had to offer. One minute they were up, and the next they were down. They may have lived thousands of years ago, but like them, we face challenges that appear insurmountable at first glance. And sometimes dealing with these hurdles chips away at our resolve, making us feel weary, as if we can no longer continue.

Isaiah's words offer a powerful solution, calling for patience and prayer. We must be willing to persevere and be prayerful in order that God might bless us with the infusing of His magnificent strength. God promises to enable us to fly like an eagle, to run without becoming weary, and to walk through this life free from spiritual exhaustion.

....

My God, I want to thank You for all You do for me by the might and power of Your Holy Spirit in me. I need You every hour. At times I feel weak and helpless. Thank You for giving me patience today in spite of the challenges set before me. In Jesus' name, amen.

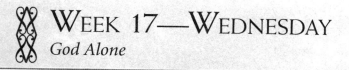

WEEK 17—WEDNESDAY
God Alone

My soul, wait silently for God alone, for my expectation is from Him. He only is my rock and my salvation; He is my defense; I shall not be moved. In God is my salvation and my glory; the rock of my strength, and my refuge, is in God.

PSALM 62:5–7

We can learn from the psalmist who addressed his own soul. Wisely, he understood the benefits that come from prudent introspection.

What God really wants us to know is that during the process of continual self-assessment, we must make sure our worship of Him is supported down at the very point of our salvation. As our Rock, God alone is our sure foundation for life. And because He lies at the very heart of our lives, we can rejoice in being steadfast, able to stand firm regardless of what comes our way.

Thank God heartily that you have given your life to Jesus and that He owns your soul as Savior. What a joyful thing to know!

....

Dear God, by Your Holy Spirit, I affirm my salvation in You and through You. Because You are my fortress, I shall not waver, and "I shall not be moved." I take my stand on You, my Rock, as I journey through life. In Jesus' name I pray, amen.

DR. DON WILTON, FIRST BAPTIST CHURCH, SPARTANBURG, SC

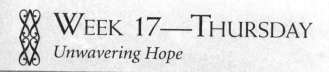

WEEK 17—THURSDAY
Unwavering Hope

Let us hold fast the confession of our hope without wavering, for He who promised is faithful. And let us consider one another in order to stir up love and good works.

HEBREWS 10:23–24

This great passage of Scripture reveals something profound—God's promises are absolutely reliable in every way. And central to His promises is the absolute assurance that salvation is for all time and all eternity. What gives us hope and strength is not our own self-reliance or thinking we can earn our salvation, but rather God's seal of salvation in us through His Holy Spirit. Despite all we may face in this world, remember that God is faithful to His word—and to us. Encourage others today as you stir up love and good works as outward manifestations of God's faithfulness.

Dear God, I thank You for the promise of my eternal security in You. I am so grateful that, because You are faithful and true, I can rely on You for anything and everything. I thank You that You hold me in the palm of Your hand and that nothing can pluck me from that spot of safety and security. Regardless of my circumstances I will strive "to stir up love and good works" as my response to Your grace. In Jesus' name I pray, amen.

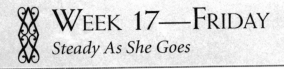

WEEK 17—FRIDAY
Steady As She Goes

We have become partakers of Christ if we hold the beginning of our confidence steadfast to the end.

HEBREWS 3:14

My grandfather, Captain Roderick Murdo McDonald, sailed the seas all his life. Like every sea captain, he knew what it meant to say, "Steady as she goes," especially when the seas threatened the lives of all on board the ship. The writer to the Hebrews reminded all believers that we can have every confidence in Christ no matter how vicious the storm that rages around us.

Salvation in Christ brings God's stamp of eternal security and makes it possible for all to have confidence in what happens at the end of our earthly existence. Abiding in Christ, regardless of what life offers, is the ultimate evidence of a life that has become one with Christ through His death, burial, and glorious resurrection from the grave. Remaining steadily true to the Lord confirms the authenticity of a person's relationship with Him and serves as a wonderful beacon of hope in the midst of a lost and dying world.

....

Precious God and heavenly Father, I thank You for saving me from my sin in and through Jesus Christ. As I journey through life, I will remain faithful to You because You are the Lord of my life. I am Your servant and belong to You. My life is in Your hands. In Jesus' name, amen.

DR. DON WILTON, FIRST BAPTIST CHURCH, SPARTANBURG, SC

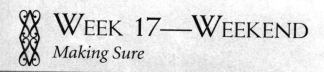

WEEK 17—WEEKEND
Making Sure

Beware, brethren, lest there be in any of you an evil heart of unbelief in departing from the living God; but exhort one another daily, while it is called "Today," lest any of you be hardened through the deceitfulness of sin. For we have become partakers of Christ if we hold the beginning of our confidence steadfast to the end.

HEBREWS 3:12–14

With the Great Commission (Matthew 28:18–20), Jesus sent all believers out into the lost and dying world to share the good news that Jesus died for our sins, was buried, and then, by the power of God, was raised from the grave. No one who believes in Jesus' name will die for eternity because He gave His life as a ransom.

Although Jesus' death did pay the ransom, we are still reminded in this passage to be careful not to deceive ourselves through our own sin and actually end up not living lives pleasing to the Lord. One way to know for sure where we stand is to examine our own steadfastness truthfully. Are we only faithful when things are going well for us? If we are fair-weather Christians, then we will have trouble finding our footing on shaky ground. The key is to stand firm until the end, regardless of our circumstances.

....

Gracious God, create in me a clean heart and show me any sin I should repent of before You. I do repent with all my heart. You are my Savior. Amen.

Week 18—Monday
The Great Escape

No temptation has overtaken you except such as is common to man; but God is faithful, who will not allow you to be tempted beyond what you are able, but with the temptation will also make the way of escape, that you may be able to bear it.

1 Corinthians 10:13

Every person is tempted. Whatever temptation we face, others have faced before us. Even Jesus was tempted. If the devil tempted the very Son of God, he will tempt you, too! Temptation is not a sin. Yielding to that temptation to do wrong is sin.

Paul was constantly tested and tempted, but God was faithful to provide a "way of escape." God knows our limitations, strengths, and weaknesses. He know how much pressure we can bear, and He will always provide an exit!

We can count on Satan's tempting, but we can also count on God's faithfulness. Daniel was tempted, but he refused to compromise (Daniel 1:8). Joseph was tempted, but he ran (Genesis 39:11–12). What are we to do? Here are five steps:

Feed on the Word of God.

Flee youthful lust and do not toy with or persist in sin.

Fight the devil. This *is* a spiritual battle.

Fellowship with the right people and stay away from the wrong crowd.

Follow our Lord's example and say, "Get behind Me, Satan!" Reject in the name of Jesus thoughts, attitudes, and feelings that do not please God.

....

Lord, help me look for the "way of escape" when I am tempted to do wrong. Thank You that You are faithful to provide a way out in every circumstance.

WEEK 18—TUESDAY
Walking in the Spirit Versus Walking in the Flesh

Walk in the Spirit, and you shall not fulfill the lust of the flesh. For the flesh lusts against the Spirit, and the Spirit against the flesh; and these are contrary to one another, so that you do not do the things that you wish. But if you are led by the Spirit, you are not under the law.

GALATIANS 5:16–18

The word *flesh* refers to our carnal nature. It is also called the "old man" or the "natural man." Romans 7:18 says that "in me (that is, in my flesh) nothing good dwells." We are born with this fallen, depraved nature, but when we are born again, we receive a new nature called the "new man" or the "spiritual man."

Within every believer are these two natures (good and evil) that are in constant conflict. How do we know when we are walking in the flesh? Galatians 5:19–21 describes the work of the flesh as "adultery, fornication, uncleanness, lewdness, idolatry, sorcery, hatred, contentions, jealousies, outburst of wrath, selfish ambitions, dissensions, heresies, envy, murders, drunkenness, revelries, and the like."

How do we know if we are walking in the Spirit? Galatians 5:22–23 says, "The fruit of the Spirit is love, joy, peace, longsuffering, kindness, goodness, faithfulness, gentleness, self-control."

If you have been redeemed, you have been set free. You are no longer a slave to sin. Still, every day you must yield to the lordship of Jesus Christ. Pray the Holy Spirit will lead, guide, and direct you as you walk through the day.

....

Lord, thank You that You have set me free from sin! Lead, guide, and direct me throughout this day, and as I follow You, may the fruit of Your Spirit be evident in my life.

Week 18—Wednesday
The Blame Game

Blessed is the man who endures temptation; for when he has been approved, he will receive the crown of life which the Lord has promised to those who love Him. Let no one say when he is tempted, "I am tempted by God"; for God cannot be tempted by evil, nor does He Himself tempt anyone.

James 1:12–13

I read about this guy who prayed, "Lord, so far today, I haven't lost my temper, gossiped, been greedy or grumpy or selfish. I haven't complained or cursed. But in a minute I have to get out of this bed—and I need all the help I can get!"

Every day we are tempted to do all those things our still-in-bed friend listed—and more. Yet the Bible makes it clear that we are not to play the blame game when it comes to our sin. Today, people blame their environment, parents, teachers, and genetics. We either try to justify our sin, or we simply don't want to take responsibility for it. However, each of us is totally responsible for our own behavior.

The devil knows what bait or hook to use for each one of us. James 1:14 explains that we are "drawn away" by our own lust. The real problem is not external; it is the heart.

I've heard people say, "But, Preacher, God knows my heart." You're right, but to suggest that you know your heart is wrong. Jeremiah said that the heart is so wicked no man can know it (17:9).

Remember, God is not the cause of sin, but He is the cure.

....

Lord, I confess that my heart is sinful. Please forgive me. Help me to remember that You are not the one tempting me, but You are the solution to my sin problem.

DR. GRANT ETHRIDGE, LIBERTY BAPTIST CHURCH, HAMPTON, VA / SUFFOLK, VA

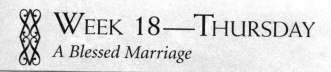

WEEK 18—THURSDAY
A Blessed Marriage

Drink water from your own cistern, and running water from your own well. Should your fountains be dispersed abroad, streams of water in the streets? Let them be only your own, and not for strangers with you. Let your fountain be blessed, and rejoice with the wife of your youth.

PROVERBS 5:15–18

Not one of us would be here if it weren't for sex. Sex is the plan of our holy God. He—the Author of all life—created us male and female. If you believe God is pro-life, then you must believe that God is pro-sex!

So how did sex become taboo, repulsive, and dirty? The fall perverted everything. Satan tries to get you to have sex before marriage, and then he does everything he can to keep you from having sex with your spouse after marriage. Biblical sex is not for a man and a man or for a woman and a woman. It is also not between any man and any woman. Sex is for a husband and wife. Sex outside of marriage is sin.

Sex is not something to be endured, but something to be enjoyed. Nothing bonds a couple in oneness like sex. They are united physically, chemically, emotionally, and spiritually. God's plan is one couple, living in one house, sleeping in one bed, attending one church, worshipping the one true God.

If you don't want to fall down, don't walk in slippery places. You should never seek sex or offer it to anyone other than your spouse. Guard your eyes from all temptation. Keep all the vows you made on your wedding day. A God-honoring marriage is exciting and fulfilling.

....

Lord, help me to honor You and honor my spouse. Thank You that marriage, the way You designed it, is exciting and fulfilling.

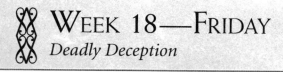

Whoever commits adultery with a woman lacks understanding; he who does so destroys his own soul. Wounds and dishonor he will get, and his reproach will not be wiped away. For jealousy is a husband's fury; therefore he will not spare in the day of vengeance. He will accept no recompense, nor will he be appeased though you give many gifts.

PROVERBS 6:32–35

Are you living a secret life of sin? Of porn? Or involvement with a co-worker? Stop immediately and fight for your marriage!

If you've had an affair, come clean. Expect your spouse to be angry. It will take time to gain back trust. Cut off all ties with the other person and ask your mate what boundaries he or she would like you to establish and honor. Do whatever it takes to rebuild trust! Your marriage is worth it.

If you are the innocent party, remember that you have imperfections. Admit the specific ways in which you are responsible for letting the marriage become dull. Tell your spouse, "I love you" every day and in every way. Get to know each other all over again.

David committed adultery. His affair led to a pregnancy, a murder, and the death of his child. Yet David is remembered as "a man after God's own heart." People can change; you can forgive.

Realize that, in this case, the grass looks greener on the other side of the fence because a septic tank is leaking over there. If that grass looks greener, start watering your own grass! *If you don't have an ongoing affair with your spouse, someone else will.*

....

Lord, help me to love and honor my spouse like You want me to. Help me to say "I love you" every day and in every way.

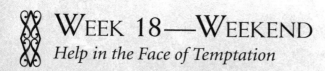

WEEK 18—WEEKEND
Help in the Face of Temptation

Keep my commands and live, and my law as the apple of your eye. Bind them on your fingers; write them on the tablet of your heart. Say to wisdom, "You are my sister," and call understanding your nearest kin, that they may keep you from the immoral woman, from the seductress who flatters with her words.

PROVERBS 7:2–5

All adults face sexual temptation, often in the form of pornography. If you bring pornography into your marriage, you are essentially bringing in another person—a real person with a soul—not some object on a screen.

Temptation often begins with the eyes. Our response to it reveals our heart. These three steps can help us stand strong:

Scripture: We hide God's Word in our heart—so that we "might not sin against [Him]" (Psalm 119:11). There is power in the Word. Jesus quoted Scripture to overcome Satan, beginning each time with "It is written."

Separation: Avoid places, movies, or shows that advocate immorality. Never travel alone. Have your computer screen facing the door. Give your passwords to a family member. This is war! Deal with sin swiftly, or it will destroy you.

Salvation: Overcoming sexual addiction takes more than willpower and more than promising you will never do it again. It will take Jesus. He who began a good work will continue it until the day of Jesus Christ (Philippians 1:6).

. . . .

Lord, help me memorize Your Word, separate myself from temptation, and look to You for help overcoming my sin.

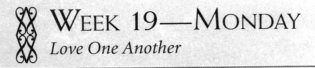

WEEK 19—MONDAY
Love One Another

"A new commandment I give to you, that you love one another; as I have loved you, that you also love one another. By this all will know that you are My disciples, if you have love for one another."

JOHN 13:34–35

Outward symbols are no indication of a true follower of Jesus Christ. The attitudes of our heart—that has been transformed by the redeeming grace of God—are what reveal that we are His children. This inner transformation results in a changed life, the external fruit of which is seen in a believer's words, attitudes, and actions. At its most basic level, this fruit can be summed up in one word: love!

In one sense, the Lord's charge to the eleven apostles was not new: God has called for obedience from His people since the garden of Eden. This commandment was new, however, in the sense that it presented a higher standard of love, one based on the example of Christ Himself whose ultimate act of love was dying on the cross for sinful human beings. Remember that this call to love is not an option, but a commandment.

"Because the love of God has been poured out in our hearts by the Holy Spirit who was given to us" (Romans 5:5), believers can love as Jesus commanded. The impact is that all humanity will know the power of God's love. Because God's love has transformed believers' hearts, they are able to extend His love to others. If the church consistently loved as Jesus loved, that love would have a powerful impact on our lost and sin-filled world.

Lord God, give me the ability to love as Jesus loved, with compassion, grace, and forgiveness. May His love flow through me to others. In Jesus' name, amen.

DR. ROB ZINN, IMMANUEL BAPTIST CHURCH, HIGHLAND, CA

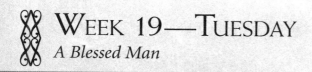

A good man deals graciously and lends; he will guide his affairs with discretion. Surely he will never be shaken; the righteous will be in everlasting remembrance. He will not be afraid of evil tidings; his heart is steadfast, trusting in the LORD.

PSALM 112:5–7

Our passage describes a blessed man, one who loves God, loves His Word, and seeks to obey what the Lord commands him to do. I have often said that the hardest thing to do as a Christian is to obey God, and yet the easiest thing to do is obey God—as soon as you decide He *is* God.

Today's passage pays tribute to those "good" individuals who are gracious, generous, and compassionate, who live justly and carefully. The results of living like this, of living God's way, are threefold: you "will never be shaken" because you are trusting the Lord's plan for your life. You will be remembered forever because of your faith in God. And you are not afraid of what you might hear because your heart is fixed in the Lord and you are trusting Him with every aspect of your life.

Have you come to the understanding that what matters at the end of your days is not what you did, but what the Lord did through you? God is faithful, and you can trust Him! Surrender to His Word and His will and be blessed! Be fruitful and know that God has your best interest in His heart.

. . . .

Lord, help me be generous, not selfish. Help me remember it is more blessed to give than to receive. In Jesus' name, amen.

WEEK 19—WEDNESDAY
To Obey Is Better . . .

It shall be that if you earnestly obey My commandments which I command you today, to love the LORD your God and serve Him with all your heart and with all your soul, then I will give you the rain for your land in its season."

DEUTERONOMY 11:13–14

I am reminded of what Samuel said to King Saul: "Has the LORD as much delight in burnt offerings and sacrifices as in obeying the voice of the LORD? Behold, to obey is better than sacrifice" (1 Samuel 15:22 NASB).

During my ministry I've noticed an odd thing: many people are a lot more willing to do things they believe are a sacrifice ("I'll sacrifice the football game and go to church") than to simply do what God tells them to do. Realize, though, that God doesn't bless effort; He blesses obedience. Sunday is not a time to "sacrifice" watching a football game; Sunday is a time for "Let's go to church and worship the Lord with His people." Likewise, it's not, "I have to give," but rather "I want to give."

Yet we human beings want all of God's blessings at no cost. But God promises His blessings to those who obey. Jesus said, "If you love Me, keep My commandments" (John 14:15). My heart to yours—to love Jesus is not to be a sacrifice but a joy, and the more you fall in love with the Lord, the easier it will be for you to do what He says.

....

Lord, give me an obedient heart. Teach me that Thy will is better than my will. I yearn to love and please You. In Jesus' name, amen.

DR. ROB ZINN, IMMANUEL BAPTIST CHURCH, HIGHLAND, CA

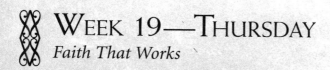

WEEK 19—THURSDAY
Faith That Works

What does it profit, my brethren, if someone says he has faith but does not have works? Can faith save him? If a brother or sister is naked and destitute of daily food, and one of you says to them, "Depart in peace, be warmed and filled," but you do not give them the things which are needed for the body, what does it profit?

JAMES 2:14–18

A basic question about Christianity is "Are you saved by faith or works?"—and the answer is "Yes!"

There is no contradiction between James 2 (above) and Ephesians 2:8–9, "For by grace you have been saved through faith, and that not of yourselves; it is the gift of God, not of works, lest anyone should boast." The simple and great truth is that genuine faith produces genuine works! If your faith in Jesus is something you only talk about, that faith is dead. As James emphasized, the Word of God teaches that what we do reveals who we are.

A true disciple of Christ will obey His commands: "He who has My commandments and keeps them, it is he who loves Me" (John 14:21). A continually disobedient life is proof of false discipleship and dead faith: "He who does not love Me does not keep My words" (v. 24). Head knowledge about God or the Bible won't save you. How we live proves who we are—or are not—in God's sight. The faith that the Lord graciously gives His people will always manifest itself in good deeds.

....

Lord, may my faith shine through my life in what I do and say. In Jesus' name, amen.

May these words of mine, with which I have made supplication before the LORD, be near the LORD our God day and night, that He may maintain the cause of His servant and the cause of His people Israel, as each day may require, that all the peoples of the earth may know that the LORD is God; there is no other.

1 KINGS 8:59–60

Solomon had prayed for and overseen the construction of the temple. After the ark was brought in, the king stood before the altar with his hands spread toward heaven and blessed all the assembly. He thanked God for His faithfulness: every promise that God made had come to pass just as He had said. Solomon asked for God's continued presence with Israel and to help His people and their king to have hearts inclined to walk in His ways and keep His commandments. Then, in the words quoted above, Solomon asked the Lord to remember the prayer that he had spoken with his lips and from his heart.

Our spoken words are but breath and sound, so they vanish almost immediately. What an encouragement to know that no prayer spoken in faith to the Lord is ever forgotten. God hears our prayers, remembers them, and answers in His time and in His own way. Solomon's prayer was not selfish. He wanted the people of Israel to be faithful to the Lord, so that all the nations might come to know and trust God. God still wants His church to be a place of prayer for all the nations.

Lord, help me to have a heart for the world. Help me to live and love people so that they may come to know You. In Jesus' name, amen.

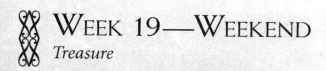

WEEK 19—WEEKEND
Treasure

"Lay up for yourselves treasures in heaven, where neither moth nor rust destroys and where thieves do not break in and steal. For where your treasure is, there your heart will be also. The lamp of the body is the eye. If therefore your eye is good, your whole body will be full of light."

MATTHEW 6:20–22

In these verses, Jesus was addressing two main sources of temptation that the Christian deals with: the flesh and the world.

Later, the apostle John wrote this about those who live in relationship to the Father: "Do not love the world or the things in the world. If anyone loves the world, the love of the Father is not in him. For all that is in the world—the lust of the flesh, the lust of the eyes, and the pride of life—is not of the Father but is of the world." (1 John 2:15–16).

Jesus emphasized that our heart and our treasure are inseparable. Our values and our character are intertwined, the first informing the second. What you love most is where your heart is! We aren't talking simply about being rich! *Treasure* is an all-inclusive word. It is not wrong to possess things; it is wrong for us to allow those things to possess our heart and therefore possess us. We need to concentrate not on the things of this world, but on the things of God that will last!

Jesus warned against our investing in pleasures that wear out, that can erode away, that can be stolen. Security is not found in such things or possessions. Security for the present and for eternity is found in Jesus and in Him alone! May God enable you to believe and live that truth.

Lord, help me live with You as my treasure. Help me know that in You I am secure. Thanks for loving me. In Your name, amen.

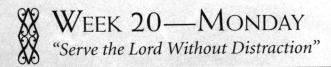

Week 20—Monday
"Serve the Lord Without Distraction"

This I say for your own profit, not that I may put a leash on you, but for what is proper, and that you may serve the Lord without distraction.

1 Corinthians 7:35

Deadlines, pressure, anxiety, stress—do these characterize your life? Are you immersed in a pressure-cooker world that never seems to let up? Distractions are a part of everyday life, but the urgent press of things to do can often feel overwhelming and—worse—capture your attention to the exclusion of everything else. This level of stress is not only harmful to your physical health, but it can also derail your spiritual life.

The apostle Paul knew that losing focus leads first to inconsistency in thought and action, but ultimately results in on-again/off-again service to the Lord. So to the Philippians Paul wrote, "One thing I do . . . I press toward the goal" (3:13–14). Paul's primary focus was the Lord, and he let nothing distract him.

How do you handle the everyday pressures that threaten to derail your service to the Lord? Do you prioritize your activities so that your day begins and ends with the Lord and includes space for Him throughout? If not, then try beginning with a small step: as you get out of bed, simply thank God for another day to serve Him. Throughout the day, talk with Him; send silent "tweets" of prayer, praise, or thanksgiving. Soon you will discover that your mind is less preoccupied with distractions and more focused on the Center of your being.

....

Teach me, Almighty Lord, to be still despite deadlines, pressure, anxiety, stress, and noise and to know that You are God, my strength, my sufficiency, my hope.

TIM DETELLIS, NEW MISSIONS, ORLANDO, FL

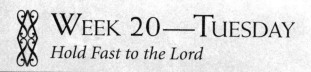

Week 20—Tuesday
Hold Fast to the Lord

You shall walk after the LORD your God and fear Him, and keep His commandments and obey His voice; you shall serve Him and hold fast to Him.

DEUTERONOMY 13:4

Think of three things that are always dependable and never changing. Does your list include things like the sunrise and sunset, a career, the universe, or the directions (north, south, east, west)? Or maybe your list is entirely different.

As we go through life, we understandably need something to steady us, a compass to guide our way and keep us on track. The problem is most things we choose are unable to provide the guidance or stability that we yearn for and need.

Moses declared to the children of Israel their need to hold fast to God. Only God in three Persons—Father, Son, and Holy Spirit—never changes. Does your list include God?

After Moses' death, Joshua was charged with leading the Israelites into the promised land. The Lord told Joshua three times that He would always be with him and would never leave or forsake him. Jesus told the disciples the same thing: "I will not leave you orphans; I will come to you" (John 14:18).

God will never let go of you, and nothing can separate you from Christ's love. Those two dependable, never-changing truths can keep you steady and on track through life, freeing you to wholeheartedly "serve [God] and hold fast to Him."

....

Thank You, Lord, for being my compass and my guide, my strength and my stability. In this ever-changing world I am truly blessed to be a child of the never-changing God.

GOD IS FAITHFUL

WEEK 20—WEDNESDAY
Love the Lord Your God

Take careful heed to do the commandment and the law which Moses the servant of the LORD commanded you, to love the LORD your God, to walk in all His ways, to keep His commandments, to hold fast to Him, and to serve Him with all your heart and with all your soul.

JOSHUA 22:5

Jesus said, "If you love Me, keep My commandments" (John 14:15). When we love Jesus, obeying Him comes more easily.

Consider, for instance, that a person's passion for something is often tied to giftedness in that area. You may be a gifted artist who first sees in your mind an image taking shape on a blank canvas, and who then uses your brushes and paints to make it appear on the canvas. Hours may pass before you realize how long you have been painting because you are captivated by your passion and absorbed in its expression. Your love of painting—and your giftedness in that area—causes time to be of little consequence.

Similarly, when you love another person, you yearn to spend time with her or to help him any way you can. Your love for them takes precedence over your wants and desires, and you see that their needs are met before yours. When they love you in return, your joy is full.

When you choose to love the Lord your God and devote your life to Him, you quickly discover that His love for you far exceeds anything you could have expected. And your response of obedience comes more easily than you could have imagined.

....

Heavenly Father, thank You for loving me and for making Your love for me more real through Your people. Teach me to, in response, love You with all that I am.

TIM DETELLIS, NEW MISSIONS, ORLANDO, FL

Week 20—Thursday
Serve the Lord Your God with All Your Heart

Now, Israel, what does the LORD your God require of you, but to fear the LORD your God, to walk in all His ways and to love Him, to serve the LORD your God with all your heart and with all your soul, and to keep the commandments of the LORD and His statutes which I command you today for your good?

DEUTERONOMY 10:12–13

What does the phrase *with all your heart* mean? And what exactly constitutes your heart anyway?

In today's scripture, *heart* refers to the center of your being, the seat of your emotions, and the primary source of your devotion rather than to the physical organ. So when God says to serve Him with all your heart, He wants you to serve Him with all your mind, all your will, and all your emotions.

By nature, our mind, will, and emotions do not want to serve God! We want to do what we want to do. That sinful tendency changes, though, once we recognize our self-centeredness as sin, ask Jesus for forgiveness, and recognize Him as our Savior and Lord. At that point God begins the work of transforming our mind and our heart. The apostle Paul wrote: "Let this mind be in you which was also in Christ Jesus" (Philippians 2:5). In other words, your thinking will become more like Christ's. And according to Ezekiel 36:26, God replaces your heart of stone with a heart of flesh.

With a renewed mind and a new heart, you can serve God with your entire being!

Thank You, Almighty Lord, that what You command, You enable us to obey. Thank You for Your transformative work in my heart that I may, in obedience to Your call to love, truly love You with my entire being!

Week 20—Friday
Serve the Lord with Gladness

Make a joyful shout to the LORD, all you lands! Serve the LORD with gladness; come before His presence with singing. . . . Enter into His gates with thanksgiving, and into His courts with praise. Be thankful to Him, and bless His name.

PSALM 100:1–2, 4

Serving the Lord with gladness is an outward demonstration of the joy of the Lord in your heart. Conversely, serving begrudgingly reveals disgruntled resentment. Which of the two do you think God honors?

The key to serving with gladness is having a thankful heart. When thankfulness resides within your soul, it permeates every part of your existence, and you cannot help but be grateful for what you have in your life. Thankfulness that flows from you to other people around you has a multiplying effect. They, in turn, begin to express their thankfulness.

The apostle Paul wrote: "Rejoice always, pray without ceasing, in everything give thanks; for this is the will of God in Christ Jesus for you" (1 Thessalonians 5:16–18). Rejoicing always becomes more possible as you develop an attitude of gratitude. Giving thanks also demonstrates to the Lord that you appreciate His provision and the security of His protection. Gladness also comes more easily when we master a lesson that Paul did: he had "learned in whatever state I am, to be content" (Philippians 4:11). This contentment comes with faith that God will meet your every need.

Today, will others be able to see in you a thankful heart and desire the same for themselves? God can use your heart of gratitude and your attitude of contentment to reveal His goodness and draw others unto Himself. Will you be one of His truth-bearers?

....

Lord, by the power of Your Spirit, may I choose gratitude. May I choose joy.

TIM DETELLIS, NEW MISSIONS, ORLANDO, FL

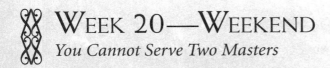

WEEK 20—WEEKEND
You Cannot Serve Two Masters

"No one can serve two masters; for either he will hate the one and love the other, or else he will be loyal to the one and despise the other."

MATTHEW 6:24

Today's scripture makes it very clear that we must choose our master. When Joshua told the Israelites that they had to choose whom they would serve, Joshua declared: "As for me and my house, we will serve the LORD" (Joshua 24:15). That goal seems simple enough, but is it really?

After all, serving the Lord means not serving self: our choice is between God's will and self-will. When God created us in His likeness, He placed within us the capacity to make decisions and then gave us the freedom to do exactly that. This ability to choose is part of our will, which works in concert with our mind and can be influenced by our emotions. Unless all three are fully submitted to God—mind, will, and emotions—we might choose to continue to be our own master.

When Lucifer rebelled against God, his bold words clearly illustrated his choice to be his own master: "I will ascend into heaven, I will exalt my throne above the stars of God; I will also sit on the mount of the congregation on the farthest sides of the north; I will ascend above the heights of the clouds, I will be like the Most High" (Isaiah 14:13–14). Any time we say, "I will," we must be sure that our choice is in line with God's will. Otherwise, like Lucifer, we may be exalting ourselves above God.

....

> *Holy God, please show me where I am living according to "I will" rather than Your will. Please forgive me and reorient my heart. I want to submit to Your good and perfect will.*

WEEK 21—MONDAY
"That You May Know"

This is the testimony: that God has given us eternal life, and this life is in His Son. He who has the Son has life; he who does not have the Son of God does not have life. These things I have written to you who believe in the name of the Son of God, that you may know that you have eternal life.

1 JOHN 5:11–13

Doubt is a great weapon of the flesh that eliminates our usefulness for Christ. The reality is this: *when we doubt, we don't.* Think about it. If I *doubt* a chair will support me, I *don't* sit in it. And when we *doubt* we have a relationship with Jesus, we *don't* walk in the freedom from death and victory over sin that are ours in Christ. So the apostle John wrote to us to eliminate doubt so that we could *know* that we have eternal life.

Too often when believers are looking for assurance about their relationship with Jesus, they look to the past. They try to remember some event from years ago when they prayed to receive Christ. Don't misunderstand me. Everyone who has a relationship with Jesus had a moment when that relationship began. But John didn't point us there to eliminate doubt and find assurance. Instead he pointed us to the present: "I have written to you who *believe.*" Present tense, not *believed* past tense. The real evidence of salvation is not an experience in the past; it is a relationship with Jesus in the present.

Lord, thank You for the freedom and victory that are mine in You. As I walk with You today, may You overwhelm me with the eternal security of my relationship with You. Thank You, Jesus, for saving me!

VANCE PITMAN, HOPE CHURCH, LAS VEGAS, NV

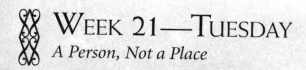

We know that we are of God, and the whole world lies under the sway of the wicked one. And we know that the Son of God has come and has given us an understanding, that we may know Him who is true; and we are in Him who is true, in His Son Jesus Christ. This is the true God and eternal life.

1 JOHN 5:19–20

If you were to ask the average person, "Where does eternal life happen?" the overwhelming response would probably be "In heaven." And in one sense that's true. But in the verses above, John pointed out that eternal life is not as much about a place as it is about a Person. And John was simply restating what Jesus Himself said: "This is eternal life, that they may know You, the only true God, and Jesus Christ whom You have sent" (John 17:3).

Did you hear it? Jesus defined eternal life: "Here it is . . ." that we *know* God. It's the same thing we read in 1 John: "that we may know Him who is true." And John does not mean merely knowing *about* something or someone. This *know* is a relational term: it means knowing someone personally and intimately.

So eternal life is not just about a place you go when you die; eternal life is about a Person whom you know in this life as well as in the life to come, and His name is Jesus. Heaven is not simply living forever in paradise; it's living with Jesus now and with Him forever in paradise!

....

Lord Jesus, thank You for eternal life! What a joy to know You now by faith. What a joy to know that one day I'll know You by sight. Lord Jesus, come quickly!

GOD IS FAITHFUL

Week 21—Wednesday
The Way to Heaven

For God so loved the world that He gave His only begotten Son, that whoever believes in Him should not perish but have everlasting life. For God did not send His Son into the world to condemn the world, but that the world through Him might be saved.

John 3:16–17

Growing up in small town in Alabama, I never dreamed that one day I would call Las Vegas home.

Where I now live is almost two thousand miles from where I grew up. But if you want to travel from Las Vegas to my hometown, you can drive south from Las Vegas to Arizona, hit I-40 all the way across the country until you get to Memphis, and then head east on Highway 72 into my hometown of Muscle Shoals. Or you could simply drive to McCarran International Airport and board a plane that would get you there eventually. If you wanted to get real crazy, you could drive to San Diego, charter a boat, and . . . I think you get the point: there are several ways to get from Las Vegas to Alabama.

Some of those ways to Alabama are easier and faster than others, but they all work. Unfortunately, many people think they can also choose from several ways to get to heaven. According to the June 24, 2008, *Washington Post,* "Seventy percent of those affiliated with a religion believe that many religions can lead to eternal salvation."[9]

The Bible teaches something radically different. God's Word teaches that He made a way to spend eternity with Him, and that way is through His Son. Jesus is the way—the *only* way—to eternal life.

....

Thank You, God, for the gift of salvation through Your Son. Thank You for Your amazing love.

VANCE PITMAN, HOPE CHURCH, LAS VEGAS, NV

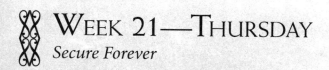

Week 21—Thursday
Secure Forever

"My sheep hear My voice, and I know them, and they follow Me. And I give them eternal life, and they shall never perish; neither shall anyone snatch them out of My hand. My Father, who has given them to Me, is greater than all; and no one is able to snatch them out of My Father's hand. I and My Father are one."

JOHN 10:27–30

Jesus was a masterful Teacher who used ordinary examples to communicate extraordinary truth. Here, for instance, He referred to one of the most ordinary jobs in His day—the shepherd. And the shepherd's responsibilities were to feed the sheep, look after their health, and protect them from danger. Sheep are timid and defenseless creatures that any predator can quickly overtake and kill. The basic goal of a shepherd, then, was to return to the owner the sheep entrusted to his care.

The imagery in these verses teaches us that, as our Shepherd, Jesus knows us by name and has everything about our lives under control. He bought us with His blood and made possible our reconciliation with the holy Father. Furthermore, nothing ever can and nothing ever will snatch us from His hand. For just as shepherds in His day were faithful to protect and defend their sheep, Jesus is faithful to give us the security that only He, as our Good Shepherd, can offer. We are His for eternity, and we will be with Him for eternity.

....

Lord, today I choose to live in the light of Your faithfulness. I trust in Your unchanging promise to be my Shepherd—and I praise You for being my Good Shepherd.

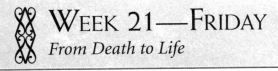

WEEK 21—FRIDAY
From Death to Life

"Most assuredly, I say to you, he who hears My word and believes in Him who sent Me has everlasting life, and shall not come into judgment, but has passed from death into life."

JOHN 5:24

The New Testament was originally written in Greek, and one distinctive characteristic of the Greek language is the importance of the verb tense. Today's verse provides a great example as Jesus revealed three things that happen the moment we first believe in Him.

First, Jesus taught that the new believer *has* everlasting life. This present tense verb indicates action that is both continuous and happening now. So we have everlasting life now! We aren't waiting to get it when we die. Eternal life is a present possession.

Second, Jesus said that we *shall not come into judgment*. This present tense means that today we don't have to fear the judgment of God. Christ fully satisfied the wrath of God for your sin and mine. We don't merely hope that we won't face God's judgment; we *know* we won't because of our forgiveness in Christ.

Third, Jesus taught that a believer *has passed from death to life*. This, however, is the perfect tense, not the present tense, and the perfect tense indicates an action completed in the past that has ongoing results. In other words, I would have experienced eternal death—eternal separation from God—but I chose to receive forgiveness of sin through the past action of Jesus' death on the cross. I now anticipate eternity with God, and that is a gift from Him, nothing I earned or deserve.

....

Lord, You brought me from death to life. I did nothing to deserve or earn it. Thank You, Jesus, for giving me eternal life.

VANCE PITMAN, HOPE CHURCH, LAS VEGAS, NV

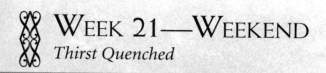

Jesus answered and said to [the woman at the well], "Whoever drinks of this water will thirst again, but whoever drinks of the water that I shall give him will never thirst. But the water that I shall give him will become in him a fountain of water springing up into everlasting life."

JOHN 4:13–14

W hen Jesus decided to travel through Samaria, the disciples were frightened. When He decided to talk to a woman at the well, they were shocked—but no one was more shocked than she was. A man talking to a woman was radical enough, but a Jewish man speaking with a Samaritan woman? Unheard of!

From a human perspective, these two had no reason to have a conversation. The tension grew when Jesus asked her for a drink—from her dipper! The one that she herself had probably drunk from earlier! Jesus took extreme steps to help her recognize her need for God and realize she was made in His image. She needed to learn how she could have access to her Creator. She needed the truth of the gospel, and that is exactly what Jesus gave her. "Drink the water I give, and you will never thirst again. This water leads to life everlasting," He said.

Like the woman at the well realized that day, we know that only Jesus can give everlasting life and that there is no life apart from Him. The drink that we first take on the day of our salvation becomes a never-ending fountain of life-giving water. We never thirst again. And our eternity is secure.

Lord, thank You for quenching my thirst. Your water satisfies my every desire here on earth, and I rejoice knowing that my eternity with You is settled and sure.

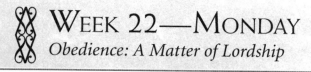

WEEK 22—MONDAY
Obedience: A Matter of Lordship

"This is what I commanded them, saying, 'Obey My voice, and I will be your God, and you shall be My people. And walk in all the ways that I have commanded you, that it may be well with you.'"

JEREMIAH 7:23

Obedience is key to the Christian life. To God our obedience is a matter of His lordship over our life, as Dr. Graham Scroggie (1877–1958) clearly understood.

Scroggie had been speaking at the Keswick Convention in England when a young woman approached him. With concern she said, "I want Jesus to be Lord of my life, but I'm afraid God will send me overseas as a missionary—and I don't want to go!"

Taking her Bible, Scroggie turned to Acts 10. God had given Peter a vision of a sheet: "In it were all kinds of four-footed animals of the earth, wild beasts, creeping things, and birds of the air. And a voice came to him, 'Rise, Peter, kill and eat.' But Peter said, "Not so, Lord!" (Acts 10:12–14). Scroggie explained to the woman, "A slave never dictates to his master; therefore, to say, 'Not so, Lord' was impertinent." He then encouraged her, "I want you to cross out the two words *Not so* and leave the word *Lord*—or else cross out the word *Lord* and leave *Not so*."

Later, looking over her shoulder, he saw a tear-stained page with the words *Not so* crossed out. With joy in her eyes, she repeated with heartfelt passion, "Lord, Lord, Lord!" She was now Jesus' disciple, and He was her Lord and Master.[10]

Are you crossing out *Not so* or *Lord* with your life?

....

Jesus, be Lord over my day and over my life. Speak to me and I will obey!

DR. FRANK COX, NORTH METRO FIRST BAPTIST CHURCH, LAWRENCEVILLE, GA

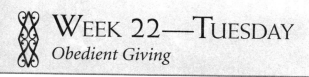
*Through the proof of this ministry, they glorify God for the obedience of your confession
to the gospel of Christ, and for your liberal sharing with them and all men, and by
their prayer for you, who long for you because of the exceeding grace of God in you.*

2 Corinthians 9:13–14

A true disciple of Jesus is a giver. Not just any kind of giver, but a generous giver! The motivation for the believer should always be the example demonstrated by our Savior, Jesus Christ. Just as Jesus gave of Himself to meet our spiritual needs, we should always be quick to give generously to meet the needs of others.

When the apostle Paul wrote the words above, the Jerusalem church was experiencing deep poverty. The Corinthian believers had promised to give to help alleviate some of the Jerusalem believers' pain. Other churches had given, and now it was the Corinthians' time to contribute. Paul admonished them to be generous. He wanted their generosity to prove their faith.

The Corinthians gave joyfully at this time to assist those in need, and their giving brought tremendous results. Jewish believers who had been skeptical of the Gentiles' faith saw by their actions that their faith was genuine. These Jewish believers also knew heartfelt gratitude to God for those who, in the spirit of Christ, had helped meet their needs. God was glorified.

As the Corinthians obeyed God by generously giving, they proclaimed the life-changing power of the gospel. Do people see Christ's generous nature and the gospel's power in your life?

How good a giver are you?

. . . .

*Lord, thank You for Your example of giving. Help me to be a generous giver so
others will see You and You will be glorified. Amen.*

GOD IS FAITHFUL

Bondservants, be obedient to those who are your masters according to the flesh, with fear and trembling, in sincerity of heart, as to Christ; not with eyeservice, as men-pleasers, but as bondservants of Christ, doing the will of God from the heart, with goodwill doing service, as to the Lord, and not to men.

EPHESIANS 6:5–7

B ondservant always means "slave," a definition we don't like very much because of its connotations and history. Yet as believers we are slaves to Jesus our Master, so we are to relate in a Christlike manner to all those in authority over us.

Most of us are in the workplace and find ourselves under the authority of others. Our Master commands us that we are to be obedient. This word *obedient* carries the idea of one who jumps at the sound of the master's voice and does what he is told to do without argument or complaint (v. 5). The word speaks of willing, attentive service, an attitude that is rare today, even among Christians.

Whatever we do as believers, we are to see it as a ministry unto the Lord. And whatever our work, we should carry it out "with fear and trembling." This command doesn't mean that we fear the people we work for; it means instead that we strive to do what is right out of fear of disobeying God.

There will always be people who are hard to work for. As best as you can, look past the person, set your eyes on the Lord, and serve Him. After all, you and I will answer to our Master when this life is over.

....

Lord, You have called me to be a servant. As I serve others today, may they see You in me and my actions. Amen.

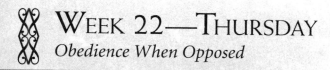

WEEK 22—THURSDAY
Obedience When Opposed

You shall be careful to do as the LORD your God has commanded you; you shall not turn aside to the right hand or to the left. You shall walk in all the ways which the LORD your God has commanded you, that you may live and that it may be well with you, and that you may prolong your days in the land which you shall possess.

DEUTERONOMY 5:32–33

Christ's followers will inevitably face defining moments.

Consider Shannon Wray, salutatorian of her senior class at Hollidaysburg Area High School in Pennsylvania. As salutatorian, Shannon earned the opportunity to speak at graduation. The school asked her to speak about the past, including how friendships helped her get through high school.

A dedicated Christian, Shannon wrote about her best friend, Jesus Christ. Shannon said, "He has always been there for me, encouraging me to stretch my limits and strive for the best He has to offer. He is my greatest friend." She continued, "It is because of Him that I have achieved and succeeded. No matter how much knowledge Hollidaysburg High School has bestowed upon me, I would know nothing if I didn't know Him."

The school censored the above statements and prohibited Shannon from making other religious references. So it was decision time. Shannon chose to obey God. She would not deny her Lord.

After winning a hard-fought battle in court over an attempt to censor religious references from her speech, Shannon Wray delivered her non-censored salutatorian speech during her graduation ceremony. She obeyed, stayed true to her convictions, and God blessed her.[11]

....

Dear Lord, may I do all that You command me today even if it invites opposition. I want to stand for You and be approved by You! Amen.

WEEK 22—FRIDAY
Obedience Through Suffering

Though He was a Son, yet He learned obedience by the things which He suffered. And having been perfected, He became the author of eternal salvation to all who obey Him, called by God as High Priest "according to the order of Melchizedek."

HEBREWS 5:8–10

Adversity is one of life's greatest teachers. Even Jesus faced adversity and "learned obedience" through suffering (v. 8). Later, when Jesus spoke of His death, He asked, "What shall I say? 'Father, save Me from this hour'?" Then Jesus made it known that He had come for this purpose. Yet in the midst of His suffering that resulted from His obedience, He cried out, "Father, glorify Your name!" (John 12:27–28). Jesus knew He could trust His Father to fulfill His purpose for His life through His suffering and death. Because of His obedience, we can receive the blessings of forgiveness and eternal life.

Like Jesus, we all face adversity. In 1986, at the age of twenty-seven, my first wife lost her two-year battle with a malignant brain tumor. During this period of suffering, we learned God had a purpose for us. We did cry out, "Father, save us from this hour!" All He asked from us was to trust and obey.

Charles H. Spurgeon reminded us, "God is too good to be unkind, too wise to be mistaken, and when I cannot trace His hand, I can always trust His heart!"[12] We can trust our heavenly Father to fulfill His good purpose in our lives just as He did in the life of His own Son.

....

Lord, I know You can be trusted even in the crucible of suffering. Not my will, but Your will be done! Amen.

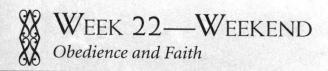

Week 22—Weekend
Obedience and Faith

"Come now, and let us reason together," says the LORD, "Though your sins are like scarlet, they shall be as white as snow; though they are red like crimson, they shall be as wool. If you are willing and obedient, you shall eat the good of the land; but if you refuse and rebel, you shall be devoured by the sword"; for the mouth of the LORD has spoken.

ISAIAH 1:18–20

When has God loved you through one of His people? We are to be channels of God's love, loving Him first and loving others as ourselves. We can only love the way God wants us to love if we are cleansed of our sin. That's why the Spirit of God issues this glorious invitation—for all people—to come and reason with God!

God starts with man's sin, describing it as being "like scarlet . . . and red like crimson!"

Then, acting out of love, God promises to make our sin as white as snow. He promises to cover our sins with His wonderful grace. God stands ready to forgive us and cleanse us whenever we turn from our sin. If we are willing to turn from our sins and obey God, we will receive His blessings!

Also, our loving God not only invites us to seriously consider His offer of grace but also to think through the consequences of refusing to repent of our sins and obey Him. Always faithful to His Word, God promises that our rebellion will surely bring His judgment on our lives.

....

Thank You, Lord, for Your grace that washes away my sin. Now enable me to be to everyone I encounter a witness to Your forgiveness! Amen.

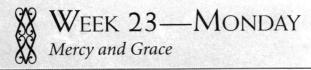

WEEK 23—MONDAY
Mercy and Grace

We do not have a High Priest who cannot sympathize with our weaknesses, but was in all points tempted as we are, yet without sin. Let us therefore come boldly to the throne of grace, that we may obtain mercy and find grace to help in time of need.

HEBREWS 4:15–16

The Incarnation—God becoming man in Jesus—is a marvelous truth on many levels.

In this particular passage, the author of Hebrews reminded us that Jesus knows what we go through in this life because He was tempted in every way imaginable—yet He remained sinless throughout His life. So when He runs to our side—and He is faithful to do exactly that—He is able to offer the perfect assistance, guidance, and comfort because He has felt what we are feeling. Jesus knows being misunderstood, mocked, forsaken, and betrayed; He knows loneliness, frustration, and necessary confrontation.

But Jesus' compassion is not merely passive. He humbled Himself and became obedient to death in order to rescue us from the dominion of darkness, the dominion of punishment for our sin and death. Jesus now ministers mercy and grace to those who go to Him for help.

Mercy means that God does *not* give us what we do deserve; *grace* means that He gives us what we do *not* deserve. Because of the Lord's mercy and grace, we can boldly and confidently enter His throne room and receive His help in our time of need. Take some time to do exactly that today.

....

Thank You, Lord of mercy, Lord of grace, for Your willingness to walk on this planet—to the cross. Thank You that, as a result, You can sympathize with our weaknesses, help us stand strong against temptation, and offer comfort when the temptation is to despair.

CHRIS DIXON, LEAD PASTOR, LIBERTY BAPTIST CHURCH, DUBLIN, GA

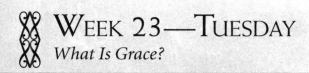
By grace you have been saved through faith, and that not of yourselves; it is the gift of God, not of works, lest anyone should boast.

EPHESIANS 2:8–9

Our US Constitution protects us from being tried for the same crime twice. That so-called double jeopardy clause appears in the Fifth Amendment, and the principle is spelled out in each of the fifty state constitutions. And God operates on this very principle: people are not punished for the same crime—or for the same sin—twice.

Two thousand years ago, Jesus stretched His arms out on a rough wooden cross and took the punishment for your sins and mine. He took on Himself the fullness of God's holy wrath against sin. He paid the price for you, buying you passage from hell to an eternity in heaven. Jesus stood in your place and paid your death penalty for your sin. "The wages of sin is death" (Romans 6:23), and Jesus paid that price by dying for you.

As Paul says, "Scarcely for a righteous man will one die; yet perhaps for a good man someone would even dare to die. But God demonstrates His own love toward us, in that while we were still sinners, Christ died for us" (Romans 5:7–8). And that is a picture of grace. We were dead spiritually, rebels against God and in bondage to sin and Satan. Yet, while we were in that condition, God saved us and God blessed us with the greatest possible gift—forgiveness for our sin and eternal life through Jesus Christ our Lord!

Simply put, grace is "**G**od's **R**iches **A**t **C**hrist's **E**xpense."

....

Thank You, Jesus, for paying the price for my sin and thereby sharing with me the riches of eternity with You and the Father.

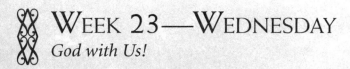

Week 23—Wednesday
God with Us!

The grace of the Lord Jesus Christ, and the love of God, and the communion of the Holy Spirit be with you all. Amen.

2 Corinthians 13:14

Too often we miss the "little big" phrases of Scripture. Never heard that expression? I use it to refer to the Bible's brief, little statements of very big truths!

One such "little big"" phrase is found in 2 Corinthians 13:14. The three-word phrase simply says, "be with you." Did you notice it the first time you read the verse above?

Read today's verse slowly: "The Lord Jesus Christ . . . the love of God . . . the communion of the Holy Spirit *be with you*." Now, what if that verse read, "The Lord Jesus Christ . . . the love of God . . . the communion of the Holy Spirit *exists*"? Would that wording make a difference? It definitely would!

And that difference is one of proximity. Oh, it would certainly be some comfort to know that God actually exists, that He *is*, that He is somewhere out there as opposed to being nonexistent and therefore nowhere at all.

But this verse goes way beyond a statement of mere existence. "Be with you" speaks of a God who longs to be close to you, who wants to identify you as His and who wants you to identify Him as your God.

And as this verse also says, your God is a God of power, love, and grace, all of which are available to you today. Whatever circumstances you may find yourself in today, God is with you!

....

Teach me, Almighty God and heavenly Father, to live in the reality that You, the God of grace and love, are with me always.

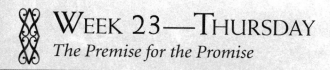

WEEK 23—THURSDAY
The Premise for the Promise

The LORD God is a sun and shield; the LORD will give grace and glory; no good thing will He withhold from those who walk uprightly.

PSALM 84:11

D id you see that? The Bible says, "No good thing will He withhold," but I wonder how many of us reading this devotional today feel like God actually *is* withholding. Maybe He's withholding financial assistance, healing, restored relationships, or a fulfillment of our dreams or desires.

If you're frustrated because God seems to be withholding blessings, look at the last part of this verse: "No good thing will He withhold *from those who walk uprightly*" (emphasis added).

There is the premise we so often miss when we think about God's promises. God is the Promise Keeper, but the premise for His promises is our responsibility. Simply put, obedience brings blessings; disobedience doesn't. Ask God to show you what disobedience you need to address.

And one more thing to notice. Even when we who are clothed in the righteousness of Christ are doing our best to obey God's commands, we still may not receive all that we want. Notice that word *good*. God, the promise reads, won't withhold any *good* things from His people. And, yes, His idea of what is good may require a paradigm shift on our part. After all, our holy God defines *good* from an eternal perspective and according to a set of values far different from what a twenty-first-century postmodern culture preaches. What seems like God's withholding may actually be His protection.

....

Lord, show me my disobedience so I may change my ways and help me understand good from Your perspective, that I may see in my life evidence of Your faithful and wise Psalm 84:11 love for me.

GOD IS FAITHFUL

Concerning this thing I pleaded with the Lord three times that it might depart from me. And He said to me, "My grace is sufficient for you, for My strength is made perfect in weakness." Therefore most gladly I will rather boast in my infirmities, that the power of Christ may rest upon me.

2 CORINTHIANS 12:8–9

Have you personally experienced what Paul wrote about here? Have you asked something of God—have you pleaded with Him—but not experienced the resolution you desperately desired? I've been there and have scars to prove it.

So how do we—like Paul—get from "God did not answer me" to "I'm content with my life and looking forward to seeing God's grace be more than sufficient in my life"?

Let's look at the apostle's example. Paul had a problem (commentators aren't in agreement as to what it was), maybe poor vision, maybe epilepsy or a different chronic illness; he took it to God three times, and through this process he experienced God's grace in the circumstances. This experience taught Paul that God's grace would always be enough for him to be able to deal with whatever circumstances he'd rather not have to deal with. The moral of the story? If there is no problem encountered, then there is no lesson learned. It was Paul's problem that revealed to him that God's grace would be enough for whatever he encountered in life. God wants you to learn that lesson too: "My grace is sufficient."

....

Lord, only life experience will teach me in my heart of hearts that Your grace truly is sufficient for me, whatever the circumstances. Enable me to thank You for those hard circumstances so then I may wholeheartedly praise You for a greater understanding of Your amazing grace.

CHRIS DIXON, LEAD PASTOR, LIBERTY BAPTIST CHURCH, DUBLIN, GA

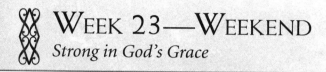

WEEK 23—WEEKEND
Strong in God's Grace

You therefore, my son, be strong in the grace that is in Christ Jesus. And the things that you have heard from me among many witnesses, commit these to faithful men who will be able to teach others also. You therefore must endure hardship as a good soldier of Jesus Christ.

2 TIMOTHY 2:1–3

Yes, you are reading someone else's letter. The apostle Paul was writing young Timothy, his close friend and partner in ministry, to encourage him to live the life God has called him to live. This three-part charge is God's call to all of His followers throughout time:

The person: Be strong in grace.
The task: Share the good news of the gospel with others, who will in turn teach others as well.
The price: Endure hardship.

God has given all of His followers the privilege and blessing of living a life of significance. He has entrusted us with the greatest story the world will ever know, the true account of God's grace made available to sinful people through Jesus Christ. Once we have experienced God's awesome grace in our lives, He calls us to invest our lives in others by sharing it with them.

Life in this fallen world will always be difficult for God's people. This world is not our home, but we are to endure life's hardships like soldiers and continue to take this live-saving, transformational message of grace out into a dark and lost world. Who will you tell today?

....

Lord, enable me, I pray, to be strong in the grace You provide me, to teach others clearly and effectively the truth about Jesus, and to endure life's hardships like a soldier.

Do not believe every spirit, but test the spirits, whether they are of God. . . . By this you know the Spirit of God: Every spirit that confesses that Jesus Christ has come in the flesh is of God, and every spirit that does not confess that Jesus Christ has come in the flesh is not of God.

1 JOHN 4:1–3

The spirit of the Antichrist is at work today—and *antichrist* means exactly what it says: "against Christ." This spirit attacks the unity of believers and hinders the work of the church. This spirit questions the authority and relevancy of God's Word, just as Satan prompted Eve to do in Eden: "Has God indeed said, 'You shall not eat of every tree of the garden'?" (Genesis 3:1). A spokesman for the Father of Lies, this spirit of the Antichrist has spun his web of lies into the very fabric of our society as well as into the philosophy and teachings of many churches. And this spirit of the Antichrist can be a subtle philosophy masked by a word like *tolerance* and an invitation to tolerate what God calls sin.

For more than two thousand years, there has been no shortage of false prophets preaching and teaching another Jesus and another gospel (2 Corinthians 11:3–4). Jesus said it would be this way just before He returned (Matthew 24:4–5, 14). So how do we know what is truth from heaven and what are Satan's lies from hell? How do we "test the spirits, whether they are of God"? We open the Word of God and ask Jesus, who is truth (John 14:6), to teach us.

．．

Lord, thank You that I don't face the deceiver on my own. By the power of Your Spirit, Jesus, please keep me strong in Your truth.

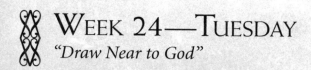

WEEK 24—TUESDAY
"Draw Near to God"

Submit to God. Resist the devil and he will flee from you. Draw near to God and He will draw near to you. Cleanse your hands, you sinners; and purify your hearts, you double-minded.

JAMES 4:7–8

One reason God commands us to submit to Him and draw near to Him is because He knows that we will be tempted by Satan. The closer we are to God, the less likely we are to buy what Satan is selling.

Temptation is a fact of everyday life, which is why Jesus instructed us to pray, "Give us this day our daily bread" (Matthew 6:11). Jesus is the Bread of Life (John 6:48), and when we have Him, we have everything we need. Yet one of Satan's greatest ploys is to tempt us with things *we think* we need and then offer cheap substitutes for an authentic walk with God. Satan's wares ultimately cannot replace what God provides us through our relationship with Christ.

Also, when we spend time in God's presence, we allow God to purify our hearts, more firmly establish Him as our Lord, and enable us to walk daily in the awareness of Jesus' lordship. Then we will have an easier time obeying the command of Romans 6:12—"Do not let sin reign in your mortal body, that you should obey it in its lusts." We aren't to let sin have control of us, we can't allow sin to sit on the throne of our hearts, and we must resist the urge to let anything in our life come ahead of God (see Exodus 20:3, 5).

. . . .

Almighty King, thank You for the privilege of being able to draw near to You. And thank You that the Prince of Darkness flees when I stand in Your glorious light.

Pay Attention or Pay the Consequences

Be sober, be vigilant; because your adversary the devil walks about like a roaring lion, seeking whom he may devour. Resist him, steadfast in the faith, knowing that the same sufferings are experienced by your brotherhood in the world.

1 PETER 5:8–9

I love documentaries about animals in the wild, and lions are especially fascinating.

Initially, a stalking lion doesn't get too close to a herd. Just near enough to see and to be seen, but not close enough to disturb the potential prey. The herd gets used to seeing the lion around and comfortable in its presence. But then one of the grazing animals, head down, begins to move away from the safety of the herd, unaware of the imminent danger. The lion, which had appeared to be lazily napping and uninterested, stares at the unsuspecting creature, and the hair on its back begins to bristle. Then, in a flash, the lion that was nearer than its victim realized, pounces, claims its prey, strangles it, and devours it.

What a picture of how Satan works! Our enemy walks around "like a roaring lion," but we get used to seeing and hearing him. We pay him little attention, and preoccupied by the affairs of life, we can stray from community with other believers and their godly counsel. We waver in our faith, and Satan pounces. His goal is to destroy and devour our testimony of God's goodness and our salvation in Jesus. So we need to "be sober, be vigilant," for there is a lion on the loose!

....

Thank You, Lord Jesus, for this wake-up call! Please show me the lions lurking in my life that I don't even see. And thank You, Lion of Judah, that Satan is no match for You!

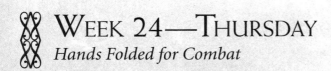

Week 24—Thursday
Hands Folded for Combat

Though we walk in the flesh, we do not war according to the flesh. For the weapons of our warfare are not carnal but mighty in God for pulling down strongholds, casting down arguments and every high thing that exalts itself against the knowledge of God, bringing every thought into captivity to the obedience of Christ.

2 Corinthians 10:3–5

One thing is for certain: we Christians are fighting a spiritual war, and prayer is our primary weapon. Lack of prayer means losing ground to the enemy.

Prayer for people who do not know Christ as their Savior is one battlefront. Satan has set up strongholds in their lives, and he holds them captive to lies by keeping them blind and deaf to God's truth. Our role is to pray, speak God's Word in love, and believe that God will cast down strongholds, open eyes, unstop ears to His truth, and overcome the arguments that have kept unbelievers unaware that they are sinners in need of a Savior.

Our role is not to debate, but to struggle in prayer. We can speak the truth of the gospel in love and pray that God will capture the heart of the lost. We must remember that the war we wage is against Satan and his lies. We have been enlisted and commissioned by Jesus to follow His lead and to pray. He will show us those He desires us to influence, to speak His Word to, and to bless in His name.

May Jesus capture our thoughts today and lead us into battle for those whom He is calling to Himself.

....

I take for granted the powerful weapon of prayer, Lord. Please forgive me—and please give me a passion for fighting for the lost and against Satan and his lies.

God, who is rich in mercy, because of His great love with which He loved us, even when we were dead in trespasses, made us alive together with Christ (by grace you have been saved), and raised us up together, and made us sit together in the heavenly places in Christ Jesus.

EPHESIANS 2:4–6

What a treasure this passage of Scripture is! These verses remind us that before we came to know Christ, we were dead in our sin. Think of what *dead* means: without life, without hope, buried. Yet God knows we are dead without Him, and He is so "rich in mercy" that it overflows the banks of heaven and pours out on those of us who are humble enough to recognize our helpless, hopeless condition.

Consider also God's love, a love so great that heaven cannot contain it. He has lavished us with the riches of His love: For God so loved . . . He gave us Jesus. God sent the Crown Jewel of heaven to earth for us: Jesus came to give His life for ours. By His mercy, grace, and love we are saved!

Because we have received His great salvation, we will one day be privileged to sit with Him in heavenly places. Until then, what a joy to share God's grace, His mercy, and His love with a hurting world.

....

Lord God, I am humbled and grateful as I think about the mercy, grace, and love You have shown me in Jesus. Yet You didn't stop there: You bless me, Your child, with Your presence, Your guidance, Your wisdom, Your hope, and, yes, Your love. Thank You.

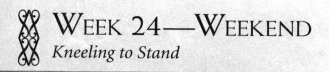

Week 24—Weekend
Kneeling to Stand

Stand therefore, having girded your waist with truth, having put on the breastplate of righteousness, and having shod your feet with the preparation of the gospel of peace; above all, taking the shield of faith with which you will be able to quench all the fiery darts of the wicked one. And take the helmet of salvation, and the sword of the Spirit, which is the word of God.

EPHESIANS 6:14–17

None of us can stand before God unless we have first kneeled before Him. When we kneel in His throne room, God equips us for spiritual battle. Then we are able to obey God's command to stand.

Stand—and not yield any ground to Satan. Stand, holding the shield of faith, when the wicked one hurls fiery doubts at you. Stand, when others are fleeing, fainting, and failing. Stand, when your world seems to be falling down around you. Stand, when you are fearful and tempted. Stand, in the power of the One who is your strength.

And "take the helmet of salvation," because a major battleground for Satan's attacks is our minds. Satan assaults us with fear, thoughts of past failures, present temptations, and worries about our future. When we have on our helmet of salvation, however, we know that we know Him.

We can also respond to Satan's assault just as Jesus did: by picking up the sword of the Spirit, the Word of God, and telling Satan, "Thus saith the Lord." Jesus stood on God's solid truth, and Satan fled. Let us follow our Lord's example. Let us kneel—open God's Word—and then stand!

. . . .

God, thank You for Your mighty Word and for its power against our enemy. May I at least daily kneel before Your Word so I may stand.

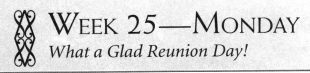

WEEK 25—MONDAY
What a Glad Reunion Day!

The Lord Himself will descend from heaven with a shout, with the voice of an archangel, and with the trumpet of God. And the dead in Christ will rise first. Then we who are alive and remain shall be caught up together with them in the clouds to meet the Lord in the air. And thus we shall always be with the Lord. Therefore comfort one another with these words.

1 THESSALONIANS 4:16–18

All of us have suffered the loss of someone we held dear. That separation is one of the most difficult of all life experiences. Sometimes the grief can debilitate a person for great lengths of time.

The Thessalonian believers were concerned about family members and friends who had died. Paul addressed their deep need for hope, their desperate longing to know that they would see their loved ones again.

In today's passage, God's Word addresses that very pointedly: Paul declared that the Lord Jesus *is* going to return one day. It could be soon. Today could be the day.

Whenever Jesus comes, our loved ones who placed their faith in Him will return with Him. When that happens, we will experience a supernatural event, a metamorphosis of our bodies: "this corruptible must put on incorruption, and this mortal must put on immortality, and we shall be changed" (1 Corinthians 15:53). At that moment we will be reunited with our loved ones "in the clouds" and forever be with the Lord.

....

Thank You, Lord, for the comfort I find in Your promises! Thank You that I will in fact see again those people I love—who have gone ahead of me to be with You—and that when I do, I will never experience another separation from them.

DR. MIKE WHITSON, FIRST BAPTIST CHURCH INDIAN TRAIL, INDIAN TRAIL, NC

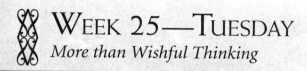

Week 25—Tuesday
More than Wishful Thinking

Beloved, now we are children of God; and it has not yet been revealed what we shall be, but we know that when He is revealed, we shall be like Him, for we shall see Him as He is. And everyone who has this hope in Him purifies himself, just as He is pure.

1 John 3:2–3

I am told that an ermine, a furry animal native to northern Europe, is extremely protective of its white fur. Apparently it would rather die than dirty its fur.

God's Word teaches that if we maintain a posture of expectancy knowing that the Lord's return is imminent, we can—like the ermine—remain spotless despite the attempts of the flesh and our enemy to stain our character or trip us up on our walk with Christ.

The apostle John declared, "Now we are children of God." I am so thankful that the Lord is not ashamed to call me His child. Yet as great as that blessing is, our adoption as His children doesn't compare to the fact that, Jesus says, we will one day be like Him.

When will that be? Whenever He returns for us! Read in Mark 13 about signs of the Lord's return. We are living in that era today!

Yet consider the young woman who wanted so desperately to be married that she bought a dress, ordered a wedding cake, set the date, called the church—even though she had no fiancé. Is that hope? No, that is wishful thinking.

Written in God's Word is the promise that one day we will see Jesus face to face. Now, *that* is hope.

....

Lord God, when storms rage, temptations loom, and heartache comes, I am especially grateful for the see-Jesus-face-to-face hope You give me.

"There will be signs in the sun, in the moon, and in the stars; and on the earth distress of nations, with perplexity, the sea and the waves roaring; . . . Then they will see the Son of Man coming in a cloud with power and great glory."

LUKE 21:25, 27

When our first child was on his way, Kathy and I were so excited about the arrival of our firstborn son. The anticipated joy was even greater than we expected—but that was after the labor pains.

The Bible compares the second coming of Christ to a mother's labor. After the contractions begin, they grow in frequency and intensity until the birth of the child. Hold that thought!

God established parameters around creation—the law of gravity and the law of motion, for instance—that would rule the universe. What astounds the scientific mind is the consistency of these laws. As believers we know this consistency exists because God upholds these laws by His divine will.

But God says that, one day and at His direction, changes will come. Like labor pains, these changes will become more frequent and more intense until the Lord Jesus Himself does return as He has promised.

Today, in the world around us, natural disasters are happening more often and bringing greater destruction and loss of life. In addition, wars across the globe are endangering and claiming lives. If these are indeed signs of the Second Coming, how much closer, then, is the Rapture?

As Luke 21:28 says, let's "lift up [our] heads" and shout with joy!

....

Lord, we do shout with joy in anticipation of Your return, of Your vanquishing sin and death, the enemy, and evil!

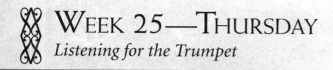

"He will send His angels with a great sound of a trumpet, and they will gather together His elect from the four winds, from one end of heaven to the other."

MATTHEW 24:31

Often in scriptures that point to the end times, it is difficult to determine which refer to the rapture of the church and which to the second coming of Christ. Many scholars contend the Rapture will take place seven years prior to Christ's return to the earth. The events mentioned in our passage today appear to happen after the Tribulation, those final three and a half years of excruciating suffering on the earth.

What a surprising turn of events that will one day occur upon the earth. Yet people today go about their daily lives, raise their children, earn their paychecks, make their plans, and enjoy their hobbies as though no such day is approaching. We are very much like those in the days of Noah, secure and careless and failing to heed the warnings. Little thought, if any, is given to this certain and coming day when the trumpet will sound.

One day soon, when the trumpet blasts, everyone will know in their heart, "It is the Lord!" Then the messengers of God will go to the four corners of the world, and the Lord will gather His own to Himself.

Are you ready? Are you watching for signs of the Second Coming? The Rapture is ever closer. Prepare with anticipation the joy of His appearing!

....

Lord Jesus, thank You for Your Word that points us to You and reminds us of the big picture, of Your coming again as Redeemer and King! Raising children and earning paychecks are opportunities to serve and glorify You, but may they never so distract us that we forget Your eternal purposes!

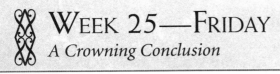

WEEK 25—FRIDAY
A Crowning Conclusion

I have fought the good fight, I have finished the race, I have kept the faith. Finally, there is laid up for me the crown of righteousness, which the Lord, the righteous Judge, will give to me on that Day, and not to me only but also to all who have loved His appearing.

2 TIMOTHY 4:7–8

Assuredly a day is coming when millions of people will disappear from the face of the earth in a great event called the Rapture. It will affect everyone who has placed their faith in Jesus Christ.

After a period of suffering called the Tribulation, we who follow Jesus will be called to the judgment seat of Christ, not to be judged for our sins—that was done at Calvary—but to be rewarded for our faithfulness. We will receive "the crown of righteousness" from the only One qualified to distribute such a reward, "the Lord, the righteous Judge."

Now consider who merits that gift: "I have fought a good fight." One doesn't have to be told that the Christian life is difficult. Anyone who has been saved for five minutes is aware that it is not a playground, but a battleground.

Also blessed are those who finish the race well. That should be our constant prayer, "Lord, let me not fall before I finish what You have given me to do." It is crucial that we remain faithful to the end.

Last, this reward is given to all who joyfully look forward to the return of the Lord Jesus.

Are you in line for a crown of righteousness?

....

Lord, as I anticipate Your glorious return, enable me to fight the good fight, finish the race well, and keep my faith in Jesus! What joy it will be to celebrate Christ's return!

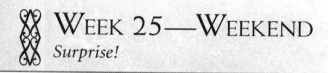

"And [those alive in the days of Noah] did not know until the flood came and took them all away, so also will the coming of the Son of Man be. . . . Watch therefore, for you do not know what hour your Lord is coming."

Matthew 24:39, 42

As I write this devotional, a big blockbuster movie about Noah is opening in theaters across the country. Although the movie depicts Noah's contemporaries being utterly surprised at God's promise being fulfilled, I am quite certain it does not do justice to how utterly caught unaware the people really were. After all, even though God gave the people of Noah's time one hundred years to get ready for the flood, only eight people truly were prepared for that deluge.

All of us are caught off guard from time to time, but we don't need to be surprised by the second coming of Christ. This week we have looked at signs today that point to Jesus' return, an event preceded seven years by the rapture of the church. Although no one knows exactly when the Bridegroom will appear, we certainly have in God's Word a barometer by which to gauge the world conditions that will prevail just prior to His coming.

God commands His people to *watch*, and that means more than just gazing heavenward. It means instead that we are to faithfully seek to share the gospel with as many people as possible before it is too late.

Jesus' return is certain. It is soon. Stay faithful.

. . . .

Lord God, may I live out my expectation that Christ will come at any moment by being sensitive to the spiritual condition of people around me and about how effectively I am sharing the truth about Jesus!

Week 26—Monday
The Courage to Trust

Trust in the LORD with all your heart, and lean not on your own understanding; in all your ways acknowledge Him, and He shall direct your paths.

PROVERBS 3:5–6

At certain points in life we come face-to-face with the reality that we can't do this journey on our own. Each of these moments can be a thing of beauty as we place everything at God's feet, receive His peace, and hear God's promise afresh: "Trust in the LORD with all your heart . . . and He shall direct your paths."

Embracing this promise takes both trust and courage. The two are inseparable. *Trust* is the choice to believe that God loves us and is committed to guiding us according to His perfect will. *Courage* is the decision to then do what God reveals is best for us. It takes courage to stop leaning on our own understanding. Trust asks us to stop pursuing our dreams and goals, to stop depending on our own ability, and to follow God's direction instead of our own.

Trust and courage are required if we are to say no to our predictable habits and limited understanding. Trust asks us to risk a journey into the unknown, into areas we've not walked, on unfamiliar paths beyond our comfort zone. We need to remind ourselves that we can safely choose—day by day, moment by moment—to trust God with all of our ways, because the promise is certain: He will direct our path.

....

Heavenly Father, as I stand on the edge of the unknown, I long to trust You. Enable me to lean the full weight of my life on Your ability to guide my steps.

DAVID EDWARDS, DAVID EDWARDS PRODUCTIONS INC., OKLAHOMA CITY, OK

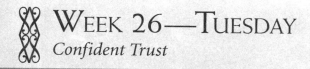

WEEK 26—TUESDAY
Confident Trust

I have called upon You, for You will hear me, O God; incline Your ear to me, and hear my speech. Show Your marvelous lovingkindness by Your right hand, O You who save those who trust in You from those who rise up against them. Keep me as the apple of Your eye; hide me under the shadow of Your wings.

PSALM 17:6–8

God hears!

And this is no trivial truth. Regardless of our status, education, culture, language, income, or color, God hears us. Whether we are succeeding or surrounded by unimaginable trouble, He still hears us. We may be walking in purity or choosing sin's darkness. Still, God hears. He hears prayers spoken from a cathedral as well as from the darkest jail cell. God hears.

But there is more! God hears *and* He responds with "lovingkindness, by [His] right hand." The right hand symbolizes authority and power. Jesus sits at God's right hand (Mark 16:19), and Jesus cares for us with His right hand. So the message of these verses is "When you call, God hears and responds . . . always."

Furthermore, David described us in this psalm as the apple of God's eye, as the object of His great love. The Almighty promises to hide you under His wings, a place of safety where not one of the enemy's schemes can harm you. Hear the Father God's assurance that nothing will ever take place in life that is beyond His ability, power, and willingness to rescue and redeem.

....

Thank You, Lord, for faithfully hearing and responding to my prayers. Thank You, Savior, for always welcoming me when I come running to You. And thank You that I find peace in the fact that You extend Your lovingkindness to me always.

WEEK 26—WEDNESDAY
Comfort of Trust

The Lord is my rock and my fortress and my deliverer; my God, my strength, in whom I will trust; my shield and the horn of my salvation, my stronghold. I will call upon the Lord, who is worthy to be praised; so shall I be saved from my enemies.

PSALM 18:2–3

There are moments in life when we need God to be a heavenly Father in whose lap we can crawl for comfort and safety. But at other moments we need Him to be our Rock.

It was such a moment David thought about as he wrote Psalm 18. After a long period of battle, God had given him victory. It had come at great price, but it had come: God had delivered David. Reflecting on all that God had saved him from, David sang his praise: "The Lord is my rock and my fortress and my deliverer." God's past faithfulness meant David's greater trust in the present.

I'm sure you know the heat of the battle, when you are in survival mode, living one moment at a time, all the while offering feeble prayers. Then God gives you victory. We look back and see His hand more clearly than we did in real time, and we praise God, "my strength and shield." When we think back to an instance of God's deliverance, we find our trust in Him reborn in the present.

....

Dear Lord, today I remember all the times I was overpowered with waves of worry, when I faced seemingly impossible situations, when everything was crashing down on me. You always delivered me. You have been—and I am blessed that You always will be—my Rock.

DAVID EDWARDS, DAVID EDWARDS PRODUCTIONS INC., OKLAHOMA CITY, OK

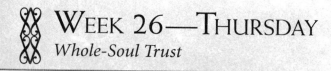# WEEK 26—THURSDAY
Whole-Soul Trust

Commit your way to the LORD, trust also in Him, and He shall bring it to pass. He shall bring forth your righteousness as the light, and your justice as the noonday.

PSALM 37:5–6

Committing your way to the LORD is not for the faint of heart. As we saw earlier this week, trust—in this verse, "committing your way to the LORD"—and courage go hand-in-hand. Courage is acting on what God reveals as His will and His direction for us: courage is trust with shoes on! And we choose to trust God based on His love for us made evident in Jesus Christ who hung on the cross as payment for our sins.

So, again, when we act with courage and trust, when we commit our way to God, we roll the whole weight of life's burdens and decisions onto Him. Then the challenge to "trust also in Him" intensifies as He makes clear which way we should go. Trust is not an abstraction or merely a mental exercise at this point, but a whole-soul choice. This kind of ferocious trust means believing that God will bring good out of our circumstances as He guides us to do the right thing.

Now consider how God honors this ferocious trust. First, God gives us both the insight and the will to make right choices. Second, He leads in order to bring forth "righteousness as the light" from deep in your soul. Finally "your justice [will be] as the noonday": others will clearly see that the Lord has done His work in you and in your life.

....

May, Lord God, my whole-soul trust reach the point where I'll never hesitate to commit to Your way and never dream of not trusting You.

WEEK 26—FRIDAY
A Life of Trust

The LORD also will be a refuge for the oppressed, a refuge in times of trouble. And those who know Your name will put their trust in You; for You, LORD, have not forsaken those who seek You.

PSALM 9:9–10

Trusting is not easy. Trust isn't merely a grit-your-teeth intellectual exercise. Instead, trust develops gradually as we see God bring us through trials and troubles.

Young warrior-king David wrote Psalm 9 after experiencing times of victory and despair. Now when danger threatened, David needed to remind himself of God's promise to be "a refuge for the oppressed, a refuge in times of trouble." A warrior's term, *refuge* refers to a place of safe retreat while the battle rages. For us this is not a physical place; instead, our refuge is our relationship with God. We enter that relationship by trust.

And trust is confidence in God's love and His guided-by-His-love plans for our lives. Ultimately we trust Him because we know Him. To know His name means that when we hear it, we remember all that God is—the Source of life, the Giver of His Holy Spirit, the One to whom we speak and who speaks to us, the One who is Lover, Liberator, and Life-Bringer. We enter the refuge of God's presence as we read and study, believe and obey, pray and worship.

Living a life of trust gives us stories of God's faithfulness to share, often inspiring others to a greater trust in God. Those Christ-followers who know God best are those who trust Him most, and their trust is a strong testimony of His faithfulness.

....

Today I seek refuge in You, Lord God. For when I'm in Your presence, I find my hope, my peace, and my confidence renewed.

DAVID EDWARDS, DAVID EDWARDS PRODUCTIONS INC., OKLAHOMA CITY, OK

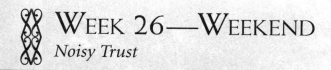

WEEK 26—WEEKEND
Noisy Trust

Let all those rejoice who put their trust in You; let them ever shout for joy, because You defend them; let those also who love Your name be joyful in You. For You, O LORD, will bless the righteous; with favor You will surround him as with a shield.

PSALM 5:11–12

Trust is noisy! Just look at King David! In the heat of battle, David was deeply dependent on God for his victories. In his times of worship, David shouted, sang, and danced—and embarrassed his wife Michal (2 Samuel 6). But David did not stop rejoicing; he did not stop his noisy trust. But too many of us have.

We have allowed skeptical people and struggling people to push back against our joyful trust and unabashed praise for all God does. But we are to trust noisily, for trust is not a peripheral component of our faith. Trust is the heart and center of our commitment to Jesus, so trust lifts its voice and shouts joyfully. Trust calls forth praise and triggers real joy. And as David did, when we experience victory, we are to shout about it. How can we do less!

Notice that David's shout of joy gave way to confidence that God would "surround him as with a shield." And this was no small shield, like one used to block an arrow. This shield was the size of a door that covered the whole body like armor. For you, this shield is God's favor on you, strong and unfailing.

Noisy trust, unfettered joy, blessed confidence: let's learn from David!

....

Help me to pay attention to protection, blessing, and provision and to shout. Let me be more aware that You are the source of my victory and that I'm surrounded by Your favor.

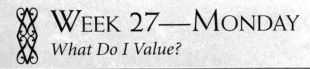

WEEK 27—MONDAY
What Do I Value?

For all that is in the world—the lust of the flesh, the lust of the eyes, and the pride of life—is not of the Father but is of the world. And the world is passing away, and the lust of it; but he who does the will of God abides forever.

1 JOHN 2:16–17

I s there anything that you value more than God? What gets in the way of your walking in God's will?

I once heard about a young couple who returned home one day to find that their house had burned down. As difficult as that was, the couple was able to take a deep breath and say: "That's just a material thing, Lord, and what's ours is Yours."

But then the couple learned the tragic news: their children had been inside. This couple had never thought they would have to give their children over to God.

Certain litmus tests—and that was definitely one—help us identify what we really value. What things make us angry when they don't go our way? This might be something we value more than God. Where are we spending most of our money? We may value that item or activity more than God.

The beauty of our gracious God, however, is that He *never* stops pursuing us. When you are God's child, you know that He loves you unconditionally. He loved us while we were yet sinners. He loved us first: before we lived, before we sinned, before we asked Him for forgiveness. And He will always be faithful in showing us that love.

....

Heavenly Father, I want to always value You above all else. I love You, Jesus. Thank You for loving me first. Amen.

CAZ MCCASLIN, UPWARD SPORTS, SPARTANBURG, SC

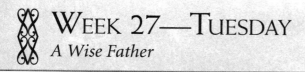

WEEK 27—TUESDAY
A Wise Father

My son, keep your father's command, and do not forsake the law of your mother. Bind them continually upon your heart; tie them around your neck. When you roam, they will lead you; when you sleep, they will keep you; and when you awake, they will speak with you.

PROVERBS 6:20–22

My dad had a distinctive way of parenting. One particular series of events while I was growing up really helped me understand and appreciate his approach.

Over a short span of time, I was invited to go to Six Flags with a friend's family on a Sunday (this was significant because Dad's only rule was "Never on Sundays"). I was also invited to two different parties at the same friend's house (he was bad news) and then a different friend invited me on a weeklong beach trip that conflicted with a family vacation.

And my dad treated each situation differently. Sometimes he said yes; sometimes he said no; and sometimes he said, "I'm leaving it up to you."

"Wait a minute! You're not parenting me very consistently!" I said. But my dad explained that his reasoning was based on what he *knew* my decisions were going to be. In those formative years his "no" *protected* me, his "leaving it up to you" *tested* me, and his "yes" came because after I'd made some good decisions, he *trusted* me.

Isn't that the way God parents? He knows us perfectly, better than we know ourselves, and He knows when we need protection, testing that produces growth, and freedom to make our own decisions.

....

Heavenly Father, please help me walk in Your ways and make decisions that honor You. I love You, Jesus, thank You for loving me first. Amen.

WEEK 27—WEDNESDAY
Let the Search Begin

Search me, O God, and know my heart; try me, and know my anxieties; and see if there is any wicked way in me, and lead me in the way everlasting.

PSALM 139:23–24

Remember when you were a kid and had great hiding places for your stuff? When my wife can't find something, she likes to say, "I hid that thing in such a wonderful place that I can't find it!"

Are you like many, if not most, people? Do you have something in a dusty ol' box at the back of the closet? Often we do the same thing with the unseen things of our heart. We put things way back in the darkest closet of our lives; we don't even want to admit they're there. Things like an unsolved relationship, an unconfessed sin, an unfulfilled commitment, or an unforgiven act of another.

We all have areas of our lives that are only visible to God and to us. When we ask God to "search" and "know" our hearts, we're asking Him to come into the most intimate parts of our lives, those parts no one else knows about. We're inviting Him to shine a light into the darkness of our hearts and reveal the things that we've held onto but need to let go of in order to let His light shine in us and through us.

Have you ever hidden a sin so well that you rarely even think about it? Ask God to reveal it so that you can confess it and be forgiven.

....

Heavenly Father, please shine Your light into the darkness of my heart. Come into every aspect of my life and lead me in the way of everlasting life. I love You, Jesus. Thank You for loving me first. Amen.

CAZ MCCASLIN, UPWARD SPORTS, SPARTANBURG, SC

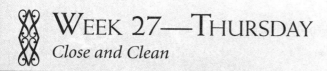

WEEK 27—THURSDAY
Close and Clean

You know what commandments we gave you through the Lord Jesus. For this is the will of God, your sanctification: that you should abstain from sexual immorality; that each of you should know how to possess his own vessel in sanctification and honor.

1 THESSALONIANS 4:2–4

Years ago, before Upward Sports began, I was on staff at First Baptist Spartanburg under Dr. Alastair Walker, and I still consider him one of my most influential mentors.

Dr. Walker always challenged us to remain "close and clean," to stay connected to God's Word so that we would always be walking in His will and staying pure in thought and action. Dr. Walker also encouraged us to find accountability partners who could speak into our lives and counsel us in making wise, responsible decisions

On occasion Dr. Walker would also call an unplanned meeting, and when you got there, you would hear the frustration and anger in his voice.

He would come in, with all the ministers on staff, slam his fist down on the table, and say, "Boys, we've lost another knight from the round table." He would usually be referring to someone he knew who had fallen into some form of unfaithfulness to his spouse.

Dr. Walker was angry at the way Satan puts us in comfortable situations and then slowly but steadily turns up the heat, until sin has crept into our lives and, among other things, caused us to lose all credibility needed to minister.

God is faithful! In Christ Jesus, we are more than able to resist those things in the world that cause us or others to stumble.

....

Heavenly Father, please help me to stay "close and clean." I love You, Jesus. Thank You for loving me first. Amen.

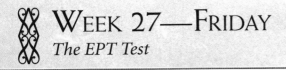

WEEK 27—FRIDAY
The EPT Test

All the ways of a man are pure in his own eyes, but the LORD weighs the spirits. Commit your works to the LORD, and your thoughts will be established.

PROVERBS 16:2–3

Don't worry. It's not the EPT test you're probably thinking of! We'll get to "EPT" in a minute.

The title of this book is *God Is Faithful*. The question is do you *truly believe* that God is faithful *to you*?

When we look at the eternity timeline that encompasses all the past and all the future, the *E* in this EPT test represents all of our past, our *experience*—and when we look back, our *experiences* demonstrate that *God is faithful*.

The *P* stands for *patience*. When we look ahead, why do we so often need to be reminded that the same faithful God in our past will be with us in the future? First Corinthians 1:9 says, "God is faithful." Not God *was* or *will be* or *could have been* faithful, but that God *is* faithful. Be patient: God will prove Himself faithful in the future just as He has in the past.

Then there's the *T*: if we know that God has been faithful to us in the past, and if we patiently await His faithfulness going forward, then we can more easily *trust* Him in the present!

Trusting God in our daily life allows us to continually walk in His will. We will all have peaks and valleys in our spiritual journeys, but our past experiences and our commitment to being patient should help us remember that God is always faithful. Will you trust Him today?

....

Heavenly Father, thank You for Your constant faithfulness. I love You, Jesus. Thank You for loving me first. Amen.

CAZ MCCASLIN, UPWARD SPORTS, SPARTANBURG, SC

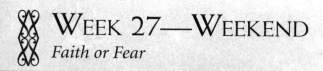

WEEK 27—WEEKEND
Faith or Fear

Submit yourselves to every ordinance of man for the Lord's sake, whether to the king as supreme, or to governors, as to those who are sent by him for the punishment of evildoers and for the praise of those who do good. For this is the will of God, that by doing good you may put to silence the ignorance of foolish men.

1 PETER 2:13–15

Have you ever found yourself torn between doing what man says and doing what God says? God commands us to submit to the laws of our rulers, but not to our fears. We need to step out in faith!

One time Jesus called Peter, the author of today's passage, to step out of the boat and walk across the water to Him. Peter was torn between stepping over the side of the boat in an act of faith and staying in the boat because of his fear.

When Peter walked out on that water, he was stepping out in faith.

My favorite definition of the word *faith* is "the belief that something you cannot see is going to happen."

My favorite definition of *fear* is "the belief that something you cannot see is going to happen."

No, that wasn't a typo: the definitions are the same! Are you going to listen to the voice of your ever-faithful God or to the voice of fear?

When Jesus extends His hand and says, "Come," will you walk with Him? Will you step out in faith—or stay back out of fear?

....

Heavenly Father, thank You for being faithful in always calling me to You. I love You, Jesus. Thank You for loving me first. Amen.

Week 28—Monday
Bitter or Better?

Let all those who seek You rejoice and be glad in You; let such as love Your salvation say continually, "The LORD be magnified!" But I am poor and needy; yet the LORD thinks upon me. You are my help and my deliverer; do not delay, O my God.

PSALM 40:16–17

Fifth-century theologian Augustine once observed, "God only had one Son who never sinned, but He never had any who never suffered."

Even we who are God's people cannot avoid suffering and trouble forever. That is a fact of life in this fallen world. The question is never "Will I face trouble?" The issue is "How will I deal with suffering when it comes?"

The saying that trouble makes you either bitter or better applies to the psalmist. Psalm 40 was written by a man in distress, a man who had trouble on every side! He was aware of his personal sin (v. 12), his life had been stuck in "a horrible pit" and depressed (v. 2), and he was harassed by critics (vv. 14–15). In spite of those troubles, however, the psalmist had a great faith in God! He grew stronger during this hard season by praising God for other believers and by trusting God for his eventual deliverance (vv. 15–16). The psalmist could have been bitter, but God's faithfulness made him better! If the psalmist was made better by trusting God, the same can happen to you! God can be trusted through the trouble!

....

Precious Lord, when trouble comes, remind me that I am not alone. I have Christian friends, and I have You, O Lord, who will deliver me in Your perfect time!

DR. J. KIE BOWMAN, HYDE PARK BAPTIST CHURCH, AUSTIN, TX

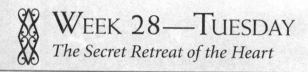

Week 28—Tuesday
The Secret Retreat of the Heart

Our soul waits for the LORD; He is our help and our shield. For our heart shall rejoice in Him, because we have trusted in His holy name. Let Your mercy, O LORD, be upon us, just as we hope in You.

PSALM 33:20–22

Have you ever been so busy, distracted, and fragmented by deadlines or pressures that you found yourself longing for a retreat, for an opportunity just to get away from it all?

The psalmist may have been in that exact frame of mind. The demands of life coming at him were so furious that he felt as if he needed a shield to protect himself from the onslaught (v. 20)! Apparently, getting away from it all wasn't an option for him at the time, and it usually won't be for us either. We are busy raising children, building a career, caring for our parents, managing our households, going to school—there isn't always time for a getaway. But the psalmist had discovered the mercy of a secret place where he could be alone with God. The psalmist described the inward journey of a retreat for his "soul"(v. 20) where he could "wait" and rest in God. He also knew that real joy comes from within from the "heart" (v. 21).

A week in the mountains or a few days at the beach can do wonders for us, but in our busy lives, a few minutes each day of personal worship, of seeking God from our hearts and souls, can also build our joy, our hope, and our trust in the midst of our busy lives.

···

Lord, today I want to retreat to a secret place of worship so You can do a fresh work in my heart and soul.

"You are My friends if you do whatever I command you. No longer do I call you servants, for a servant does not know what his master is doing; but I have called you friends, for all things that I heard from My Father I have made known to you. You did not choose Me, but I chose you and appointed you that you should go and bear fruit."

JOHN 15:14–16

George Whitefield and John Wesley were two preachers who had known each other since college, and God used both of them mightily to share the good news of Jesus Christ.

Historians report that Whitefield had a bigger impact on colonial America and was probably a more gifted preacher than Wesley. Yet today more people are familiar with Wesley. Why? Like Whitefield, Wesley had a heart for God, but he also had a mind for organization. He organized new believers into discipleship groups which were later known as Methodists.

Whitefield tried something similar, but he lacked the organizational gifts to sustain a movement. He once confided to Wesley that his "converts" had become "a rope of sand." Whitefield led thousands to the Lord and helped ignite the first Great Awakening in the colonies, but he wondered if he had failed in long-term discipleship.

Perhaps Whitefield was too hard on himself. After all, God had used him in a mighty way, but Whitefield's concern that God's truth take root and bear fruit should be our concern as well. Jesus promises that when we serve Him, we will see fruit—we will see results—from that service. Normally, fruit spoils quickly, but God can bless the fruit of our work for Him and make it last!

....

Lord, allow my service to You to have a lasting impact for Your glory!

DR. J. KIE BOWMAN, HYDE PARK BAPTIST CHURCH, AUSTIN, TX

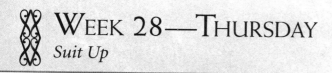

WEEK 28—THURSDAY
Suit Up

"I am the LORD, and there is no other; there is no God besides Me. I will gird you, though you have not known Me, that they may know from the rising of the sun to its setting that there is none besides Me. I am the LORD, and there is no other."

ISAIAH 45:5–6

You have clothes for different purposes, don't you? We all do. Some we work in, some we play in, and some we wear around the house and hope only our family ever sees us in them!

When God's people were facing international trouble from the powerful nations around them, God assured the powerful foreign king Cyrus that He would "gird" him with just the right equipment for every struggle so that, in turn, he could help God's people.

In those days men wore long, flowing robes. The style made it difficult for them to run, do strenuous work, or fight, because their legs got tangled in the robes. So the men would tuck their long robes into a belt around their waist in order to free their legs and gain mobility for any challenge. This process—called girding—is used in Scripture as a metaphor for vitality and strength.

And girding is at the heart of this good news: when God calls you to a task, when you face difficult circumstances that require action, God prepares you. He clothes you with everything you need. He makes sure you don't go into battle unprepared. If the Lord would do that for a pagan king who did not know Him, imagine how much more prepared He will make you because you are His child!

....

God, by faith I know that You have given me everything I need to do Your will today.

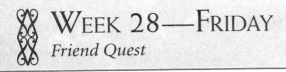

Week 28—Friday
Friend Quest

A man who has friends must himself be friendly, but there is a friend who sticks closer than a brother.

Proverbs 18:24

As a result of social media, *friend* is now a verb! We "friend" and "unfriend" people we may have never talked to in person. The value of a friend on social media may, at times, be pretty insignificant, but a real friend is worth his or her weight in gold!

It's interesting to note that the first part of this passage is translated differently from the second. The Hebrew word for *friend* in the first part of the verse refers to close associations. The second word refers to a loving friend.

Furthermore, the overall meaning of the passage has been debated. The King James family of translations views this proverb as common-sense advice about being friendly in order to make friends. Modern translations, however, view it as a warning about false friends or bad companions. Nevertheless, all translations agree that the second half of the verse teaches there is one Friend above all others!

Each of us needs to *have* a good friend, and each of us needs to *be* a good friend. As Christians, we have all discovered a new family of friends, but our best friend is our Lord Jesus!

....

O Lord, thank You for my friends! Help me be a good friend. Most of all, thank You for "friending" me.

DR. J. KIE BOWMAN, HYDE PARK BAPTIST CHURCH, AUSTIN, TX

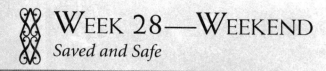

WEEK 28—WEEKEND
Saved and Safe

The salvation of the righteous is from the LORD; He is their strength in the time of trouble. And the LORD shall help them and deliver them; He shall deliver them from the wicked, and save them, because they trust in Him.

PSALM 37:39–40

If you were to ask the average church member in America what it means to be saved, what do you suppose that person would say? Would most church members mention eternal life, the forgiveness of sins, and a relationship with Jesus? I hope so!

Eternal life, the forgiveness of sins, and a relationship with Jesus are all components of salvation, but another important aspect of salvation is drawn from the Old Testament: God *saves* us from trouble here and now!

And I have a great example from when I was a boy. My brother fell through thin ice into a freezing cold river, and my father pulled him out before he was swept away by the current. My dad literally saved my brother.

In a similar way, our Almighty God and heavenly Father saves us from disaster because He loves us. We are His children, and He is our *strength*, a Hebrew word that means He provides us with security and personal protection whenever trouble comes. God has promised to help us, save us, and deliver us in times of stress and when we are under personal attack, because we have faith in Him. In Christ we are saved forever, and we are safe today!

....

Lord, You alone are my salvation and my strength, and I trust in You!

WEEK 29—MONDAY
Jesus Is the Word

In the beginning was the Word, and the Word was with God, and the Word was God. He was in the beginning with God. All things were made through Him, and without Him nothing was made that was made. In Him was life, and the life was the light of men.

JOHN 1:1–4

Just who is Jesus? The Nicene Creed states Jesus is "Light of Light, very God of very God; begotten, not made, *being of one substance* with the Father by whom all things are made" (emphasis added). The Council of Nicea made this declaration based on one letter in the Greek language: *iota,* the letter *i.* The difference between the Greek word for *similar* and *same* is the letter *i.* Seem trivial? One letter or even one comma can have a great impact on one's life.

Back in the days of the telegraph, a woman touring Europe cabled her husband asking to buy a beautiful bracelet for $75,000. The husband cabled back: "No, price too high." But the cable operator missed the comma and instead sent this message: "No price too high." She bought the bracelet. The happy ending is the husband sued the company and won his money back.

Jesus is not just *similar* to God; He is the *same* as God. He is the incarnate Word who in the beginning created this world with His spoken word. Jesus shines light, gives life, and dispenses love to all who worship Him as God of very God. Everything, including your very self, has stamped on it "Made by Jesus!"

....

Lord Jesus, when I read the written Word, I am reading You, the living Word. You are the Light who dispels the darkness and the Life who defeats death. Forever and ever You are God!

DR. JAMES MERRITT, CROSS POINTE CHURCH, DULUTH, GA

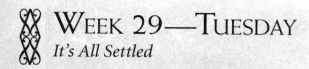

Forever, O L<small>ORD</small>, Your word is settled in heaven. Your faithfulness endures to all generations; You established the earth, and it abides. . . . Your testimonies are wonderful; therefore my soul keeps them. The entrance of Your words gives light; it gives understanding to the simple.

P<small>SALM</small> 119:89–90, 129–130

There is an old saying that "the only permanent thing in this world is change." Someone else said, "Change is inevitable . . . except from a vending machine." There is much truth in both statements—as life experience teaches us—but neither statement is totally accurate.

The truth is, one thing is absolutely permanent. One thing is completely indestructible. One thing is here to stay both for time and eternity. One thing is always going to be both in this world and the world to come—the Word of God.

The Hebrew word for *settled* is a word that means "absolutely, irrevocably fixed," and two things are definitely settled in heaven: the God of the Word and the Word of God.

In a lifetime the average person will speak 370,110,001 words (I have no idea who figures these things out!). In eternity most of those words will be forgotten, never to be heard or remembered again. But the Word of God will still be shining its light and truth one trillion years from now. It is immutable, indestructible, and, yes, infallible. Of course it is, for it is *God's* Word.

....

Father, Your Word is settled forever in eternity. I ask You to daily settle it in my heart that I may walk in its light and bathe in its truth.

WEEK 29—WEDNESDAY
Above All Else

I will praise You with my whole heart; before the gods I will sing praises to You. I will worship toward Your holy temple, and praise Your name for Your lovingkindness and Your truth; for You have magnified Your word above all Your name.

PSALM 138:1–2

Dale Carnegie once wrote, "A person's name is to that person the sweetest and most important sound in any language."[13] This statement may or may not ring true for you, but it is very true of God. Names are very important to our God. He has, for instance, given Jesus "the name which is above every name." Indeed, "at the name of Jesus every knee [will one day] bow . . . every tongue [will] confess that Jesus Christ is Lord" (Philippians 2:9–11).

And there's more evidence that names are important to God: the first job assigned in all of history was the charge to Adam to name the animals. Names in Scripture served a number of functions in addition to identifying a person. A name could tell about a person's birth (*Moses*, "drew him out of the water" [Exodus 2:10]), reveal a parent's reaction to the birth of a child (*Isaac*, "laughter"), or communicate God's message (*Jesus*, "Jehovah saves"). Even in eternity names will be significant: we are told we will all be given new names (Revelation 2:17). And one of the Ten Commandments warns against taking God's name in vain (Exodus 20:7). Yet Scripture says God has magnified His word even above His name! Why? Because if one's word cannot be trusted, then one's name becomes worthless. So here is a thought: You can honor God's name by hearing and obeying His Word.

....

Father, I praise Your name and honor Your Word. I am grateful I can call on one and rely on the other!

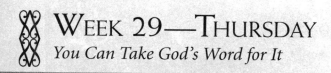

WEEK 29—THURSDAY
You Can Take God's Word for It

By faith we understand that the worlds were framed by the word of God, so that the things which are seen were not made of things which are visible.

HEBREWS 11:3

To echo the author of Hebrews, by faith we see that the world was called into existence by God's word.

It is amazing to me that what scientists have taken centuries and volumes to *try to* explain—the origin of the universe—can be explained in two words: "God said." Look at the first chapter of Genesis, and you'll find "God said" eight times, and every time God spoke, He spoke something into existence. He created.

God spoke . . . and the universe lit up like a Roman candle. God spoke . . . and mountains began to rise and oceans began to roll. God spoke . . . and the sun began to shine, stars began to twinkle, and the moon began to glow. God spoke . . . and birds began to fly and fish began to swim. God spoke . . . and man began to walk.

The Almighty God spoke this world into existence, but we can only understand that truth by faith. Hebrews 11:3 goes on to say, "Because of our faith, we . . . also know that what can be seen was made out of what cannot be seen" (Hebrews 11:3 CEV).

And that is a good definition of real faith: believing that everything you can see comes from nothing that you can see. Anybody can take something and use it to create something else, but no one except God can take nothing and make something out of it.

All that we can see teaches us to trust the God that we cannot see.

....

Father, the world we can see invites us to trust in You for those things we can't see.

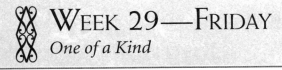

Your word is very pure; therefore Your servant loves it. . . . My eyes are awake through the night watches, that I may meditate on Your word.

PSALM 119:140, 148

Google undertook the impressive task of trying to determine how many books have been written throughout history, and they concluded that approximately 130 million books have been written. And that means you have a decision to make: either the Bible is just another book—one of 130 million books, one more example of human beings putting words to paper—or the Bible is unlike any other book ever written, because God Himself provided the words.

The Bible is inspired—every word on every page of this Book is the very breath of God. Simply put, that means that men wrote what God told them to write. Phrases like "God said," "God spoke," and "The Word of the Lord came" occur over seven hundred times in the first five books of the Old Testament and more than four thousand times in all of the Old Testament.

We believe that the entire Bible, in its original form, was breathed by God so that a writer could record precisely what God wanted him to write. Unlike the other 129,999,999 books that are filled with the words of men, this Book contains the Word of God. Put simply, men wrote the Bible, but God authored the Bible. When we read the Bible and meditate on it, we are hearing God speak.

....

Father, may the purity of Your Word purify my heart as I meditate today on its unadulterated truth.

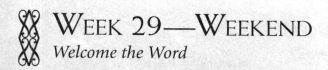

Lay aside all filthiness and overflow of wickedness, and receive with meekness the implanted word, which is able to save your souls. But be doers of the word, and not hearers only, deceiving yourselves.

JAMES 1:21–22

The Greek word for *receive* literally means "to make welcome." It is the picture of receiving a guest with open arms.

Many homes have a welcome mat at the front door. It says upfront to anyone who knocks that this home will eagerly receive you and treat you like royalty. And this is exactly the kind of attitude you and I ought to have toward God's Word. We need to have a welcome mat at the front door of our heart, and every chance we get, we want to throw the door open wide, welcome God's Word into our heart and soul, and make God's Word a part of our daily life.

But the word *receive* doesn't just mean "to welcome." *Receive* can also mean allowing someone to come in and totally influence and dominate your home. Just imagine if the president of the United States requested to spend the night in your home. You wouldn't treat him like any other guest; you likely would go above and beyond to give him full access to your home. When you welcome God's Word into your heart, you must have that same attitude of acceptance and give the Word of God full access to your life.

One more thing. God sees that His Word is welcome in your hearts when you obey it.

....

Father, I welcome Your Word into my life today. I want to do whatever it tells me to do. Please enable me, empower me to be a doer of Your Word.

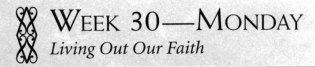

Week 30—Monday
Living Out Our Faith

Watch, stand fast in the faith, be brave, be strong. Let all that you do be done with love.

1 Corinthians 16:13–14

Near the end of Paul's letter to the church at Corinth are wonderful words for us believers today. Here are three exhortations to live out our faith:

Watch. As we watch the events taking place in our world today, we see a continual drift away from the Word of God as the guide for decisions made by governments, organizations, and individuals. The saddest note is that some of these who are drifting name Jesus as their Savior.

Don't waver in obedience to Christ; don't compromise biblical beliefs in order to accommodate the world. Every person must decide who or what will be the authority in his or her life. Will it be the philosophy of the day, or will it be the Bible with truth that has been proven and unchanging for thousands of years?

Remember that you stand in the power of Christ; you do not stand alone. Put differently, Christ stands with us when we stand for Him. His power enables us to share His love even when we are oppressed, threatened, or abused for our faith in Jesus.

....

Father, throughout history Your followers have stood strong in their commitment to follow You. I know I won't have that strength if I stand apart from You. Help me today to be unwavering in my faith and my obedience to You. Help me to show Your love to other people and use me to help individuals place their faith in You.

DR. MARTY JACUMIN, BAY LEAF BAPTIST CHURCH, RALEIGH , NC

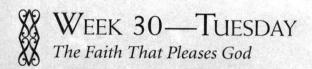

WEEK 30—TUESDAY
The Faith That Pleases God

Now faith is the substance of things hoped for, the evidence of things not seen. . . .
Without faith it is impossible to please Him, for he who comes to God must believe that
He is, and that He is a rewarder of those who diligently seek Him.

HEBREWS 11:1, 6

Apparently men and women today are in great need of motivation. A quick Google search reveals thousands of motivational speakers, some of whom charge exorbitant fees to speak energy and direction into people's lives. Life coaches have also become popular, and they encourage individuals to look within themselves to identify dreams and possibilities they could pursue in quest of fulfillment.

Motivational speakers and life coaches often teach that nothing is impossible for a person who works hard enough. This philosophy is appealing, and it may prompt people to strive harder to reach their goals. The problem, though? This teaching is not biblical. We may want to believe that no goal is impossible for us to achieve, but Hebrews 11:6 teaches that one goal is absolutely impossible for us to do on our own: it is impossible to please God without faith. We will never please the Lord unless we live in a way that demonstrates that we trust Him.

All human beings place their faith in something. For some, it is reason. For others, it may be finances. We who follow Jesus must put our faith in Him alone. If we truly desire to please the Lord, we must understand that we can place our trust only in Him—and only then do we please our Lord.

....

Heavenly Father, help me live in a way that pleases You. May my life be a wonderful testimony of what it means to walk with You.

WEEK 30—WEDNESDAY
Faith for the Battle

"If you have faith as a mustard seed, you will say to this mountain, 'Move from here to there,' and it will move; and nothing will be impossible for you. However, this kind does not go out except by prayer and fasting."

MATTHEW 17:20–21

Absolutely critical to understanding a passage from the Bible is placing it in the context of Scripture. Today's verses, for instance, appear in a discussion of spiritual warfare. Attempting to cast out demons in their own power rather than in the power of the Lord, the disciples of Jesus had been unable to cure an epileptic boy. The disciples' experience illustrates that in our own strength, we are no match for the devil and his demons. The Bible describes Satan as a roaring lion seeking whom he may destroy (1 Peter 5:8). The Bible also teaches that the devil is very cunning, and history shows he is the great deceiver.

Knowing full well what the devil is capable of and what we are capable of, God never asks us to stand against Satan in our own power. The only way that we can resist Satan is in God's power, and we experience that power by faith. We must believe that, with the Lord's help and by the power of His Spirit that indwells His people, we can resist the devil. On the cross Jesus secured our victory over Satan, sin, and death, yet spiritual warfare continues. But we don't fight alone!

Father, thank You for not leaving me to engage in spiritual warfare in my own strength. Thank You for supplying not only Your spiritual armor but also the strength I need to fight the enemy.

DR. MARTY JACUMIN, BAY LEAF BAPTIST CHURCH, RALEIGH , NC

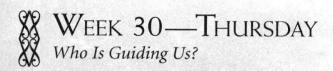

WEEK 30—THURSDAY
Who Is Guiding Us?

He who has prepared us for [eternal life] is God, who also has given us the Spirit as a guarantee. So we are always confident, knowing that while we are at home in the body we are absent from the Lord. For we walk by faith, not by sight.

2 CORINTHIANS 5:5–7

When I was in college, I had a blind classmate who made his way around campus with the help of a seeing-eye dog. It was amazing to watch Billy and his dog work together. Billy crossed busy streets and parking lots with the help of his dog. They were a great team because Billy trusted his dog to lead him in the right direction and keep him away from danger.

Before Jesus returned to heaven after the resurrection, He promised His followers that He would not abandon them, that His Spirit would come and indwell them. Jesus knew that fallen human beings could not walk by faith if left to themselves, so He sent His Holy Spirit to be our guide.

But are you allowing the Spirit of God to lead you as you live out your faith each day? Trouble comes when we seek to make our own decisions rather than following the leading of God's Spirit. It would have been disastrous if Billy had decided he didn't need his dog and simply walked wherever he wanted to walk. Why would deciding that we don't need God's Spirit as a guide be any less disastrous?

....

Heavenly Father, I still have not mastered walking by faith and not by sight. Help me to trust You more every day and to deepen my dependence on You. I long for the day when faith will be sight, when I will be with You in heaven.

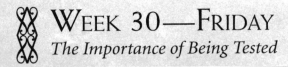

WEEK 30—FRIDAY
The Importance of Being Tested

Count it all joy when you fall into various trials, knowing that the testing of your faith produces patience. But let patience have its perfect work, that you may be perfect and complete, lacking nothing.

JAMES 1:2–4

I have been blessed to coach young Pop Warner football players, major college athletes, and every skill level in between. Because of this background, I love the athletic metaphors found in Scripture. The apostle Paul, for instance, reminded us believers to run well the race of life (1 Corinthians 9:24), and today's verses sound like a coach's pep talk.

Now I know of no coaches who would want to skip practices and simply compete. We need practices in order to prepare our athletes for when the opposing team comes and offers stiff competition. And just as a coach prepares his players, God prepares His followers for the tasks He has for us. God knows He must test us so that we will grow in our faith so that we will more willingly and more consistently depend on Him and obey Him.

As someone has rightly observed, a faith that hasn't been tested is a faith that can't be trusted.

Sovereign God and heavenly Father, it amazes me that You use made-of-dust human beings to carry out Your heaven-sent and eternally significant work. I do want to serve You—and serve You well, so may I not resist Your testing and may I not grow faint when trials come. I want to cooperate with this process as You grow me and shape me into a follower You can use.

DR. MARTY JACUMIN, BAY LEAF BAPTIST CHURCH, RALEIGH , NC

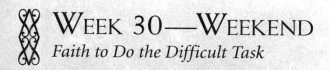

Week 30—Weekend
Faith to Do the Difficult Task

Jesus . . . said to [His disciples], "Have faith in God. For assuredly, I say to you, whoever says to this mountain, 'Be removed and be cast into the sea,' and does not doubt in his heart, but believes that those things he says will be done, he will have whatever he says."

MARK 11:22–23

I teach preaching at Southeastern Baptist Theological Seminary, and every semester I have each of my students preach three sermons. When I make that announcement, some students look at me as if I have asked them to fly to the moon. That's when I remind them that Jesus doesn't ask us to preach in our own strength but to rely on Him.

Now I have to wonder if Jesus saw the same kind of wide-eyed astonishment on His disciples' faces when He described this mountain-moving faith. Jesus wanted His followers—then and now—to know that apart from Him they could do nothing and that with Him, they could do what seemed impossible.

So what is God asking you to do? Go on a mission trip? Share the gospel with your neighbor? Start a Bible study in your neighborhood or at work? If God's will for your life seems impossible, remember that He isn't asking you to do it alone. God simply desires for you to have faith enough to step out in obedience and to believe that He can do the impossible through you. That's mountain-moving faith.

· ·

Father, help me trust You; help me believe that You can use me and work through me to accomplish Your will. Strengthen my faith so that I'm prepared to obey You no matter how impossible the task may seem.

Week 31—Monday
The Power of Faith

For I am not ashamed of the gospel of Christ, for it is the power of God to salvation for everyone who believes, for the Jew first and also for the Greek. For in it the righteousness of God is revealed from faith to faith; as it is written, "The just shall live by faith."

ROMANS 1:16–17

We are made right with God—He declares us just—not because of anything we have done, but because of what Jesus did for us when He died on the cross. When we acknowledge our sinfulness and then accept the sacrificial death of sinless Jesus on our behalf, God declares us righteous. Our righteousness is God's gift to us; we have done nothing to deserve it.

And this remarkable truth makes the Christian gospel different from every other religious teaching. All other religions are built upon what we human beings must do to reach God, nirvana, or whatever the objective may be. But the gospel—the good news of Jesus—is about what God has done for us. We aren't following seven paths or five pillars; we aren't climbing a ladder to reach heaven. Instead we trust Jesus—we trust that His death on the cross opened the door to a relationship with God and eternity with Him. The way to God isn't a path we Christians walk; it is a Person we know. Jesus didn't come to show us the way; He proclaimed, "I am the way" (John 14:6). This simple gospel truth—when it is shared, when it is believed—possesses divine power to change lives.

God of grace, thank You for calling me to know Jesus, to know the righteousness He purchased with His life, to be in relationship with You now and forever.

DR. WILLIAM RICE, CALVARY CHURCH, CLEARWATER, FL

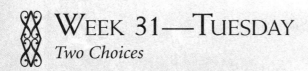

[Jesus] came to His own, and His own did not receive Him. But as many as received Him, to them He gave the right to become children of God, to those who believe in His name: who were born, not of blood, nor of the will of the flesh, nor of the will of man, but of God.

JOHN 1:11–13

Two people—maybe even from the same family—sit in the same room and hear the same message. But these two different people have two different responses. One hears and believes; one hears and dismisses.

Jesus came to His very own people. They knew about God. They had the law, the prophets, the temple, the sacrifices, and the promise that the Messiah was coming. Yet many, even most of God's chosen people, missed God's Son when He came. They dismissed Jesus as crazy, presumptuous, unwanted—and that still happens today. People hear and walk away, dismissing Jesus and missing God.

But something wonderful and spiritual happens to those who hear and believe. The apostle John said we are "born" spiritually, born according to God's will and plan. By God's intentional design, a person who trusts in Jesus becomes a child of God, and He becomes that person's Father.

Sometimes we forget just how radically Jesus changed everything. Jesus came so that we could be born in a new way and know God in a close personal relationship. Jesus came to make life new, richer, more significant—for those who believe, not those who dismiss. In which group are you?

....

Thank You, Lord God, for enabling me to see the truth about Your Son Jesus and about my need for a Savior. Thank You for embracing me as Your child. Your grace is truly amazing.

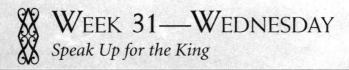

WEEK 31—WEDNESDAY
Speak Up for the King

We are ambassadors for Christ, as though God were pleading through us: we implore you on Christ's behalf, be reconciled to God. For He made Him who knew no sin to be sin for us, that we might become the righteousness of God in Him.

2 CORINTHIANS 5:20–21

God is doing something in the world and He wants you to be involved. The something God is doing is reaching out to the people He loves with an offer of reconciliation. We sinful human beings are separated from our pure and holy God, but He wants a relationship with each of us. And God wants you to share that message as His ambassador on this earth.

Think about an ambassador's unique position. Ambassadors live in one country but are citizens of another. They live under one king but are loyal to another. Back when messages could take days or weeks to arrive, an ambassador quite literally had to speak for an absent king.

Similarly, we live in one place, but our greater loyalties lie with another. We serve a heavenly King whom much of our world still needs to know. Who will speak for our King today? Who will represent His kingdom today? How about you?

God is working to draw people to Him and to their eternal home with Him, but God makes His appeal through you. What will happen to lost people you meet today if you are silent today and don't tell others what they need to know?

. . . .

I pray, Lord, give me courage and faith to talk openly about You, my King. Use me as Your ambassador, so I can share the truth about You with those who have yet to hear or accept it.

DR. WILLIAM RICE, CALVARY CHURCH, CLEARWATER, FL

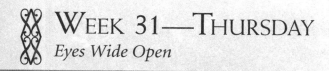

Week 31—Thursday
Eyes Wide Open

He who is spiritual judges all things, yet he himself is rightly judged by no one. For "who has known the mind of the LORD that he may instruct Him?" But we have the mind of Christ.

1 CORINTHIANS 2:15–16

You've probably seen a stereogram, one of those pictures that contains a second picture that appears if you stare long enough. At first the stereogram may look like some graphic design, and then suddenly a 3-D image jumps out at you. Maybe it's an animal, a house, or a person's face.

Spiritual truths can be like that. Plenty of people see without seeing, hear without hearing. After all, in our natural mind we simply can't comprehend certain spiritual realities. But Jesus gives us new eyes to see. The person who has met Christ and in whom the Holy Spirit dwells sees things differently; they now see what they never saw before.

Several years ago a friend of mine recognized his wickedness and accepted Jesus as his Lord. Early one morning a few days later, he called to his wife. "Quick! Come outside and look at the colors in the sky!" Of course he had seen the sun rise many times, but that day he saw it with new eyes. What a symbol of the work God was doing in his life!

On our own we can never understand the things of God, but when Christ lives within us, He gives us new eyes to see His truth.

....

Lord Jesus, I praise You for giving me new eyes to see Your truth and a new heart to receive it. May I now use those new eyes to see the people around me the way You see them, that I might reach out with Your love, compassion, and truth.

WEEK 31—FRIDAY
One of a Kind

There are diversities of gifts, but the same Spirit. There are differences of ministries, but the same Lord. And there are diversities of activities, but it is the same God who works all in all.

1 CORINTHIANS 12:4–6

Look around today and you'll see that people are magnificently diverse. God apparently loves variety.

Diversity is also found in the church, the body of Christ. Even though we Christ-followers have the same Lord, same faith, same baptism, and same convictions about foundational issues, we are still quite different from one another.

The same Spirit of God dwells within each believer, but His presence looks different in each believer's life. One is gifted one way, someone else another, and that is a good thing: God's work requires different people with different gifts.

Now here's the big point: God made you to be you. You aren't like others. You don't have the gifts that others have. You aren't supposed to because, according to God's plan, there are people only you can reach and things only you can do. And if you don't do it, who will?

The comparison game is a trap and a lie. If you spend your life comparing yourself to others, you may very well miss God's unique plan for your life. So don't try to be like someone else. Instead focus on becoming more like Jesus, and as you do, you will more fully become the unique person God created you to be.

....

Thank You, Creator God, for this reminder that You made me who I am, with specific gifts and for specific reasons. May I keep my eyes not on others, but on You so I don't miss an opportunity to reach out to someone in Your name.

186   DR. WILLIAM RICE, CALVARY CHURCH, CLEARWATER, FL

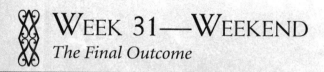

WEEK 31—WEEKEND
The Final Outcome

[God] put all things under [the Lord Jesus'] feet, and gave Him to be head over all things to the church, which is His body, the fullness of Him who fills all in all.

EPHESIANS 1:22–23

From the beginning God has had a plan for rescuing a fallen race and a fallen planet, and His Son Jesus was key to that plan. Jesus died on the cross to pay for our sins, but then He triumphed over death by rising from the grave. Jesus ascended into heaven, but He has promised to return and reign over all things forever.

The unfolding of this sovereign plan may be hard to imagine as the world around us rages with unbelief and sin. Military empires march with cruelty and oppression; entertainment empires produce filth and mock God; financial empires grow as greedy men pursue greater wealth at the expense of others; and political empires vote as if God does not matter. Many people live thinking they won't be held accountable for their choices. But God will judge, and He will accomplish His great purpose. He will place all things under the authority of Christ, and He will reign forever.

The Bible also speaks of the day when "the knowledge of the glory of the LORD" will cover the earth "as the waters cover the sea" (Habakkuk 2:14). Never doubt God's ultimate and complete victory, a victory accomplished and a promise fulfilled as Jesus takes the throne for His eternal reign.

....

O Sovereign God, what a breath of fresh air for a weary soul! It is good to be reminded that You are in control, that Jesus will return, that He will reign forever and ever over a kingdom that glorifies, celebrates, and praises You. Come quickly, Lord Jesus.

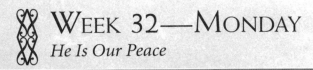
[Jesus] Himself is our peace, who has made both one, and has broken down the middle wall of separation, having abolished in His flesh the enmity, that is, the law of commandments contained in ordinances, so as to create in Himself one new man from the two, thus making peace.

EPHESIANS 2:14–15

You know one problem with laws and rules? They always need enforcement. And if you've ever gotten a speeding ticket (or weaseled out of one), you know that enforcement can become subjective, tricky and—let's face it—a bit mean.

And of course laws and rules never change anybody's heart. If anything, laws just build resentment, encourage sneakiness, and cause my fallen soul to wonder just how much I can get away with and still smugly consider myself "innocent." Laws make us conniving; they gum up our relationship with God and our relationships with one another. ("Lawbreaker versus Enforcer" is not a great model for any relationship!) And laws sure don't help us in "making peace."

But sacrificial love? That's an entirely different matter. Sacrificial love brings us closer to God and to one another. It was sacrificial love that brought God near. It's sacrificial love that holds us close to His heart. It's sacrificial love that has brought us peace with Him. On this side of the cross, followers of Jesus have no need for clever interpretation of complicated rules. And enforcement? It's off the table (Romans 8:1). The wall between holy God and sinful you and me has been demolished. Jesus is our peace.

....

Lord, thank You for freeing me from the burden of complex and burdensome rules. The wall between holy You and sinful me is gone, and You have invited me to know You, to know Your peace, and to follow You.

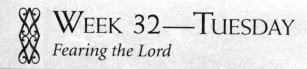

Week 32—Tuesday
Fearing the Lord

Who is the man that fears the LORD? Him shall He teach in the way He chooses. He himself shall dwell in prosperity, and his descendants shall inherit the earth. The secret of the LORD is with those who fear Him, and He will show them His covenant

PSALM 25:12–14

The Man Upstairs. My Co-Pilot. The pop-culture god acknowledged for touchdowns and Emmy awards.

What do these versions of god have in common? For one thing, they're never scary. They are helpful, nice, and accommodating; they have a reputation for helping people out of tough spots. These versions of god are very easy to deal with. Even a bit cuddly.

Oh, and one other thing—these gods don't exist.

See, the God who Is, who calls Himself *I Am*, is scary. His power is scary. His knowledge of me is scary. His capacity for wrath is scary. And His absolute commitment to holiness may be His scariest trait of all.

In fact, if we don't take God seriously enough to be very afraid of Him, we are not worshipping the God of the Bible.

But when we approach this powerful, holy God in honest fear, an amazing thing happens. God sees us through Jesus' death on the cross. The Almighty exhausted His righteous wrath toward us there. He is no longer angry at those of us who fear Him.

And to those who fear God, He is Teacher, Provider, and Lord, and He has made a covenant commitment to be with us now and for eternity.

Are you *not* afraid of God? Then you've not truly met Him. Afraid, yet forgiven? You are blessed to be one of His covenant people.

....

Lord, thank You for teaching me to fear You that I might live fearlessly.

> *He is the Mediator of the new covenant, by means of death, for the redemption of the transgressions under the first covenant, that those who are called may receive the promise of the eternal inheritance.*
>
> HEBREWS 9:15

Mediators play an important role in many difficult legal cases, and mediation is tricky business. A mediator has to listen to and thoroughly grasp two vastly different viewpoints. A mediator has to bridge the gap between two parties who are incredibly far apart.

"Holy God vs. Sinful Man" was the toughest mediation case of all time. On the one hand was the Living God, dwelling in absolute holiness, justice, and purity. On the other hand were we humans who, at our best, produce only "filthy rags" (Isaiah 64:6) or "rubbish" (Philippians 3:8).

Talk about a gap! How could any mediator resolve such a case? How could any mediator possibly grasp the righteous demands of a Holy God while understanding the struggles of our life in a fallen world? Only One could . . . and He did.

The miracle of Jesus' mediation is this: God came in the flesh, walked through a lifetime of what it's like to be a man, and then died in the role of Penalty-Bearer for our sins. And on the cross, Jesus' mediation succeeded. It is finished! Mediation is complete! The empty tomb proves that the case has been settled! And now Jesus calls. To the weary. To the hurting. To the broken. To the ones who have no hope. To all the ones who are trapped under more guilt than they can lift. And the risen Jesus offers the astounding "promise of the eternal inheritance."

....

Lord, thank You that You paid my overwhelming debt and settled the case. Thank You for welcoming me into Your family. What overwhelming grace!

DR. RICHARD A. POWELL, MCGREGOR BAPTIST CHURCH, FORT MYERS, FL

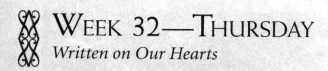

Week 32—Thursday
Written on Our Hearts

"Behold, the days are coming, says the LORD, when I will make a new covenant with the house of Israel and with the house of Judah . . . I will put My law in their minds, and write it on their hearts; and I will be their God, and they shall be My people."

JEREMIAH 31:31, 33

When LuAnne Rousey and I were first dating, there was a lot I needed to learn.

Does she like flowers? If so, what kind? What sort of movies? What restaurants? What's her favorite color? When's her birthday? Her curfew? (Dare not mess that one up!)

But . . . LuAnne Powell and I have been married for thirty-five years. Of course, I still pay attention to her needs and her wants, but I don't dwell on the minutiae nearly as much as I once did. You see, I've had her in my heart for a long time. (And there is no curfew!)

Well, according to Jewish tradition, the Torah (the Old Testament) contains 613 different commands. That's a lot to learn!

And no one can perfectly obey all those laws. It's an unbearable weight. In fact, the true purpose of God's Old Testament Law was to drive people to cry out for the mercy of the Savior!

So Jesus came. And since then He has provided those who follow Him with the very presence of His Holy Spirit. It is the Holy Spirit of God in every believer who inscribes God's Word on our hearts and minds.

....

Lord, sometimes it seems that the harder I try to obey, the more I fail. Thank You that Your faithfulness, not mine, makes me and keeps me Your child.

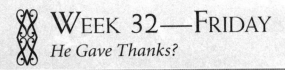

WEEK 32—FRIDAY
He Gave Thanks?

Then [Jesus] took the cup, and gave thanks, and gave it to [His disciples], saying,
"Drink from it, all of you. For this is My blood of the new covenant, which is shed for
many for the remission of sins. But I say to you, I will not drink of this fruit of the vine
from now on until that day when I drink it new with you in My Father's kingdom."

MATTHEW 26:27–29

I t's a holy moment. Years of ministry are drawing to a close. Now comes death on the cross. Jesus gathered His closest followers. How can we even begin to understand His state of mind at that moment? It's hard to imagine His heart as He took the cup in hand, knowing that He was about to illustrate one of Christianity's most significant messages: the cup's contents stand for His soon-to-be-shed blood.

And Jesus "gave thanks."

Why?

We know what Jesus was about to face: the agony of the garden. The pain of betrayal. The denial by one of his three closest followers. The scourging. Crucifixion. The undiluted outpouring of His Father's wrath. For us, death has lost its sting. For Him, death would sting hard. Indescribably hard.

So why was Jesus thankful? I believe that there is only one possible answer: because of us. Hebrews 12:2 essentially says that Jesus looked down through time, saw you and me, and decided that, although the cross was a nightmare, forgiving us was worth the pain.

....

Lord, life isn't always easy. Sometimes I feel I have every right to be ungrateful
for the hard times. But You weren't. So, on my dark days, when endurance is
hard, teach me to, like You, look ahead and know that one day the pain will all
be worth it.

DR. RICHARD A. POWELL, MCGREGOR BAPTIST CHURCH, FORT MYERS, FL

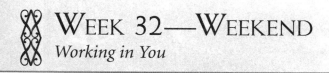
Now may the God of peace who brought up our Lord Jesus from the dead, that great Shepherd of the sheep, through the blood of the everlasting covenant, make you complete in every good work to do His will, working in you what is well pleasing in His sight, through Jesus Christ, to whom be glory forever and ever. Amen.

HEBREWS 13:20–21

The part of Florida where I live has some of the most beautiful water anywhere. We have the Gulf, bays, marshes, birds, dolphins, manatees, and some of the best wildlife anywhere!

But I don't have a kayak. Slowly paddling around until my arms are really tired has never sounded like fun.

My friend, are you tired of paddling? Is life just too hard? Do you feel that you have to work really hard to paddle to where God wants you, to where life will be great?

A few years back I bought a jet ski. That purchase meant power—and I rejected forever the thought of having to paddle to the point of exhaustion.

The power to please God by doing His will doesn't come from your effort. It comes from the fact that He bought you and is now working within you to make you more like Christ. So you aren't reduced to kayaking. You have a jet ski! You have, in Almighty God and apart from your own effort, everything you need to be "well pleasing in His sight." The power you need to please God came when He purchased you on Calvary. Now, stop paddling!

Lord, sometimes I've thought—and acted like—pleasing You is all up to me. Thank You for today's reminder that I am well pleasing in Your sight because of Jesus and that You are doing the hard work of making me more like Him.

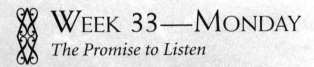

WEEK 33—MONDAY
The Promise to Listen

For I know the thoughts that I think toward you, says the LORD, thoughts of peace and not of evil, to give you a future and a hope. Then you will call upon Me and go and pray to Me, and I will listen to you. And you will seek Me and find Me, when you search for Me with all your heart.

JEREMIAH 29:11–13

O ne of the greatest hurts we will ever experience is the pain of not being heard when we bare our soul to another. Such breakdowns in communication occur between married couples, families, friends, and coworkers. Wouldn't it be tragic if you thought your heavenly Father didn't listen to you! You would feel abandoned and ignored; you would be frustrated and angered. If you shared your secret dreams and deepest heartaches with your Father and He didn't listen, you would certainly feel that He didn't care about you.

The promise of this passage is that God does listen because He deeply loves you just as He loves His chosen people, Israel. Having been carried off into captivity, Israel was in the midst of intense hurt, wondering if God cared. He spoke to them through the prophet Jeremiah and assured them that He had good plans for them. He encouraged Israel to call on Him, and He promised to listen to their cry if they sought Him with all their heart.

You may wonder if God has forgotten you. He hasn't. He has good plans for you. So, in the midst of your pain and loneliness, call out to Him and know that He hears you. He may not explain everything to you or give you what you want, but you will experience His loving concern and assurance.

....

Thank You, Jesus, for listening!

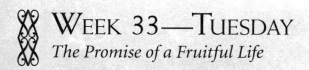
"I am the vine, you are the branches. He who abides in Me, and I in him, bears much fruit; for without Me you can do nothing."

JOHN 15:5

Every human being wants to live a life of significance. So what can you do to make your life on earth have a far-reaching, positive, lasting impact? Life is brief and busy, so it is easy to become preoccupied. Jesus made a very clear promise, though: your life *will* bear much fruit. And He was referring to fruit that is significant. Jesus promised that your life will be significant and have eternal value. But there is one condition.

Not everyone will make a difference of eternal value. Jesus clarified the necessary position and condition for bearing that kind of fruit. Simply put, Jesus is the Source, and we are the conduits. He is the Power, and we are the vessels through which His power flows into the world. In and of ourselves, we will do nothing of eternal value. Only God can do that. We will make a significant difference only if we "abide" in Christ and allow His power to flow through us. There is nothing mystical here. *Abiding* simply means recognizing both my place and His vastly superior place. As I abide, He bears the fruit. *I am not the cause of the fruit; I am the conduit of God-given fruit.* But I must abide!

The key is to abide in Christ: to breathe, walk, live, think, dream, plan, and respond with Jesus as the center of my universe. To abide in Jesus means to be consumed with Him. As I make Him the focus of my life, He will bear fruit through me.

....

Lord, I want to live every moment consumed with You! In Christ, amen.

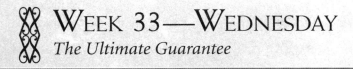

WEEK 33—WEDNESDAY
The Ultimate Guarantee

For all the promises of God in [Jesus] are Yes, and in Him Amen, to the glory of God through us. Now He who establishes us with you in Christ and has anointed us is God, who also has sealed us and given us the Spirit in our hearts as a guarantee.

2 CORINTHIANS 1:20–22

When God makes a promise, will He be true to His word? Absolutely! There is no greater truth than the trustworthiness of God. It is His glory to be faithful. He has also given us a guarantee—but a guarantee is only as good as the company backing it up! Our guarantee is spelled out by God the Father and backed by God the Son and God the Holy Spirit.

In today's passage our position in Christ—our position of salvation and redemption—is guaranteed. God the Father has established *us* in God the Son and "sealed *us* and given *us* the [Holy] Spirit." The Spirit is "in *our* hearts as a guarantee," like a deposit you make on what you want to purchase. The Holy Spirit is God's deposit in our lives, ensuring us that He will fully purchase us. If He were to default on our salvation, He would lose His deposit. But that is utterly impossible. God cannot deny Himself, and by nature He is faithful.

This passage is clear: your salvation is not dependent on you, but on the seal of the Son and on the Spirit's presence in you. So banish the thought that you could lose your salvation! God is able; He has promised; He is faithful. You are His—and He has put on you the guarantee . . . of Himself!

....

Thank You, God, for Your grace that never fails! Amen.

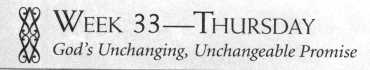

WEEK 33—THURSDAY
God's Unchanging, Unchangeable Promise

God, determining to show more abundantly to the heirs of promise the immutability of His counsel, confirmed it by an oath, that by two immutable things, in which it is impossible for God to lie, we might have strong consolation, who have fled for refuge to lay hold of the hope set before us.

HEBREWS 6:17–18

Nothing is impossible for God. He can do absolutely whatever He wants to do, but absolutely nothing that is contrary to His character. His nature is perfect and holy. Therefore, it is impossible for His counsel to change (it was perfect at the start) or His word to be violated (your holy God cannot lie).

When you look around and see constant changes in circumstances, people, yourself, and our country, it is difficult to grasp that something is unchanging. Yet, because it is impossible for God to violate or change His character, we are assured that it is "impossible for God to lie." That fact gives us "consolation" and comfort. If God could lie, we would never know which of His promises He will break. We would live in a constant state of uncertainty and unrest. However, because it is impossible for God to lie, we take comfort in His promises! Jesus' resurrection validated His claim that "I am the resurrection and the life" (John 11:25).

And this Jesus has gone before us, representing us to the Father as the perfect sacrifice for our sins. Therefore the "hope set before us" and "an anchor of the soul" (v. 19) is the assurance of that right standing we have before God in Christ.

....

Thank You, Lord God, that You are holy, Your Word is unchanging and unchangeable, and my status as Your child is secure. Amen!

WEEK 33—FRIDAY
The Promise of Newness

If anyone is in Christ, he is a new creation; old things have passed away; behold, all things have become new.

2 CORINTHIANS 5:17

Other than possibly the smile on your face and the joy in your eyes, it's likely that nothing about you visibly changed when you surrendered to the lordship of Jesus. You probably did not experience the dramatic changes the apostle Paul did at his conversion (1 Corinthians 15:9).

Despite the lack of external evidence, God promised that two things happened when you were saved. First, "old things have passed away." This verb is in the Greek aorist tense, meaning the action happened once and is completed. The "old" refers to your sin-stained heart, the stranglehold of sin on you, the darkness of your mind, your separation from God. When you were saved, God replaced your sin-stained heart with a clean heart of righteousness, and sin no longer has power over you because the power of God abides in you. God lifted the veil from over your mind and illuminated your thinking by His truth. You once were separated from God, but now you are reconciled to Him. The god of this world no longer rules your life because Jesus is your Lord and your God. Old things have definitely passed away!

Second, God's promise continues with "All things have become new." You have a new family, a new heart, a new Father, a new destiny, and a new purpose. You have a new song in your heart. And you have the Holy Spirit abiding within you, providing you with God's power so you are able to live the godly life He has called on you to live.

....

Lord, thank You for transforming me into a new creation.

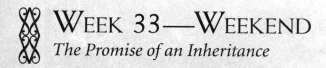

WEEK 33—WEEKEND
The Promise of an Inheritance

For as many of you as were baptized into Christ have put on Christ. There is neither Jew nor Greek, there is neither slave nor free, there is neither male nor female; for you are all one in Christ Jesus. And if you are Christ's, then you are Abraham's seed, and heirs according to the promise.

GALATIANS 3:27–29

God promises His family an inheritance, and that inheritance is our salvation! Abraham "believed God, and it was accounted to him for righteousness" (Galatians 3:6). Like this forefather of faith, we become righteous when we believe.

Fortunately, salvation is available to all. God does not discriminate. Praise the Lord that Gentiles can be included in His family. Praise Him that social standing is irrelevant when coming to Christ: "there is neither slave nor free." Gender is not an issue: "there is neither male nor female." The significance of this promise is that God makes no distinction about whom He will include in His family of faith. *All* will receive an inheritance—if!

Yes, there is an *if* in the promise. Notice verse 29: "*If* you are Christ's." That is the condition. And how do you know if you "are Christ's" or if you have been "baptized into Christ"? There is only one way: you trust that Jesus Christ is God's Son, the One who paid the price for your sins and whose resurrection validated His deity.

Being born into a Christian family will not make you a Christian. You must recognize Jesus as God's Son and trust Him as your Savior and Lord. Then you will have an eternal inheritance.

··

Thank You, Lord, that my inheritance is secure in Christ!

WEEK 34—MONDAY
A Sense of Security in Uncertain Times

The LORD knows the days of the upright, and their inheritance shall be forever. They shall not be ashamed in the evil time, and in the days of famine they shall be satisfied.

PSALM 37:18–19

One of the great struggles we face in life is insecurity. If we are honest, we all struggle, at times, with emotional insecurity. With the turmoil in the world, we are also fearful for our physical security, and we work our whole lives trying to achieve financial security. In the midst of these insecurities, the psalm for today gives a promise that brings great comfort and security. God knows. He knows every struggle, every heartache, every fear, and every trial. In fact, not only does He know what is happening right now, He knew before the foundation of the world that you would go through these struggles. God is not surprised in the least by anything that comes into your life. He is the sovereign, omniscient God.

God not only knows our trials but He sustains us. The apostle Paul said in Philippians 1:6, "being confident of this very thing, that He who began a good work in you will complete it until the day of Jesus Christ." Hardships, trials, disasters and famine will come and go. But God's faithfulness and promise to keep us are eternal. Therefore, we can rest in the security of knowing that we can trust God in everything.

Father, thank You that You have the power to keep me secure regardless of the circumstances of my life. In Jesus' name, amen.

DR. LEE SHEPPARD, MABEL WHITE BAPTIST CHURCH, MACON, GA

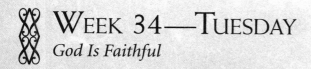

WEEK 34—TUESDAY
God Is Faithful

[Jesus] said to me, "It is done! I am the Alpha and the Omega, the Beginning and the End. I will give of the fountain of the water of life freely to him who thirsts. He who overcomes shall inherit all things, and I will be his God and he shall be My son."

REVELATION 21:6–7

Think about a wedding ring for a moment. I remember the day I put my wife's wedding ring on her finger and pledged to her my faithfulness. Did you know that the wedding ring originated in ancient Egypt, and was formed into a circle as a symbol of eternal love? It symbolizes that true love has neither beginning nor end. In real life, however, relationships do sometimes struggle and end. Marriages are dissolved through divorce or death. While we would like to claim that our love is eternal, human love is painfully finite.

God's love, however, is eternal. The book of Revelation gives us an amazing vision of the eternal God who has no beginning and no end. He is the God of yesterday, today, and forever. He has always existed and will always be with us. He is the Alpha and Omega. He is faithful to His people and we can rest in His continual presence. We are His "people," and He is our God.

Friend, our God is not a distant God that only exists in the farthest realm of outer space, or worse, only in our imagination; He is an up close and personal God who will never leave us or forsake us. He works all things for His glory and our good, and in the end we will inherit eternal life.

....

Father, I am grateful that Your love and Your faithfulness endure forever. In Jesus' name, amen.

WEEK 34—WEDNESDAY
It's Not about Me!

For by Him all things were created that are in heaven and that are on earth, visible and invisible, whether thrones or dominions or principalities or powers. All things were created through Him and for Him.

COLOSSIANS 1:16

When things don't go your way, do you react or respond? Think carefully about how you answer that question. Every day of our lives we are confronted with circumstances that squeeze one of those actions out of us, and the behavior that manifests itself is telling.

When we react, it is usually not good. Reaction is often guided by the flesh. We want what we want, when we want it. We want our plans to come to fruition. We want our way, and when we don't get it, we react. Sometimes our reaction is manifest in anger, frustration, pouting or a bad attitude. When we react, we are putting our selfishness on full display.

However, when we respond, it is often guided by the Spirit. When we respond, it says that we are thinking biblically. Paul said that God created all things and that all things were created through Him and for Him. Where do you see your way in this verse? God created all things, including us, for Himself. So when we don't get our way, it may be painful, and it may not be the road of our choice, but He is right there with us. He is giving us the opportunity to trust Him with our circumstances and display our faith in Him. We need to remind ourselves daily that it's not about us; it's all about Him.

Father, thank You that You are ever-present—regardless what the circumstances of my life suggest—and that You are always working out Your good plan for me. In Jesus' name, amen.

DR. LEE SHEPPARD, MABEL WHITE BAPTIST CHURCH, MACON, GA

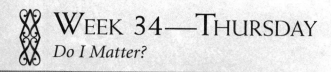

Week 34—Thursday
Do I Matter?

When the fullness of the time had come, God sent forth His Son, born of a woman, born under the law, to redeem those who were under the law, that we might receive the adoption as sons. And because you are sons, God has sent forth the Spirit of His Son into your hearts, crying out, "Abba, Father!"

GALATIANS 4:4–6

As a parent there is something special about children. We don't just appreciate our children, we love them. I remember the first time I saw each of our three children. When they were born, my heart raced and my eyes were wide with amazement. In that instant I loved them unconditionally and accepted them into our family. There is nothing they can do that will ever make them not a part of our family.

Did you know that the same thing is true of your spiritual family? God doesn't just appreciate you—He loves you! As His children, we yearn to know this. We find ourselves, at times, asking, "God, do You know where I am? Do You even care?" If we're not careful, we let our circumstances send us the wrong message. We lose our job, are betrayed by a close friend, get a dreaded diagnosis from the doctor, or feel rejected, and we find ourselves wondering, "Do I matter?"

The Bible provides perspective with these words: "when the fullness of the time had come, God sent forth His Son, born . . . that we might receive the adoption as sons." This is God's definitive reply to our questions and struggles. God is saying, "I love you. I accept you. I have adopted you into my family." Adopted children are *chosen* children! You really do matter!

. . . .

Father, thank You that I really do matter to You. In Jesus' name, amen.

For this reason we also, since the day we heard it, do not cease to pray for you, and to ask that you may be filled with the knowledge of His will in all wisdom and spiritual understanding; that you may walk worthy of the Lord, fully pleasing Him, being fruitful in every good work and increasing in the knowledge of God.

COLOSSIANS 1:9–10

Being a member of God's family brings privileges. One of our privileges is prayer. There is awesome power in prayer. Paul gave us three ways to intercede. First, we should pray that God will fill us with the knowledge of His will. In other words, we should ask God to help us understand what He wants us to do. It is important that we understand God's Word so that God can use it to increase our knowledge of Him.

We should also pray that we will live a life worthy of the Lord, fully pleasing Him. Does our behavior reflect the Father to others? When we represent the Father in a way that honors Him, that is a life worthy of the Lord. Our chief aim should be to please God. The Bible says in Hebrews that without faith it is impossible to please God. Walking with God by faith is a life that pleases God.

A third way we can pray is that we will bear fruit in every good work. The fruit is the fruit of the Spirit: love, joy, patience, kindness, goodness, faithfulness, gentleness, and self-control. As we walk with God, growing in the knowledge of Him, the fruit of the Spirit will be a natural byproduct of our relationship with Him.

....

Father, thank You for the powerful gift of prayer. In Jesus' name, amen.

DR. LEE SHEPPARD, MABEL WHITE BAPTIST CHURCH, MACON, GA

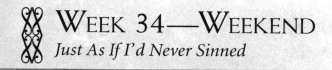

Week 34—Weekend
Just As If I'd Never Sinned

But the Scripture has confined all under sin, that the promise by faith in Jesus Christ might be given to those who believe. But before faith came, we were kept under guard by the law, kept for the faith which would afterward be revealed. Therefore the law was our tutor to bring us to Christ, that we might be justified by faith.

GALATIANS 3:22–24

The gospel is rich and fertile soil for those who want to sink their roots deep and grow in the knowledge of Christ. Before Jesus died on the cross, the Bible says we were all prisoners of sin and anchored to the law that we could not keep. However, God used the law like a funnel to direct humanity to Christ. The desire of the Father is that we will be justified by our faith in Christ alone.

Justification—I've heard it defined "Just as if I'd never sinned." In other words, the one who has surrendered their life to Jesus Christ is blameless before God and receives no condemnation. Have you paused to think of the impact justification has on our lives? Here are a few to meditate on. We are at peace with God (Romans 5:1). We rejoice, because of our standing, in the hope of sharing God's eternal glory (v. 2). We rejoice in suffering, knowing that our suffering produces endurance, which produces character, which produces hope (vv. 3–5). We are assured of a final salvation (vv. 6–11). And because we are reconciled to God, the Holy Spirit fills our hearts with great joy!

....

Father, thank You that I am no longer a prisoner to sin and that my eternal inheritance is secure in You. I now know that I will stand blameless before You one day! In Jesus' name, amen.

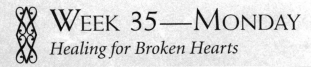

WEEK 35—MONDAY
Healing for Broken Hearts

The Spirit of the Lord God is upon Me, because the Lord has anointed Me to preach good tidings to the poor; He has sent Me to heal the brokenhearted . . . to comfort all who mourn . . . to give them beauty for ashes, the oil of joy for mourning.

ISAIAH 61:1–3

Several years ago I discovered the music of Tommy Walker and the CA Worship Band. What great music! One of my favorite songs is Ron Kenoly's "He Turned My Mourning into Dancing." The chorus says, "He's turned my mourning into dancing again. He's lifted my sorrows; I can't stay silent! I must sing, for His joy has come!"

Several Old Testament passages reflect this wonderful truth, but none better than Isaiah's word to his generation and ours. In Isaiah 61, all three Persons of the Trinity—Father, Son, and Spirit—are pictured as bringing healing to our lives. And it is Jesus Himself who comes near to us in the brokenness of life and replaces our ashes (a sign of grieving) with oil (a sign of refreshment).

Granted, the brokenness we are experiencing may be very different from the brokenness the people of Israel faced, but the cure is the same. It is the love of God revealed in His Son, Jesus, that makes it possible for us to recover from broken hearts and shattered lives. Perhaps today you feel overwhelmed by loss and heartache. Know that the Anointed One has come to exchange His beauty for your ashes and His oil for your mourning. You *will* dance again.

....

Thank You, God, that Your love is the cure for the brokenness in my life. Thank You for the hope and comfort I find in that truth. Thank You that You will enable me to dance again!

RICK WHITE, SENIOR PASTOR, THE PEOPLE'S CHURCH, FRANKLIN, TN

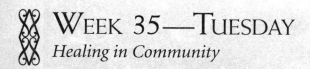

WEEK 35—TUESDAY
Healing in Community

Confess your trespasses to one another, and pray for one another, that you may be healed. The effective, fervent prayer of a righteous man avails much.

JAMES 5:16

In his book *Courageous Leadership*, Willow Creek pastor Bill Hybels wrote: "The local church is the hope of the world. There is nothing like the local church when it's working right. . . . Whatever the capacity for human suffering, the church has a greater capacity for healing and wholeness."[14]

The church is not a showplace for saints, but rather it is to be a safe place for broken and imperfect people—a category that includes all of us. The church is to be a place for all people regardless of the current condition of their life or their history. After all, God loves each of us just the way we are—but He loves us too much to leave us this way!

The local church can be a place for healing when members live out Scripture's thirty-eight "one another" commands: love one another, serve one another, encourage one another, and so on. God intends for the Christian life to always be lived out in community. Yes, we confess all our sin to God, but we find a different kind of healing when we confess our brokenness to members of a safe and caring community.

Is your church a safe community for hurting and imperfect people? The truth is that hurt people tend to hurt others while healing people help others heal.

....

Thank You, Lord God, for bringing into my life people who have helped me heal. Use me as an instrument of healing in the lives of others, I pray, for their good and Your glory.

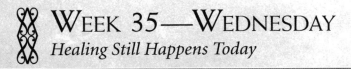

Week 35—Wednesday
Healing Still Happens Today

Surely He has borne our griefs and carried our sorrows; yet we esteemed Him stricken, smitten by God, and afflicted. But He was wounded for our transgressions, He was bruised for our iniquities; the chastisement for our peace was upon Him, and by His stripes we are healed.

Isaiah 53:4–5

It was early January 2010 when I learned that I had large B-cell, T-cell-rich non-Hodgkin's lymphoma. I had ministered to people with cancer throughout my ministry, and now I was the one battling cancer.

Can I just say I absolutely hate cancer? Perhaps no other word in the English language strikes such fear in the human heart. Cancer touches almost every family directly or indirectly. In one year I buried five young adults—all in their forties, all victims of cancer. Today, just past four years clear of cancer, I carry the title "cancer survivor."

Why are some of us healed and others are not? I don't know, but I keep in mind that all healing on this earth is temporary at best. All of us are going to die—and all of us will know ultimate healing when we are in the presence of Jesus.

My doctor termed me a "full recovery" patient. *Healing* was not a part of his vocabulary, but it was my experience. So I encourage you to always pray for healing—and always leave the results to the One who brings ultimate healing.

....

Jesus, I know You came to die primarily for our spiritual healing, but I also know that during Your earthly ministry You brought physical healing. So, Lord, I come before You grateful for the spiritual healing, boldly requesting physical healing, and willing to submit to Your good and perfect will for my life.

RICK WHITE, SENIOR PASTOR, THE PEOPLE'S CHURCH, FRANKLIN, TN

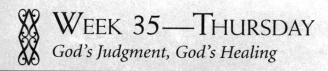

Week 35—Thursday
God's Judgment, God's Healing

"To you who fear My name the Sun of Righteousness shall arise with healing in His wings; and you shall go out and grow fat like stall-fed calves," . . . says the Lord of hosts.

Malachi 4:2–3

You might be surprised by the verse that precedes the one you just read. Hear the warning of verse 1: "The day is coming, burning like an oven, and all the proud, yes, all who do wickedly will be stubble." Yes, that description of God's judgment is juxtaposed with a reference to His healing.

A future judgment is coming for those who have rejected God's love and His provision for salvation in Jesus Christ. The day when the Sovereign Lord of this universe brings His judgment is going to be indescribably terrible.

Perhaps you remember this phrase from the opening of *ABC's Wide World of Sports*: "the thrill of victory and the agony of defeat." That is exactly what Malachi 4:1–2 describes. For some individuals, the day of judgment will be truly agonizing. For those who fear the Lord, that day will be a thrilling one of victory, healing, and God's restoration of all that is right and good. This future healing should encourage every believer even while it serves as a catalyst for us to reach our families, friends, and coworkers with the good news.

. . . .

Righteous and good God, You have established standards that none of us can meet. Thank You, Jesus, for meeting those standards and then dying for us who can't. And thank You for the thrill of Your victory over sin and death—and for the thrilling fact that I share in that with You!

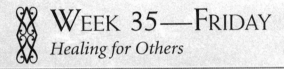

WEEK 35—FRIDAY
Healing for Others

Blessed be the God and Father of our Lord Jesus Christ, the Father of mercies and God of all comfort, who comforts us in all our tribulation, that we may be able to comfort those who are in any trouble.

2 CORINTHIANS 1:3–4

Several days ago a man walked into my office deeply troubled by the news he had just received from his doctor. The diagnosis was cancer. In fact the diagnosis was large B-cell non-Hodgkin's lymphoma, the very same cancer that I had experienced four years earlier. I was able to come alongside him and share in great detail what I had experienced. We prayed together very specifically about his health and the journey that was before him. I, who had been comforted when I walked that path, was able to bring comfort to him.

When we share with others about the healing work God has done in our lives, we are actually privileged to participate with God in their healing. And we are much more willing to share accounts of our physical healing than we are talking about our failures, hurts, habits, and hang-ups. Our pride causes us to protect our scars when God really wants to use those as well to bring hope and healing to others.

Take some time today to think about where God has brought healing in your life (marriage, finances, addictions, and so forth). Will you allow God to use your story to encourage and bring healing to another person? Is there a doctor in your house? I think so.

....

Thank You, Redeemer God, that one way You redeem life's hard times is by allowing us to come alongside others who encounter those same circumstances. Thank You that even pain beyond description is not wasted in Your economy.

RICK WHITE, SENIOR PASTOR, THE PEOPLE'S CHURCH, FRANKLIN, TN

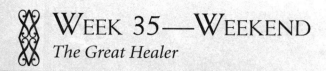

Week 35—Weekend
The Great Healer

The LORD builds up Jerusalem; He gathers together the outcasts of Israel. He heals the brokenhearted and binds up their wounds. He counts the number of the stars; He calls them all by name. Great is our Lord, and mighty in power; His understanding is infinite. The LORD lifts up the humble; He casts the wicked down to the ground.

PSALM 147:2–6

Recently I spoke on Colossians 3:15–17 and living with an attitude of gratitude. I was helped by John Ortberg's observation that gratitude involves three factors: benefits, benefactor, beneficiary—and the Latin *bene* means "good."[15]

We are to live with gratitude because in Christ we are the *beneficiaries* of many wonderful *benefits*. The psalmist reminded us to "forget not all His benefits" (103:2). According to James 1:17, every good thing and every perfect thing comes down from the Father above; He, our great Benefactor, is the One directing good things our way.

The psalmist also declared that the Lord "heals the brokenhearted and binds up their wounds" (147:3). He is the same wonderful Benefactor who created the world in which we live. He is the great and powerful God, supreme over creation, the church, and the Christian. Scientists have identified some of the stars in the galaxy, but our great God knows the name of each and every star because He created them. And our God is also the Great Healer who brings health and wholeness to all who will trust in Him.

Blessed be His name!

. . . .

Good and gracious God, taking a few minutes to consider the benefits of being Your child does lead to an attitude of gratitude. Thank You for the many blessings You faithfully, continually pour into my life. May I be mindful of them and grateful to You.

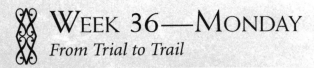
Oh, how great is Your goodness, which You have laid up for those who fear You, which You have prepared for those who trust in You in the presence of the sons of men!

PSALM 31:19

Think about it. Without affliction in our lives, there is much about God's character that we would not appreciate. In fact, one reason why God allows life's trials is to draw us closer to Him so that we might know Him better.

Pastor and writer A. W. Tozer defined the goodness of God as "that which disposes Him to be kind, cordial, benevolent, and full of good will toward men. He is tenderhearted and of quick sympathy and His unfailing attitude toward all moral beings is open, frank, and friendly. By His nature He is inclined to bestow blessedness and He takes holy pleasure in the happiness of His people."[16]

Certain aspects of God's goodness are heightened against the dark backdrop of affliction. David knew affliction, but as he drew nearer to God, he was reminded that God is good.

God has goodness stored up for us. He does not forget us in our trial, but He does allow the trial to accomplish its full work in our lives. And as the trial does its work and we find refuge in God, we can experience the full assurance of His goodness.

Like David, if you are experiencing a *trial,* choose to see it as a *trail* that leads you closer to the Lord. Patiently endure the difficulty, awaiting God to reveal to you His goodness.

....

Thank You, Redeemer God, for Your ability to turn my trial into a trail to You. As I walk toward You, may I be open to all that You want to reveal to me about Yourself.

DR. LEVI SKIPPER, CONCORD BAPTIST CHURCH, CLERMONT, GA

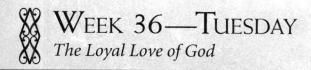

WEEK 36—TUESDAY
The Loyal Love of God

Oh, that men would give thanks to the LORD for His goodness, and for His wonderful works to the children of men! For He satisfies the longing soul, and fills the hungry soul with goodness.

PSALM 107:8–9

Think of a time when a worship leader at church truly led you to a time of praising the Lord with all your heart. Even as a pastor, I have at times struggled to worship; I've had difficulty focusing on the Lord.

Maybe that's why I like to read Psalm 107 and imagine the words being spoken by a worship leader encouraging a congregation to praise God. The leader prompted praise by reminding the people that God delivers His own from their affliction as a display of His loyal love. The worship leader talked about the Israelites' wanderings in the wilderness when they were hungry, thirsty, and without direction; when they cried out to the Lord; when God led His people to safety. The congregation had good reason to lift their voices and wholeheartedly give thanks to God!

When we face great trials, we too must remember the loyal love of God. Think about where you see it in Scripture and when you've experienced it yourself. I remind myself of times when God helped me make decisions or gave me His peace when I was afraid. God has always satisfied the hunger of my soul. God has faithfully loved me, and He will continue to faithfully love me. May your loyal God use Psalm 107 to lead you to worship!

....

Thank You, Almighty God, for Your faithfulness, Your goodness, Your loyal love. I am humbled and grateful that You are mindful of me, shepherding me along this journey of life and never letting me down.

WEEK 36—WEDNESDAY
Our Compassionate and Gracious God

The works of the LORD are great, studied by all who have pleasure in them. His work is honorable and glorious, and His righteousness endures forever. He has made His wonderful works to be remembered; the LORD is gracious and full of compassion.

PSALM 111:2–4

Uninhibited and unrestrained worship of God—like that of this psalmist—is beautiful and inspiring. The psalmist's thanks is heartwarming and a bit contagious!

In Psalm 111:1, he proclaimed, "I will praise the LORD with my whole heart." The subject of his thanksgiving to God—say the commentators—is the Lord's great work probably on behalf of Israel during the exodus. Do you remember how the people of Israel acted during the time of the exodus? They were hardhearted, obstinate, rebellious, often ungrateful—and this list goes on. But God? The psalmist wants us to remember that He is "gracious and full of compassion" (v. 4).

Think about how God has shown grace and compassion to you and the body of Christ. What patience He has toward us when we act just as those in Israel did! What grace He displays toward us even though we often only call out to Him in times of trouble—and ignore Him when things seem to be going well! May we—as the psalmist encourages us to—"Praise the Lord!" more consistently, for He is indeed gracious and compassionate.

....

Yes, may my worship of You be more consistent, Lord God, for You give me plenty of reasons to praise You! Like the psalmist, I can see Your grace, compassion, and faithfulness in my past as well as in my present as you are slow to anger and abounding in love to me! You are indeed worthy of all my praise!

DR. LEVI SKIPPER, CONCORD BAPTIST CHURCH, CLERMONT, GA

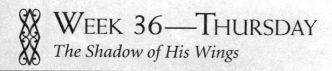

Week 36—Thursday
The Shadow of His Wings

How precious is Your lovingkindness, O God! Therefore the children of men put their trust under the shadow of Your wings. They are abundantly satisfied with the fullness of Your house, and You give them drink from the river of Your pleasures. For with You is the fountain of life; in Your light we see light.

PSALM 36:7–9

Thanks to today's technology—specifically a live feed from the web—my children spent several months watching an eagle in her nest, celebrating when they saw eggs, ecstatic when the eggs hatched, and fascinated by the tiny, helpless babies. These eaglets could barely move, and they always seemed to be chirping and crying as they stretched their tender necks toward the sky. What a tender picture of the mother feeding her young and covering them with her wings for protection.

You and I also need protection. We are citizens of God's kingdom of light, yet we are surrounded by a dark and evil culture that would consume us if possible. We must also be alert, for the great enemy lurks. And we would do well to follow the little eagles' example: keep our faces turned up toward heaven, our necks stretched out toward God's throne, and our voices crying out for His protection. Then, like the mother eagle, the Lord Himself stretches out His wings, and we are safe in their shadow.

The psalmist exclaimed, "How precious is your lovingkindness, O God!" As the psalmist acknowledged, God's attentive and protective love was priceless; how could he do anything but praise the Lord!

....

The shadow of Your wings is a place of protection—and more! There, Lord God, I am reminded of Your remarkable love for chirpy, needy me and of Your generous provision of those needs. Thank You!

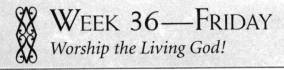

WEEK 36—FRIDAY
Worship the Living God!

May the LORD give you increase more and more, you and your children. May you be blessed by the LORD, who made heaven and earth.

PSALM 115:14–15

A few verses before today's passage, the writer mocked the false gods of his day, essentially saying, "Your god can't speak! You made his mouth out of silver! Your god can't hear! You made his ears out of gold! Your god can't see or smell either." The psalmist pointed out the ridiculousness of believing in a god made by human hands as opposed to the God who made the heavens and the earth.

I will never forget my visit to the archaeological site of Angkor Wat in Cambodia. The entire place was filled with idols made by the hands of men, and I saw many people worshipping those idols. Ironically, when Angkor Wat had been ransacked during a war many years prior, a lot of these idols had been beheaded, and some had lost their feet. I thought to myself, *Who would worship a god that can't keep its head or its feet in war?* Like the psalmist, I mocked the idols.

After all, the stones could do nothing for the worshippers, but our living God can hear and does respond when we worship Him. When you pray, you aren't speaking to a headless idol, a lifeless rock, or a golden ear. You are speaking to your Creator, the living God who knows what is best for you, who is quick to listen when you call, and who will speak back to you. What a blessing to know the living Maker of heaven and earth!

....

Living God, I am so blessed to know You, to be able to worship You, to have You as my heavenly Father, my Fortress, my Guide, my Shepherd, my King.

DR. LEVI SKIPPER, CONCORD BAPTIST CHURCH, CLERMONT, GA

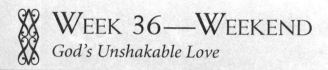

Week 36—Weekend
God's Unshakable Love

I am persuaded that neither death nor life, nor angels nor principalities nor powers, nor things present nor things to come, nor height nor depth, nor any other created thing, shall be able to separate us from the love of God which is in Christ Jesus our Lord.

Romans 8:38–39

Crescendos of praise for God's lovingkindness appear throughout the book of Psalms. And we twenty-first-century believers also have reason to celebrate God's loyal love. *But,* we may wonder from time to time, *can we ever be separated from the love of God?*

Writing to believers in Rome, the apostle Paul described God's work of salvation through His Son, Jesus, salvation we receive by faith. Even as Paul praised this gracious plan of forgiveness, he knew that when trials, affliction, temptations, and difficulties occur, his readers might conclude that the love of God had disappeared. And we understand. We've faced trials and wondered whether God really loved us.

In Romans 8, Paul put such concerns to rest when he proclaimed that absolutely nothing can separate us from God's love. Paul listed threats ranging from physical danger to spiritual attacks, not one of which is able to separate us from God's love. Of course Paul pointed to the greatest evidence of God's love: the death of His Son on the cross for our sins. So you can be at peace: enjoy God's unshakable, good, loyal, compassionate, gracious, protective love for you.

....

Heavenly Father, forgive me for letting circumstances skew my thinking about Your love. Rather than life's challenges, heartaches, and hurts, the truth of Your Word—the truth of Romans 8—needs to be the basis of my confidence in Your love for me. Help me cement this truth in my heart and mind.

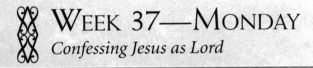
If you confess with your mouth the Lord Jesus and believe in your heart that God has raised Him from the dead, you will be saved. For with the heart one believes unto righteousness, and with the mouth confession is made unto salvation.

ROMANS 10:9–10

As Paul wrote to believers in Rome, in order to have a saving relationship with God, we must confess, "Jesus is Lord."

In our culture of cheap talk, this affirmation seems too simple to bring about such a profound relationship with God. In the first century, however, these three words represented near treason. Caesar tolerated no rival; the slightest resistance was considered a credible threat. Citizens expressed their devotion to Caesar with a verbal confession affirming his lordship. Imagine the scandal of refusing to confess Caesar as the supreme leader and replacing his name with that of an obscure Galilean Jew crucified in Jerusalem thirty years earlier.

Furthermore, the name of Jesus should have been a reminder of Rome's power. After all, whatever threat Jesus had posed was surely extinguished when He was crucified—but the name and fame of Jesus did not die with Him. His followers claimed that He was resurrected. Transformed and empowered by this truth, His humble witnesses scattered all over the planet preaching that Jesus lives and that His resurrection validated His supreme lordship. Jesus was Lord even in Caesar's Rome.

....

Lord Jesus, it's sobering to realize how easily I speak the truth "Jesus is Lord" when early believers risked their lives to say those very words. Thank You for the freedom I have to follow You. And thank You for the salvation You provide. I truly owe You, Lord God, my absolute devotion. Teach me to follow You with unrivaled devotion.

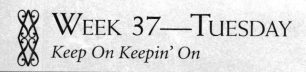

WEEK 37—TUESDAY
Keep On Keepin' On

The steps of a good man are ordered by the LORD, and He delights in his way. Though he fall, he shall not be utterly cast down; for the LORD upholds him with His hand.

PSALM 37:23–24

While a high-school freshman taking a woodshop class, I built a footpath through the woods by our school. The terrain was harsh and the grade steep, but the path allowed all to cover the distance safely and quickly. We planned every step and prepared a place for every footstep. When it was finished, we took joy in the path.

In these verses from Psalm 37, God reminds us that He plans, establishes, and appoints our steps for this journey of life. Like a general leading His troops to victory, He establishes our steps so that we can walk where He wants us to walk—and He delights in us when we do.

We are to live for God, our Creator, and His pleasure in us is maximized when we walk with Him even in the face of adversity. God knows that we are prone to wander especially when life is hard, but He promises that when we fall, He will uphold us.

God establishes our way, enjoys our way, and enables our way. Don't quit. Times will get tough. You will fall down from time to time, but you must never surrender.

....

Jesus, I want to place my feet only on the steps that You have established for me. Whenever I fall, please help me always get up and continue on the path You have for me!

WEEK 37—WEDNESDAY
Finding Hope in God

This is the will of Him who sent Me, that everyone who sees the Son and believes in Him may have everlasting life; and I will raise him up at the last day.

JOHN 6:40

You've seen those close ballgames when the lead goes back and forth until, near the end, one team bursts ahead and the other loses hope of winning. That's when they stop trying, their faces show their despair, and even some fans will head for the exits. The clock is still ticking. The game is still being televised. The plays still count in the stat books. But when hope is gone, then the drive, the energy, and the courage diminish.

Hope motivates, inspires, and energizes us for the challenges of life. The human heart needs hope, and God's promises fuel hope. Just as the aroma from the kitchen tells of a delicious meal to come, God's promises tell us of His blessings that await.

When we—like the players in the game—lose hope, we become disheartened. Life is hard, and our enemy is relentless. Yet we stay in the game because Jesus has promised us everlasting life. Not only do we have His promise that the victory is ours, but we also have hope in the fact that God wants to save us. Furthermore, He has provided a way to save us through His Son and has given us a word to cling to—His promise of everlasting life.

....

Lord God, You know this game of life is demanding. You know that I get tired and then too easily disheartened. Help me keep my eyes on Jesus, my hope for today and for eternity. He does not just give bread for life; Jesus is the Bread of Life.

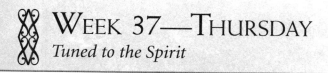

Week 37—Thursday
Tuned to the Spirit

Those who live according to the flesh set their minds on the things of the flesh, but those who live according to the Spirit, the things of the Spirit.

ROMANS 8:5

My blood runs Clemson orange.

I grew up 19.68 miles from the stadium (known as "Death Valley") and attended home games with my dad. Away games in the late 1970s meant listening to the game on radio. ESPN, college football Direct TV package, ESPN3 to watch the live streaming of the game—none of these options were available. We huddled around the radio in 1979 when Clemson beat the mighty Fighting Irish of Notre Dame in South Bend. Whenever the signal faltered, we did everything possible to tune that radio. Whenever we lost the signal, we'd be confused, worried, and discouraged. When we found the signal, then we would learn the truth and (often) celebrate.

Setting your mind on the things of the flesh is like tuning in to the flesh. When you do that, you will live according to the flesh. But when your life is tuned in to the Spirit, then you will live according to the Spirit. God commands us to fix our attention on the Spirit. The flesh will distract, defile, and depress, but God's Spirit will provide direction, reveal God's truth, and bless us with abundant life.

....

Lord God, I know that when I named Jesus my Savior, You changed the station that my heart was tuned to. But You know the reception can get fuzzy. Please continue to keep me sharply tuned to Your Spirit, that I will live, according to His leading, a life that glorifies You.

WEEK 37—FRIDAY
Saving, Life-Transforming Grace

The grace of God that brings salvation has appeared to all men, teaching us that, denying ungodliness and worldly lusts, we should live soberly, righteously, and godly in the present age, looking for the blessed hope and glorious appearing of our great God and Savior Jesus Christ.

TITUS 2:11–13

The Bible reveals different activities or types of grace: forgiving grace that saves us (Titus 2:11; Ephesians 2:8–9), forming grace that sanctifies us (1 Corinthians 15:10), and finishing grace that satisfies us (1 Peter 1:13).

Forgiving grace—the type that brings salvation—is available to all. In Colossians 1:6 Paul called the gospel "the grace of God in truth." The amazing, indescribable, unsearchable grace of God is contained in one truth: the gospel. That Jesus died for our sins, that He was buried, and that He rose again the third day according to the Scripture (1 Corinthians 15:3–4)—this is the gospel, and this is God's truly amazing grace.

And this grace of God teaches that we should live in such a way that people who hear the gospel find it credible. Our lives are associated with the gospel just as an advertising slogan is attached to a product. Of course the gospel possesses intrinsic merit and Spirit-enforced credibility, but the gospel also needs to be represented by a pure life, a righteous life, a sober life. In other words, our lives are evidence that the gospel is real and the gospel changes lives.

....

Lord God, only with Your help can I be evidence of Your saving, life-transforming grace. Enable me, I pray, to live a pure life that honors You and a joyful life that draws others to You. Use my life to reveal the power and the love of Your gospel.

DR. CLAYTON CLOER, FIRST BAPTIST CHURCH OF CENTRAL FLORIDA, ORLANDO, FL

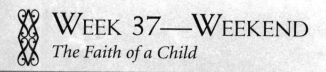

Week 37—Weekend
The Faith of a Child

"Unless you are converted and become as little children, you will by no means enter the kingdom of heaven. Therefore whoever humbles himself as this little child is the greatest in the kingdom of heaven."

MATTHEW 18:3–4

I am the greatest! trumpeted heavyweight boxer Muhammad Ali.

Jesus faced people whose egos were similar to Ali's: the Pharisees and scribes loved the praise of men, the Sadducees loved the chief seats in the synagogue, and His own disciples argued often about who would be the greatest in the kingdom. The Eleven were disputing the matter just hours before the crucifixion! Ali would have fit right in with the first-century folks Jesus encountered. I guess all of us would have.

Consider the way Jesus addressed this issue of greatness. First, He praised the desire to be great. He did not rebuke His disciples or humiliate them. In fact, Jesus even told them—and us—how to be great: humble yourselves. In God's kingdom, humility is the doorway to greatness, and little children have that gift of humility. They model for adults dependence, trust, and innocence that honors God and leads to greatness in His economy.

Childlike dependence embraces Christ as the faithful Provider of all that we need. Childlike trust takes God at His word, embracing big dreams and a limitless God, believing that God will do whatever He says He will do. And childlike innocence is a purity of heart, a freedom from deception, an ease when it comes to forgiving and moving on, and a readiness to trust.

. . . .

Work into my heart, Lord God, childlike dependence on You, childlike trust in You, and childlike innocence that honors You.

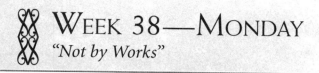

WEEK 38—MONDAY
"Not by Works"

When the kindness and the love of God our Savior toward man appeared, not by works of righteousness which we have done, but according to His mercy He saved us, through the washing of regeneration and renewing of the Holy Spirit, whom He poured out on us abundantly through Jesus Christ our Savior.

TITUS 3:4–6

The apostle Paul knew exactly what God had called him to do: "teach [God's chosen people] to know the truth that shows them how to live godly lives" (Titus 1:1 NLT). As he always did in the middle of his "do this and don't do that" passages, Paul was careful to remind his readers that it is Jesus who graciously does the transforming work in believers' hearts and lives.

Also, as Paul did elsewhere in the New Testament (see Ephesians 2:8, for instance), the apostle proclaimed in Titus 3:5 that God loves us "not because of the righteous things we have done, but because of his mercy" (NLT). Consider what our merciful God has done for us:

He revealed His kindness and love by not punishing us as our sins deserve.
He saved us from the consequences of our sin, eternal separation from God.
He forgave our sins and washed them away.
He gave us new birth.
He gave us new life.
He poured out the Holy Spirit upon us.

And God sent His Son as the Savior of the world. Is Jesus your Savior? If so, thank Him. If not, you only need to ask.

. . . .

Jesus, I recognize my sin—and I ask for Your forgiveness. I deserve to be punished—and I thank You for taking that punishment for my sins. Humbled by Your love, I receive You as my Savior and invite You to be Lord of my life.

DR. ALEX HIMAYA, THECHURCH.AT, TULSA, OK

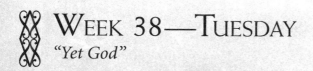

WEEK 38—TUESDAY
"Yet God"

Being justified freely by His grace through the redemption that is in Christ Jesus, whom God set forth as a propitiation by His blood, through faith, to demonstrate His righteousness, because in His forbearance God had passed over the sins that were previously committed.

ROMANS 3:24–25

Right after telling us that "all have sinned and fall short of the glory of God" (Romans 3:23), the apostle Paul proclaimed, "Yet God" (v. 24 NLT).

In our sin, we were destined for a real place called hell, a place of eternal separation from God. *Yet God*, extending us kindness we don't deserve, declared that we sinners are righteous. God did that because the sinless Jesus, by the shedding of His blood, was the perfect and pure sacrifice for our sin.

Jesus' death has huge implications for every aspect of the Christian life. As Paul put it, "People are made right with God when they believe that Jesus sacrificed his life, shedding his blood" (v. 25 NLT)—and that is the essence of Christianity. We are not made right with God by what we do or what we don't do. We are made right with God by whom we know: Jesus!

One more thing. Not only do we come to God through grace, but we walk with God all the days of our lives in grace. There is only one Person who can live the Christian life. I am not that Person, and you aren't either. Jesus is the only One capable of living the Christian life, and He wants to live it in you and through you, as your Savior.

God of grace, You sent Jesus to be my Savior and His Spirit to enable me to live the Christian life. May my life testify to Your grace and love.

WEEK 38—WEDNESDAY
"We Believe"

Then [the Samaritans of the city] said to the woman [who had met Jesus at the well],
"Now we believe, not because of what you said, for we ourselves have heard Him and
we know that this is indeed the Christ, the Savior of the world."

JOHN 4:42

Christ, the Savior of the world—this is not just the theme of this week. It is the gospel message, the good news of Jesus Christ. Like others, John proclaimed that Jesus Christ is indeed "the Savior of the world," that "God so loved the world that He gave His only begotten Son, that whoever believes in Him should not perish but have everlasting life" (John 3:16).

God's kindness toward us is utterly undeserved. There is nothing we could ever do to deserve salvation. None of us can earn our way to God, but the religious teachers of Jesus' day did not agree. They insisted on manmade paths to God; however, Jesus knew no path designed by human beings would enable us to enter into a relationship with the holy God. If there were any other option, don't you think God would have chosen it rather than allow His Son to be butchered for our sin?

God allowed Jesus' brutal death to count as payment for our sins. God allowed the blood of Jesus to satisfy His holy wrath toward sin. When we accept that truth, God declares us righteous. We don't earn it; it comes from the declaration of God. We simply choose belief—and gratitude.

....

Jesus, Savior of the world, You saved me from punishment for my sin. You
changed my life now and for eternity. Help me live in Your grace, willing and
able to share the good news with those who have yet to hear it.

DR. ALEX HIMAYA, THECHURCH.AT, TULSA, OK

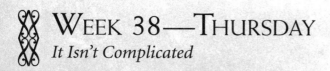
Do not be ashamed of the testimony of our Lord, nor of me His prisoner, but share with me in the sufferings for the gospel according to the power of God, who has saved us and called us with a holy calling, not according to our works, but according to His own purpose and grace which was given to us in Christ Jesus before time began.

2 TIMOTHY 1:8–9

The gospel is not complicated: we recognize our sin and accept the gift of sinless Jesus' death on the cross on our behalf. The enemy wants to complicate the simple, while God simplifies the complicated.

God saved us *and* calls us to live a holy life. Just as our gracious God oversaw the work of salvation, He is doing the work of sanctification—of making us more like Jesus—in the life of every believer. Again, His presence with us and within us is not something we deserve or can earn.

Notice one more thing that Paul told Timothy above. Paul declared that this divine plan of grace existed "before time began." It was always our sovereign God's plan to save us by grace. His plan was never "Do this and this *so that*" we might be saved or experience His blessing. We do and don't do according to His instructions out of gratitude for His grace.

God's plan isn't complicated: it is His grace played out through all of time as well as in the lives of those who recognize the gift of Jesus.

....

Lord God, Jesus offered His life in obedience to You for my salvation. In response I offer my life of obedience to You, a thanks offering made out of gratitude for Your immeasurable grace.

Week 38—Friday
The Bread of Life

"Most assuredly, I say to you, he who believes in Me has everlasting life. I am the bread of life. . . . I am the living bread which came down from heaven. If anyone eats of this bread, he will live forever; and the bread that I shall give is My flesh, which I shall give for the life of the world."

JOHN 6:47–48, 51

The chapter of John's Gospel where this statement appears is significant. Jesus has fed a large and hungry crowd. The men alone numbered five thousand, so the entire crowd may have been between ten and fifteen thousand people. The available food was a boy's lunch: two small fish and five little barley loaves. Yet when Jesus blessed those fish and loaves, the crowd ate "as much as they wanted" (v. 11), and there were twelve baskets of leftover bread. The barley loaves the boy in the crowd had shared provided sustenance for thousands of people.

Even as He provided for these people's physical needs, Jesus was more concerned about their spiritual sustenance, and that is what He was addressing when He said, "I am the bread of life." In Jesus' day, bread was the all-important commodity. In addition to being a staple in people's homes, the price of bread was the index to the economy. Physical bread was important, but not the most important. The implication here in John 6 is that our body could live better without food than our soul can live without Jesus.

....

Lord Jesus, enable me to be as concerned about what I feed my soul as I am about what I feed my body. Even as You satisfy that soul hunger, I also ask You to keep me hungry to know You better.

DR. ALEX HIMAYA, THECHURCH.AT, TULSA, OK

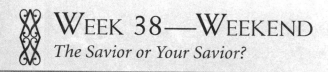

Bodily exercise profits a little, but godliness is profitable for all things, having promise of the life that now is and of that which is to come. This is a faithful saying and worthy of all acceptance. For to this end we both labor and suffer reproach, because we trust in the living God, who is the Savior of all men, especially of those who believe.

1 TIMOTHY 4:8–10

The inward man is much more important than the outward man. Don't you think Timothy already knew this just as you and I do? Yet we—apparently like Timothy—need Paul's reminder.

Paul also reminded us that living for God—serving Him by sharing the gospel—will mean not only effort but suffering. But "the living God" can and will empower us each step of the way. Yes, the *living* God: Jesus is alive, victorious over sin and death, the grave and hell! Jesus is alive—and Jesus is *the* Savior for anyone who believes.

Jesus saves us from the power of sin in our life as well as from the consequences of our sinful nature and sinful ways: those consequences would be eternal separation from our holy God. For those of us who recognize our need, Jesus is not just *the* "Savior of all men," but He is *our* Savior.

Yes, Jesus is *the* Savior, but is He *your* Savior? I pray that if you haven't accepted already, you will soon welcome Jesus as *your* Lord.

....

Lord Jesus, as each day I learn more about living with You as my Savior and Lord, keep me aware of who in my path needs to hear the life-saving, life-giving message of the salvation You offer. Use me to speak Your truth and Your love into their lives.

WEEK 39—MONDAY
The Name Above All Names

God also has highly exalted Him and given Him the name which is above every name, that at the name of Jesus every knee should bow, of those in heaven, and of those on earth, and of those under the earth, and that every tongue should confess that Jesus Christ is Lord, to the glory of God the Father.

PHILIPPIANS 2:9–11

No one has the opportunity to select his or her name. Some people change their name later in life, perhaps because they dislike the name they were given or maybe because they were married. Regardless, most people go by the name they received at birth. Scripture tells us that God Himself gave Jesus the name He received at His birth.

The Lord informed Jesus' birth parents of the special name He had for their son. Gabriel announced to Mary, "You will conceive in your womb and bring forth a son, and shall call His name JESUS. He will be great, and will be called the Son of the Highest" (Luke 1:31–32). An angel of the Lord also told Joseph, "You shall call His name JESUS, for He will save His people from their sins" (Matthew 1:21). Before His birth, Jesus was given a glorious name that pointed to His majesty as well as His purpose.

Today's passage is Paul's reminder of the divine authority of Christ's name. Every knee will one day bow and every person will one day speak of the lordship of Jesus. Whatever your circumstances today, call on the name of Jesus in faith and praise!

....

Heavenly Father, I exalt the name of Christ, a name of grace and hope, of joy and peace! May my words and my actions today bring glory to His holy, wonderful name.

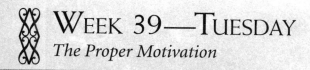

WEEK 39—TUESDAY
The Proper Motivation

Brethren, by the mercies of God . . . present your bodies a living sacrifice, holy, acceptable to God, which is your reasonable service. And do not be conformed to this world, but be transformed by the renewing of your mind, that you may prove what is that good and acceptable and perfect will of God.

ROMANS 12:1–2

What specific motivation, if any, do you have for living the Christian life? Has a family member been nagging you to attend church more frequently? Or maybe a recent health scare has let you know it's time to shape up spiritually? Whatever the case, this is a key fact: without the proper biblical motivation, your spiritual energy for living a life that honors Jesus will wane. Without that proper biblical motivation that comes with understanding the gospel of Jesus, your faith will fizzle and any spiritual movement come to a screeching halt.

This is why in today's passage, Paul appealed to us to remember the mercy of God. Under the Old Testament system, God's people brought calves, lambs, or other animals to be sacrificed for their sin. This act conveyed repentance; it served as a physical reminder of our need for God's forgiveness. But Jesus came to earth to be the perfect sacrifice for our sin. His death on the cross brought us hope, healing, and reconciliation with God. That God ordained for Jesus to die in the place of sinners is the supreme act of mercy. And Jesus' death in our place provides the greatest motivation for us to live for Him a life of holiness.

....

Lord Jesus, renew my mind today. Empower me to live obediently to You rather than in conformity with the world, that I might live a life that pleases and glorifies You.

WEEK 39—WEDNESDAY
The Temple of the Holy Spirit

Do you not know that your body is the temple of the Holy Spirit who is in you, whom you have from God, and you are not your own? For you were bought at a price; therefore glorify God in your body and in your spirit, which are God's.

1 CORINTHIANS 6:19–20

In one of His most vivid word pictures, Jesus said if your eye causes you to lust, pluck it out. Or if your hand causes you to sin, cut it off (Matthew 5:29–30). Clearly, sexual purity is a big deal to God. Perhaps nothing disqualifies a person from spiritual service faster than sexual unfaithfulness, and that's why the devil has temptation lurking on every corner.

In 1 Corinthians 6:19–20, Paul wrote the countercultural message that our bodies belong not to us, but to God. Christians—whose bodies are temples of the Holy Spirit—do not have the freedom to behave however they choose. Just as a tenant is expected to abide by his agreement with the landlord, so we Christians are called to submit our bodies to Christ, who is to be Lord over our entire being. So if you are struggling with lust, ask God to purify your heart and bless you with the spiritual fruit of self-control (Galatians 5:23). In quiet, humble submission, ask God to cleanse your mind and your heart and to use you in His service.

....

Heavenly Father, thank You for reminding me that my body is Yours, not mine, and that it is a temple for Your Holy Spirit. Reign over me today as my Master and Lord. And make me holy, I pray, as You are holy.

REV. JEREMY MORTON, CARTERSVILLE FIRST BAPTIST CHURCH, CARTERSVILLE, GA

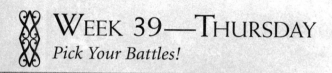

WEEK 39—THURSDAY
Pick Your Battles!

Receive one who is weak in the faith, but not to disputes over doubtful things. . . .
Each of us shall give account of himself to God. Therefore let us not judge one another
anymore, but rather resolve this, not to put a stumbling block or a cause to fall
in our brother's way.

ROMANS 14:1, 12–13

Pick your battles! If you are a parent, you may have come to appreciate the wisdom of those three words. Did you know, though, that the principle is a biblical one? It pretty much summarizes Paul's main point in his Romans 14 discussion of personal liberty.

Paul acknowledged that many people have deep convictions about eating certain foods, while others hold a certain day on the calendar in higher regard than other days. And what is to be a believer's response to these differences? Paul called each individual to both obeying God and extending kindness and patience to those they differ from. God alone is Judge, and all of us will stand before Him and give an account of why we did what we did or didn't do what we didn't do. Instead of judging a person whose opinion is contrary to yours, praise God for the variety of the people in His kingdom. Don't fight your brother on small matters, Paul counseled, but let those differences help you grow in wisdom and grace.

True Christian living always means taking into account the interests of other people. True Christian living involves the pursuit of "the things which make for peace and the things by which one may edify another" (v. 19).

....

Lord, guide my decisions that I may not be a stumbling block to others, that
I am not conforming to this world, and that I am honoring You with my life.

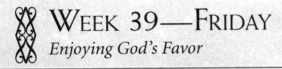

WEEK 39—FRIDAY
Enjoying God's Favor

Blessed be the Lord, who daily loads us with benefits, the God of our salvation! Our God is the God of salvation; and to GOD the Lord belong escapes from death.

PSALM 68:19–20

K ing David was well-acquainted with the highs and lows of life. As a young man, he courageously protected his flock when predators tried to run away with a lamb (1 Samuel 17:34). He fearlessly fought the nine-foot-six enemy of Israel, Goliath of Gath, when no other soldier would (v. 37). The Israelite women sang songs in praise of David's battlefield heroics (1 Samuel 18:7). Without a doubt, David enjoyed tremendous success when he walked with God. The hand of the Lord was clearly on his life. Many psalms—like the one quoted above—are simply David crediting God as the source of every blessing he enjoyed.

But this man after God's own heart was not perfect. Other psalms are pain-filled cries to God from a place of deep distress. David expressed tremendous grief and heartache as a result of his failure as a man, a father, and a king. David was guilty of adultery and murder (2 Samuel 11), which led to unspeakable family distress and unfortunate passivity in David's parenting (2 Samuel 13:21–22).

When David walked in humble obedience to God, he enjoyed God's favor. But when David disobeyed God and sinned, misery resulted. Such is the nature of the Christian walk. When we walk closely with the Lord, we walk under the umbrella of His blessed protection. But when we foolishly, pridefully turn away from the Lord, we are vulnerable to the enemy's attack.

Holy God, draw my heart into deep intimacy with You. I want to stay close to You, knowing You better each day, and resting in Your favor.

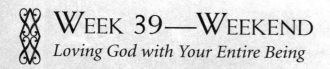

Jesus answered [the scribe], "The first of all the commandments is: 'Hear, O Israel, the LORD our God, the LORD is one. And you shall love the LORD your God with all your heart, with all your soul, with all your mind, and with all your strength.' This is the first commandment."

MARK 12:29–30

Are you able to summarize in a single sentence the Bible's call on a believer's life? Does that assignment sound intimidating or even impossible? Actually, Jesus has already done this for us. The backstory is God solving the problem of humanity's sin by sending Jesus to the cross where He bore the punishment for your sins and mine. The only proper response to this sacrificial and redemptive love for us is for us to love God with all of our being.

Referred to as the first or the greatest commandment, this call to love God is based on Deuteronomy 6:4–5, "Hear, O Israel: The LORD our God, the LORD is one! You shall love the LORD your God."

Jesus got more specific, saying we are to love God with all our heart, all our soul, all our mind, and all our strength. How can we possibly love God this deeply? The next verses in Deuteronomy 6 offer these tips: have the Word imprinted on your heart, teach God's commands to your children, have conversations about His truth at home, talk about the gospel when you're traveling, and discuss God's goodness at bedtime, mealtime, and every morning.

··

Heavenly Father, help me love You with my entire being, as You deserve. And thank You, Jesus, for loving me and going to the cross for me. May everything I do arise from my ever-deepening love for You.

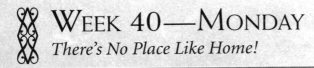

We have known and believed the love that God has for us. God is love, and he who abides in love abides in God, and God in him. . . . We love Him because He first loved us.

1 JOHN 4:16, 19

Dorothy had it right. Her time in Oz reinforced for her that there really is no place like home. The finest resorts on earth can't begin to compare to home. Only at home do we find some of life's greatest riches . . . Peace. Comfort. Security. Rest. Love.

In today's comforting passage, our heavenly Father invites us to abide in Him, to make Him our abode, to make Him our home. In Him we dwell, and in us His Spirit dwells (2 Timothy 1:14). Isn't it wonderful to think that the same qualities that can make an earthly home so special are available to us as we abide in our heavenly Father? In Him we find peace. In Him we find immeasurable comfort even as the storms of life rage around us. We find security for today and for eternity. We find rest, the soul-rest the world can't provide, and the divine peace that passes understanding. And we find love— God's love that "bears all things, believes all things, hopes all things, endures all things" (1 Corinthians 13:7).

Whatever you're dealing with today, you don't have to wonder whether you'll be accepted. Your heavenly Father loved you first and now waits for you with open arms—to come home!

....

Father, today I want to abide in You. I don't want to simply squeeze You into my life; I want You to be my life. Teach me to acknowledge You in all my ways, starting now.

BRAD BOWEN, HERITAGE CHURCH, MOULTRIE, GA

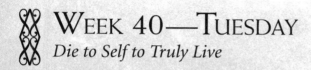

> *"These things I have spoken to you, that My joy may remain in you, and that your joy may be full. This is My commandment, that you love one another as I have loved you. Greater love has no one than this, than to lay down one's life for his friends. . . . These things I command you, that you love one another."*
>
> JOHN 15:11–13, 17

God's economy has a completely different set of rules:

To be great, serve (Matthew 23:11).

The last will actually be first (Matthew 20:16).

Small gifts can far surpass expensive ones in value (Luke 21:3).

And in today's passage from the gospel of John, Jesus shared the way to experience life at its best: lay it down! We really begin to live only when we imitate Jesus and live for others. In fact, the more intensely we pursue our own happiness, the more elusive it seems to become.

Not sure you believe that last sentence? Then put it to the test. For the next twenty-four hours, set aside your personal desires and do your best to be a blessing to every person God puts in your path. If I were a betting man, I'd say you are about to have the most rewarding, joy-filled day you've had in a long time!

....

Father, show me today people who need to be loved. Give me Your eyes to see them as You do and fill me with Your Spirit so I overflow with Your love. Empower me to love selflessly and with compassion.

WEEK 40—WEDNESDAY
The Mystery of Worship

I bow my knees to the father of our Lord Jesus Christ . . . that Christ may dwell in your hearts through faith; that you, being rooted and grounded in love, may be able to comprehend with all the saints what is the width and length and depth and height—to know the love of Christ which passes knowledge; that you may be filled with all the fullness of God.

EPHESIANS 3:14, 17–19

Have you ever entered a worship service burdened by a heavy heart, but then you soon find yourself caught up in God's powerful, loving presence? All of a sudden life's problems have shrunk to a much more manageable size. (Or maybe God seems bigger?)

At the height of Job's despair (Job 38), God painted for this man whom He loved a picture of His glory by asking Job to ponder His awe-inspiring mastery over creation. This exchange between God and Job turned out to be a much-needed reality check that helped Job realign his perspective on his circumstances. By prompting Job to reflect on all He had created and on His sovereign control over every aspect of His creation, the Almighty reminded Job in no uncertain terms that God is much, much bigger than anything Job might face, no matter how desperately he feels otherwise.

Worship can have the same effect on us. As we express our love for God by declaring His greatness, we are lifting our eyes beyond things of this earth. Hope replaces despair. Peace replaces worry. Love replaces bitterness. Today's passage is a call to remember the enormity of God's love for us, a call to worship Him.

Father, forgive me for spending so much time focusing on my problems. Today may I lift my eyes as Job did and focus on You, whose glory is breathtaking and whose goodness far outweighs anything I face.

238   BRAD BOWEN, HERITAGE CHURCH, MOULTRIE, GA

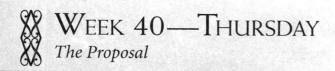

WEEK 40—THURSDAY
The Proposal

The LORD has appeared of old to me, saying: "Yes, I have loved you with an everlasting love; therefore with lovingkindness I have drawn you."

JEREMIAH 31:3

I recently had the distinct honor of performing the wedding ceremony of a couple who resisted the cultural norm and maintained their purity until their wedding day. In fact, the kiss at the altar was their very first!

The beautiful young bride shared her deep appreciation for the way her husband had fought for her heart and remained faithful to his convictions during their engagement. The result was an unbreakable sense of security in his commitment to her. "It was so worth it!" was the sentiment they both expressed.

On a much grander scale, God has fought for our hearts, and that fierce battle culminated in Jesus' brutal death on the cross. But nothing—not the excruciating pain of crucifixion, not even the more devastating pain of being separated from His Father because of our sins—would keep our Bridegroom from making a way for us, His bride. Now, with lovingkindness, mercy, and grace, Jesus patiently waits for every man, woman, boy, and girl to say yes to His proposal of forgiveness of sins and a glorious everlasting life with Him.

Reaffirm your commitment to Christ today. Start by simply thanking Him for never giving up on you.

. . . .

Holy and Perfect Father, thank You for wooing me to Your side, for capturing my heart, by Your Spirit. Thank You too for being patient with me who has said yes to You with my mouth, but too often in the course of a day, I say no to you with my thoughts, words, and actions. And thank You for the security that comes with knowing You will never leave me alone in this world.

GOD IS FAITHFUL

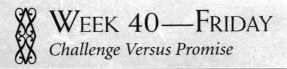

WEEK 40—FRIDAY
Challenge Versus Promise

"He who has My commandments and keeps them, it is he who loves Me. And he who loves Me will be loved by My Father, and I will love him and manifest Myself to him."

JOHN 14:21

I used to read today's passage as a challenge. My interpretation would read something like, "If you really love Me, you will do everything right." The problem? I could never seem to do everything just right, so I always felt I was disappointing God.

Since I don't always obey His commands, does this mean I don't truly love God? Am I missing out on God's love and blessings because I have fallen so short?

These are just a couple of the questions that plagued my daily thoughts as I struggled to meet all of my self-imposed expectations. Yes, *self*-imposed expectations.

If you have had similar doubts, let me encourage you today. I no longer read this passage as a challenge, for our relationship with God is not works-based at all. We have received unmerited—undeserved and unearned—favor through Christ. In light of that truth, these words from our Lord now read as an incredible promise: "Fall in love with the Father, and you will naturally obey Him!"

It is so freeing to have my spiritual "to do" list shortened to just one action item: *love Jesus.* And I have found that the more I love Him, the more I want to please Him. The challenge to obey will always leave you feeling defeated, but the promise of God's unshakable love will inspire you to pursue Him—and enable you to obey Him—like never before.

....

Father, today I want to simply fall in love with You all over again. Show me how I can express my love for You today.

BRAD BOWEN, HERITAGE CHURCH, MOULTRIE, GA

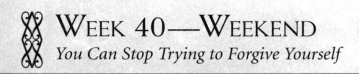
God demonstrates His own love toward us, in that while we were still sinners, Christ died for us.

ROMANS 5:8

Have you ever wished that life had an "undo" button or a "redo" feature? I cringe sometimes when I think about the foolish, sinful, harmful actions of my past. As the masterful accuser, Satan loves to remind me of my transgressions until I'm disgusted with myself and struggling to maintain a decent "pastor posture."

Not long ago, in a season of discouragement, I sought the counsel of a wise mentor. I lamented, "I just can't forgive myself!"

Her reply? She laughed! Yes, laughed. Granted, this is not the recommended response to someone's heartfelt confession, but with godly wisdom and an impeccable delivery, she spoke through her laughter: "Brad, that's not even in the Bible. If you could forgive yourself, you wouldn't need Jesus!"

Revelation! Freedom!

What used to tear me away from God—the heavy burden of shame, condemnation, and regret that I carried because of my sin—now draws me closer to Him. When I am weak, He is strong. Like the apostle Paul, I now boast about my weaknesses; I cling to the promise that His grace is absolutely and thoroughly sufficient for me!

....

Father, today I bring You my worst. You know even better than I the ugliness that lives inside of me, but I trust in Your gifts of mercy, forgiveness, and grace to me and in the truth that Your redemptive power is far greater than the damage I've done. Thank You for loving me when I am at my worst. And thank You for never giving up on me. Today I choose to walk in Your forgiveness, Your grace, and Your love.

GOD IS FAITHFUL

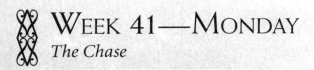

WEEK 41—MONDAY
The Chase

Pursue peace with all people, and holiness, without which no one will see the Lord: looking carefully lest anyone fall short of the grace of God.

HEBREWS 12:14–15

I f you like hunting, shopping, or collecting, you know the challenge and the thrill of the chase. Our scripture today reminds us that we Christ-followers can approach every day as just such an adventure as we "pursue peace with all people, and holiness."

God's instructions to *pursue* or *chase* peace and right living may be His way of letting us know that they will seem elusive. It's not easy to be at peace with everyone, and that "not easy" may sometimes border on the impossible. Similarly, living a pure life in a world saturated with sin and godlessness also isn't something we'll fall backward into.

Furthermore, pursuing peace with all people *and* living a life of holiness could feel contradictory at times. Trying to please God may mean believing, doing, and articulating things that cause people to have conflict with us. And yet we are to pursue both peace and holiness. God never said it would be easy.

But God does remind us that the effort is not in our own strength: we are to be careful not to turn our backs on His grace. God wants to join you and enable you in this two-pronged assignment. Expect His grace to amaze you. He just may surprise you by empowering you to overcome temptation.

. . . .

Thank You, Lord, for Your grace: when You call me to do something, for instance, You—by the power of Your Spirit—enable me to accomplish it. And may You, Spirit, give me energy and strength to live at peace with others as I seek to live a holy life that glorifies You.

MARK HOOVER, NEWSPRING CHURCH, WICHITA, KS

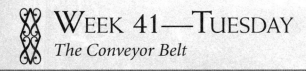

WEEK 41—TUESDAY
The Conveyor Belt

Be anxious for nothing, but in everything by prayer and supplication, with thanksgiving, let your requests be made known to God; and the peace of God, which surpasses all understanding, will guard your hearts and minds through Christ Jesus.

PHILIPPIANS 4:6–7

Whenever I read these verses, I imagine working at a conveyor belt that's moving items along. Some are intended for me, but others are meant to pass me by and stay on the belt, left for someone else's more skilled attention. If I take something not intended for me or beyond my ability to fix, I'm sure to be stressed out, and I might even do damage.

Like that conveyor belt, each day of life presents us with a variety of situations. Some will be within our power to change, and we should take those off the belt and deal with them. But when situations beyond our resources and abilities arise, we need to remember that God doesn't want us to "be anxious" about them. God wants us to let them move up the line to Him. And when, by prayer and with thanksgiving, we do that, He promises that His peace will guard our minds and emotions; will relieve us from pressure to achieve the impossible; and will comfort us with the reality that He is at work.

So powerful is this promised peace that we're assured it's even better than the ability to understand our circumstances. After all, if we understood our problems, they'd still be there. We gain nothing if we hold onto and try to fix what is beyond our ability and therefore probably not intended for us.

....

Lord, may I leave on the conveyor belt to heaven those situations which are beyond my ability to rectify—may I leave them for You to deal with—and may I receive the peace You offer me to get on with living.

WEEK 41—WEDNESDAY
Peace with God

Having been justified by faith, we have peace with God through our Lord Jesus Christ, through whom also we have access by faith into this grace in which we stand, and rejoice in hope of the glory of God.

ROMANS 5:1–2

S omeone has said that peace is a sense of well-being regardless of life's circumstances. If that's the case, it seems to me that any genuine tranquility must be rooted in peace *with* God. After all, if we are at war with God, any other peace we'd enjoy would be temporary at best. Yet if God is for us, any enemy rising against us is set for defeat. Peace with God is key!

The good news is that peace with God is a gift, available to all who receive Jesus as Savior and Lord. Our sins, which created hostility between sinful us and holy God, have been paid for by the blood of Christ. In addition, the perfect righteousness of Jesus has been applied to our personal account. Scripture says we have "been justified by faith": in the eyes of God, our legal status is "righteous." Clearly this isn't something we achieve; it's all the gracious work of Jesus.

And these wonderful theological truths have real-life significance. Specifically, those of us who live at peace with God enjoy instant and continual access to Him. And even when storms arise, even when we experience loss or pain, we can be sure that the presence of God will always be a safe place. We also enjoy the big-picture perspective and unshakable assurance that His glorious heaven awaits.

....

Gracious God, thank You for the joy, the hope, and the peace with You that I am blessed with as a result of my faith in Jesus.

MARK HOOVER, NEWSPRING CHURCH, WICHITA, KS

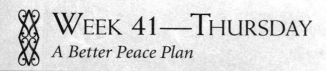

WEEK 41—THURSDAY
A Better Peace Plan

"Peace I leave with you, My peace I give to you; not as the world gives do I give to you. Let not your heart be troubled, neither let it be afraid."

JOHN 14:27

Are you facing something difficult today? Does a certain situation have your emotions churning like a stormy sea? Or maybe your world has recently been turned upside down and you're shocked about the new reality you have to deal with. What Jesus offered His disciples in John 14:27, He offers you!

The context for that verse is Jesus' final address to His disciples before His arrest and crucifixion. He knew their world would be turned upside down when they watched him be taken away and brutally executed. Even though Jesus had tried to prepare them, He knew that the unfolding of these events would still come as a shock.

Jesus did not remove His disciples then or you today from the crisis, but He did leave them (and us) His peace, which is very different from the short-lived peace the world knows.

The peace Jesus gives is lasting. And it's the kind of peace that enabled the disciples not only to survive the difficult hour, but actually to emerge stronger, empowered to fulfill their roles in the young church. So, just as you would sit confidently in a chair placed behind you by a trusted friend, you can be confident that Jesus' peace will be there!

....

Thank You, Jesus, for Your peace and for the way it transforms our lives, sustains our faith, and grows our faith. When I'm feeling unsettled or overwhelmed, please—with the prompting of Your Spirit—remind me to turn to You and receive the peace You long for Your followers to know.

GOD IS FAITHFUL

Put on love, which is the bond of perfection. And let the peace of God rule in your hearts, to which also you were called in one body; and be thankful.

COLOSSIANS 3:14–15

Conflicts and disputes are inevitable, even between people who love each other and very much want to get along. Conflicts and disputes are more likely when we have to deal with someone who seems to be trying to make our lives difficult. When that happens, we may wonder, *How am I going to approach this? Do I stand my ground and demand my rights? Do I try to compromise? Do I give in and then let it go?* Something inside of us, some internal referee, will make that call.

But today's scripture presents a great alternative to trying to sort out such a dilemma on our own. This verse challenges us to let the peace of God "rule"— meaning "arbitrate"—in our hearts.

As James 4:1–3 says, conflicts arise because people can't get what they want. But we who have the inner sense of well-being that Christ gives need never be grasping for what we feel should be ours.

We're going to be fine, not because we've carved out our spot in the world, but because of God's awesome promises to—among other things—always be with us, to guide our steps, and to supply all our needs. People who enjoy the peace of God can afford to be gracious when conflicts arise.

Good and merciful God, conflicts and potential conflicts are great opportunities for me to love others by loving them with Your love. Make me willing to die to my wishes and "put on love."

MARK HOOVER, NEWSPRING CHURCH, WICHITA, KS

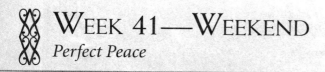

WEEK 41—WEEKEND
Perfect Peace

You will keep him in perfect peace, whose mind is stayed on You, because he trusts in You. Trust in the LORD forever, for in YAH, the LORD, is everlasting strength.

ISAIAH 26:3–4

D id you ever sail, oblivious and untroubled, through a threatening experience, blissfully unaware of any danger? When you found out later how close you came to disaster, did you reflect in amazement on how peaceful you were during that time? You were close to trouble but didn't know it. Looking back, you definitely saw it as an "ignorance is bliss" moment.

Actually, there's a bliss that's much more authentic. Isaiah wrote that the person who is focused on God is kept in genuine and "perfect peace," in divine bliss. That person is not necessarily unaware of the problems, dangers, or threats, but that person is simply not focused on them. In fact, this person is so absorbed in the presence of God, all else is insignificant by contrast.

That kind of focus away from situations implies a submission to God, a yielding up of those circumstances. Yet we humans so like having some (a lot of?) control. What is the appeal? Are we hoping to create an orderly, peaceful space to live in? We never have to try for very long before we realize just how much in life we can't control. We simply aren't able to establish or maintain a well-ordered existence.

> *Lord God, my efforts to manage and micromanage don't succeed. Yet I struggle to leave total control to You—even though You alone have accurate knowledge of what is best as well as the ability to do the impossible. Teach me to let go more readily, more completely, that I may know Your perfect peace.*

WEEK 42—MONDAY
God's Great Faithfulness

My God shall supply all your need according to His riches in glory by Christ Jesus.

PHILIPPIANS 4:19

One of the most hated subjects to broach in the local church is giving. The reason? Too many Christians love money more than God—or so it seems. But giving is part of a vibrant and growing Christian life. The Philippians were faithful givers to the work of the Lord, and Paul commended them for this partnership in his ministry.

The New Testament teaches that Christians are to give abundantly (2 Corinthians 9:6), and I am convinced that giving should begin with a tithe as the minimum standard. God always enables what He requires of us, and giving to support His church financially is no exception. Furthermore, God supplies all the needs—notice the context—of those who faithfully give to kingdom causes. God supplies "according to His riches," which means that God supplies more than enough to meet mere physical needs. In addition to that, He supplies us with rich spiritual blessings.

While I was attending Bible college, my wife and I weren't making very much money. One week we wrote out our tithe check knowing we might not have enough to get through the week. We gave anyway. The next day I prayed, "Lord, supply our need. We are trusting You." When I checked the mail that day, I found a check from someone in our home church. The amount was more than enough to cover our needs. God doesn't always use that method, but He always supplies.

Obey God and give. You can't outgive Him.

....

Lord, I trust You to supply my need as I give to kingdom causes—and I thank You in advance for Your great faithfulness.

MIKE ORR, FIRST BAPTIST CHURCH, CHIPLEY, FL

WEEK 42—TUESDAY
Trust and Contentment

I know how to be abased, and I know how to abound. Everywhere and in all things I have learned both to be full and to be hungry, both to abound and to suffer need. I can do all things through Christ who strengthens me.

PHILIPPIANS 4:12–13

Circumstances often dictate our level of joy, peace, and contentment with life. When things are good, we are content. When situations deteriorate, our contentment dissipates. Paul, however, learned to be content regardless of his circumstances. He accepted the easy times and the difficult times as areas to develop spiritually and to learn to depend more fully upon the Lord.

The apostle thrived when he experienced trial, tragedy, and torture, and he was edified by the comfortable times as well. What was Paul's secret? In all things he depended upon the Lord, who faithfully supplied strength and ability for all circumstances.

Sometimes I feel as if I will smother under the weight of projects, burdens, and deadlines. Then I remember the promise of these verses and pray over my circumstances. Hopelessness and stress turn to peace and productivity. I believe God's promise: our Lord will supply the strength we need for all things.

My mom has Alzheimer's, and her condition is rapidly worsening. My dad lovingly cares for my mom. Some days I know he feels as though he will buckle under the stress, but in such moments God gives him grace. God always gives us strength when we are weak. Whatever the scenario—difficult marriage, stressful job, health issues, a rebellious child—God always gives us strength when we are weak. Your faithful Savior, your glorious Helper, will always supply the strength you need! Praise Him!

....

Lord, I trust You in everything—and I want to trust You more.

"Most assuredly, I say to you, whatever you ask the Father in My name He will give you. Until now you have asked nothing in My name. Ask, and you will receive, that your joy may be full."

JOHN 16:23–24

One of the spiritual blessings we enjoy as God's children is the privilege of prayer. Christ's death on the cross bridged the gap between our holy God and us sinners, giving us the ability to communicate with God. Prayer and the results of prayer are a source of joy to those following Jesus. After all, as saved people, you and I have access to the God of the universe, and as His children, we can go before Him anytime and ask Him anything.

When people want to see me, they talk with my assistant, and she schedules an appointment. If I am available, I may see them immediately. My daughter, however, is another story. She arrives at my office, and unless I am with someone, she bursts through my door and says, "Hey, Dad!" Why the radical difference? Because she is my child. We are God's, with the ability—thanks to Christ—to come into His presence anytime to talk. He hears us and He answers (1 John 5:14–15). (Thankfully He always answers according to His will, for some things we ask for would not be good for us!)

We have a promise from God: communicate with Him in prayer, and He will answer. So nothing should get us down because we can talk to God about it. Pray about every anxiety, every problem, and every situation.

....

Lord, help me to practice prayer and experience its joy.

MIKE ORR, FIRST BAPTIST CHURCH, CHIPLEY, FL

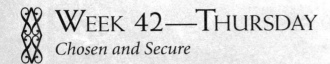

WEEK 42—THURSDAY
Chosen and Secure

Blessed be the God and Father of our Lord Jesus Christ, who has blessed us with every spiritual blessing in the heavenly places in Christ, just as He chose us in Him before the foundation of the world, that we should be holy and without blame before Him in love.

EPHESIANS 1:3–4

Next time you're at the grocery story, see if you can find a magazine cover that *doesn't* address exercise or diet. Staying fit and eating healthy are important, but they don't guarantee good health.

Similarly, the Lord does not guarantee us good physical health on the earth, but He does guarantee us eternal life. We never have to wonder if our eternal life will be lost or revoked over some action or failure to act. Prompted by God's Spirit, Paul erupted in praise for the One who has given to us "every spiritual blessing in the heavenly places."

These blessings include the fact that God knew us before He created the universe, and He chose us to be in His family (vv. 4–5). God forgave our sins (v. 7) and He guarantees our inheritance (vv. 13–14). All these blessings—and many others—are permanent realities for all of us who have been saved.

We remain in this sin-cursed world awaiting the return of Christ and the establishment of His eternal kingdom. Yet we are assured of God's promises to us. I never have to wonder when I wake in the mornings, "Am I still saved?" Nor do I have to wonder if I will remain saved throughout the day, for I am blessed by my faithful Lord with a secure eternal life! No wonder Paul praised God at the thought of these realities!

....

Lord, may I rest in Your guarantee of eternal life.

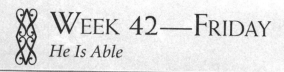

WEEK 42—FRIDAY
He Is Able

Now to Him who is able to do exceedingly abundantly above all that we ask or think, according to the power that works in us, to Him be glory in the church by Christ Jesus to all generations, forever and ever. Amen.

EPHESIANS 3:20–21

We often make two mistakes in our relationship with our all-powerful God. First, we don't depend on Him. We trust in our ability and resources to do life and serve His kingdom. But nothing great will be accomplished if we're trusting our abilities. Eternal things are accomplished by the power supplied by our Lord (John 15:5). Second, we foolishly live with a lack of genuine faith. Local church congregations miss the experience of God's great work because they make no attempt to trust God beyond their resources. Individual believers fail to be used of God in mighty ways because they do not trust God beyond their personal abilities.

Today's text is clear: there is nothing we can ask or even think that is beyond God's ability to do. He will superabundantly supply power in response to our petitions. Trusting in God, we make our requests known to Him. We must not depend on our abilities or be limited by our resources. We are to pray, always remembering that God answers according to His will to accomplish great things through us. He will get the glory.

It is amazing that our God works through us to accomplish God-sized things. I can ask much, but my petition will never exceed God's power. I can dream big dreams, but my dreams will never exceed God's capacity to do! To God be the glory for the great things He has done and will do!

....

Lord, help me to trust in Your great power and pray big prayers.

MIKE ORR, FIRST BAPTIST CHURCH, CHIPLEY, FL

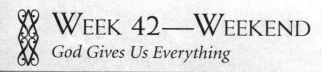

WEEK 42—WEEKEND
God Gives Us Everything

Let no one boast in men. For all things are yours: whether Paul or Apollos or Cephas, or the world or life or death, or things present or things to come—all are yours. And you are Christ's, and Christ is God's.

1 CORINTHIANS 3:21-23

The Corinthian Christians had been arguing to the point of division: one group liked Paul, another Cephas, and yet another Apollos. Paul reminded them that all spiritual leaders are gifts from God. He then listed all that is given to believers through Christ.

The people of God are to respect and follow spiritual leaders who faithfully teach the Word and live by the Word (Hebrews 13:7, 17).

Also, the world will one day be given to us. It is now "under the sway of the wicked one" (1 John 5:19), but one day we will rule with Christ on earth (Revelation 20:6).

In addition, life itself is a gift from God (Romans 6:23). There is no better way to live than to live for Christ. The abundant life we live is indeed a precious gift.

Death is also a gift to believers. We have victory over death (1 Corinthians 15:54-57).

Things present and things to come—good and bad—belong to us, yet everything we experience works for our good: God uses everything to make us more like Jesus (Romans 8:28).

All these blessings are ours because we belong to Christ and Christ, to God. How secure we are in Him, who gives all things!

. . . .

Lord, You do give Your people everything! May I live with heartfelt gratitude to You.

WEEK 43—MONDAY
In His Steps

To this you were called, because Christ also suffered for us, leaving us an example, that you should follow His steps.

1 PETER 2:21

Charles Sheldon's famous book *In His Steps* has sold more than thirty million copies and encouraged countless believers since it was first published in 1896.

The theme of the book is the question "What would Jesus do?" Do you remember the "WWJD" bracelet popular in the nineties? You may have even worn one on your wrist. Yes, that popular acronym was based on Charles Sheldon's work.[17]

This guideline that Mr. Sheldon offered Christ-followers—the reminder of which many displayed on their wrist—should actually be the guide in every believer's heart: we Christians are to be like Christ; we are to follow in His steps. Jesus left us His example to follow, and every time we read the Gospels we see the pattern. We are to love like Him. We are to serve like Him. We are to forgive like Him. We are to respond like Him. We are to be willing to put other people's interests before ours, to let ourselves be interrupted by their needs, and to be able to share our faith with and pray for those God puts in our path—just as Jesus did.

In every situation, we do well to ask ourselves, "What would Jesus do?" It's not a difficult question to answer: Jesus left us His example, and we are to "follow His steps."

....

Dear Lord Jesus, thank You for coming to this earth and showing us how to live. Empower me today to follow Your example and walk in Your steps. Amen.

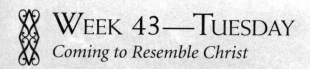

WEEK 43—TUESDAY
Coming to Resemble Christ

Be imitators of God as dear children. And walk in love, as Christ also has loved us and given Himself for us, an offering and a sacrifice to God for a sweet-smelling aroma.

EPHESIANS 5:1–2

On a wall at The Alamo in San Antonio, Texas, hangs a portrait with the following inscription: "James Butler Bonham. No picture of him exists. This portrait is of his nephew, Major James Bonham, deceased, who greatly resembled his uncle. It is placed here by the family that people may know the appearance of the man who died for freedom."

Similarly, no picture of Jesus exists. Nothing in oils or watercolor, nothing on a smartphone or Instagram. But people should be able to look at His followers and see His likeness in us.

Imitation is acting like someone; resemblance is looking like someone. When we recognize our need for the Savior and begin a relationship with God, Jesus—Emmanuel, "God with us"—moves into our life. Two thousand years ago He offered Himself up as a sacrifice and payment for your sins and mine, and what resulted was our transformation. He now lives in us and through us, and that is why we are able to imitate Him and come to resemble Him.

May we commit ourselves to live like the old song says, "While passing through this world of sin . . . let others see Jesus in you."[18]

....

Lord, I ask You to manifest Yourself in me today in such a way that others will see You in me and want to know You better. I want to imitate You and come to resemble You more and more. In Jesus' name, amen.

WEEK 43—WEDNESDAY
Taking on the Likeness of Christ

Let this mind be in you which was also in Christ Jesus, who, being in the form of God, did not consider it robbery to be equal with God, but made Himself of no reputation, taking the form of a bondservant, and coming in the likeness of men.

PHILIPPIANS 2:5–7

Recently I heard an older married couple talking, and one said, "We've been together so long, that we now think alike and sometimes even finish one another's sentences." This really does happen when you know someone well and spend a lot of time with that person.

Similarly, as we walk with Christ, as we spend a lot of time with Him, we begin to grow into His likeness. By the power of the Holy Spirit at work in us, we develop the mind of Christ. Review the fruit of the Spirit (Galatians 5:22–23) and see the Christlike qualities the Spirit wants to work into your heart, your words, your actions.

When we surrender to the Spirit's work, a great transformation begins. Our mind begins to be renewed; put differently, we begin having the mind of Christ. The next time you get frustrated and want to give someone a piece of your mind, choose instead to be like Jesus and take "the form of a bond-servant." This dying-to-self action will leave a lasting impression on the heart and mind of anyone who is watching your life.

....

Lord Jesus, I want to be like You today. May Your mind and Your heart be in me so that people will notice You in my life and want to come to know You. It's for Your glory I pray this prayer. Amen.

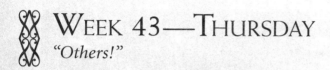
"Yet it shall not be so among you; but whoever desires to become great among you shall be your servant. And whoever of you desires to be first shall be slave of all. For even the Son of Man did not come to be served, but to serve, and to give His life a ransom for many."

MARK 10:43–45

Someone once said, "The opposite of love is not hate. It is self!"

Does that statement surprise you? Then think about what the apostle Paul wrote in his 2 Timothy 3:1–4 listing of the signs of the end times. One of those signs is people who are "lovers of themselves" (v. 2). In sharp contrast to these self-saturated people are those individuals whose hearts are saturated with the servant attitude of Christ.

Such was the heart of General William Booth, the founder of the Salvation Army. It is said that just before he died, he was scheduled to deliver the main message to thousands of his "soldiers" who had gathered together at their annual international convention. In light of his failing health and inability to attend, Booth decided to dictate a one-word telegram from his sickbed that he might inspire his many soldiers in attendance. Booth's final message was "Others!"

If you and I had to speak our last word today, what would it be—a self-word or a servant-word? The time to decide is now, while we can still change our path.

....

Jesus, thank You for giving Yourself for others. Because of what You did on the cross, my life will never be the same. Continue to make me a more wholehearted servant to You and to the "others" You place in my path. Amen.

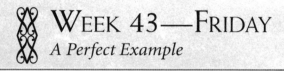

Week 43—Friday
A Perfect Example

"If I then, your Lord and Teacher, have washed your feet, you also ought to wash one another's feet. For I have given you an example, that you should do as I have done to you."

John 13:14–15

We really don't hear much about washing one another's feet these days. With the advancement in footwear and all the convenient bathing facilities of our day—not to mention various modes of transportation—there is hardly the need. But by necessity the situation was very different in Jesus' day, and this dirty duty was most often reserved for a lowly house servant.

No wonder the disciples were confused when Jesus removed His outer robe before the Passover meal, wrapped a towel around His waist, and began to work His way around the room, washing feet. Doing the work of a slave was not really the assignment these disciples had in mind for themselves. I would venture to say that doing the work of a slave is also very seldom what we have on our mind. But Jesus chose foot washing as the perfect object lesson to remind believers—then and now—that we are not to be seeking out the places of honor, but rather places of service.

After washing His disciples' feet, Jesus called them and us to serve our church, our families, our friends, our neighbors, and even our enemies. We who follow Christ must remember that we are never greater than our Master who carried the basin. Also, as Jesus told His disciples, "If you know these things, blessed are you if you do them" (v. 17).

....

Lord Jesus, humbled by Your example, I ask You to give me not only Your servant heart but also Your eyes to see those I could serve in Your name.

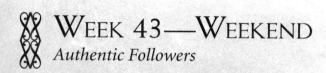
Whoever keeps His word, truly the love of God is perfected in him. By this we know that we are in Him. He who says he abides in Him ought himself also to walk just as He walked.

1 John 2:5–6

Have you ever been duped by a counterfeit? Were you embarrassed that you hadn't been able to distinguish the real from the fake? No doubt we have all been misled at one time or another.

Did you know that the United States Secret Service spends thousands of personnel hours and millions of dollars each year trying to stop counterfeit currency? Apparently some differences between the authentic and the fake are obvious giveaways. One of the things these agents check out is the portrait on the currency: Does it look lifelike and crisp? Another thing they look at is the paper itself: Are tiny red and blue fibers embedded throughout? Counterfeit currency has these markings only on the surface.

Here in 1 John, the apostle John described a similar type of litmus test to determine whether certain followers of Christ are authentic: Are we doing what Jesus Himself did? We cannot say we are Christians and then not follow Jesus' commands. We would be counterfeit disciples—and poor counterfeits at that!

To be Jesus' disciples, we must obey His word, walk as He walked, abide in Him, and let His Spirit work His character into our lives moment by moment, day by day. Only then will others know authentic Christianity!

> *Lord, I commit myself today to abiding in You and to keeping Your word that my witness to this lost world will be authentic Christianity. Amen.*

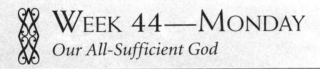

WEEK 44—MONDAY
Our All-Sufficient God

Our sufficiency is from God, who also made us sufficient as ministers of the new covenant, not of the letter but of the Spirit; for the letter kills, but the Spirit gives life.

2 CORINTHIANS 3:5–6

I recently read an article on ten ways to develop more self-confidence. The author mentioned things like dress nicely, walk more briskly, have good posture, and use positive self-talk. Most of us could benefit from more self-confidence, and all this is good advice.

However, in our text, the apostle Paul suggested a different source of confidence: instead of having confidence in ourselves, our confidence needs to be in God. Paul himself had come full circle. When he was known as Saul of Tarsus, he was prideful, arrogant, and oozing with self-confidence. He was highly esteemed as a member of the Jewish Sanhedrin, a Pharisee, and a well-educated student of Gamaliel. All of that contributed to his self-righteousness and (false) piety. After his dramatic conversion, however, Paul confessed that he found his competence in Christ and Christ alone. This competence was born out of God's Holy Spirit dwelling within him.

That kind of God-confidence is about resting in His strength and trusting His sufficiency. Remember this familiar passage? "I can do all things through Christ who strengthens me" (Philippians 4:13). It's true! You can be confident—in Almighty God!

....

Father, forgive me for the pride and pretense I cling to in order to feel more self-confident. Teach me, I pray, to develop greater confidence in You and in Your unchanging love. May I yield my weakness to You, discover Your strength, and grow in trust and God-confidence. Amen.

DR. STEVE DIGHTON, LENEXA BAPTIST CHURCH, LENEXA, KS

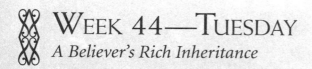

WEEK 44—TUESDAY
A Believer's Rich Inheritance

[I pray] that the God of our Lord Jesus Christ, the Father of glory, may give to you the spirit of wisdom and revelation in the knowledge of Him, the eyes of your understanding being enlightened; that you may know what is the hope of His calling, what are the riches of the glory of His inheritance in the saints.

EPHESIANS 1:17–18

When you hear the word *inheritance,* do you immediately think of what might be passed on to you when a wealthy relative includes you in the will? Or are you thinking of Paul's writing of inheritance to the believers in Ephesus? In our text Paul was praying for the Ephesians, that "the eyes of [their] understanding [would be] enlightened" and able to see the inheritance God has for His people. This inheritance is future: Jesus promised us heaven where there are "many mansions," where He has gone to "prepare a place" for each of His followers (John 14:2). "The riches of the glory of His inheritance" have a present aspect as well, one of which is the sufficiency of Christ: by His Holy Spirit we are "equipped for every good work" (2 Timothy 3:17).

Consider for a moment the value of riches like these. In 2 Corinthians 8:9, Paul wrote that "though [Jesus] was rich, yet for your sakes He became poor, that you through His poverty might become rich." Yet all too often we Christ-followers live as though we are spiritually destitute, when our present inheritance in Jesus means strength and sufficiency in Him.

....

Father, thank You for the rich inheritance that is mine through Jesus Christ, Your Son and my Lord. May I not squander the riches You have given me.

Week 44—Wednesday
God's Unchanging Love

If God is for us, who can be against us? He who did not spare His own Son, but delivered Him up for us all, how shall He not with Him also freely give us all things?

Romans 8:31–32

Called the crown jewel of this rich epistle, Romans 8 opens by saying there is "now no condemnation to those who are in Christ Jesus" (v. 1). The chapter concludes by telling us that absolutely nothing can ever separate us from God (vv. 38–39). Today's verses remind us that God spared nothing for our redemption, giving His only begotten Son to die in our place. That remarkable act reassures us of His love for us: Why would God—who held back nothing to rescue us from sin and damnation—not provide our other needs out of His abundant resources? After all, it's inherent in God's character to give (John 3:16).

Do you have confidence today that God is for you? That He who met your greatest needs of all—forgiveness of sin and reconciliation with Him—will meet your other needs as well? If you were to answer that question solely on the basis of your personal experiences, you might not be so sure. If a good day means a good God, a bad day raises doubts about His goodness. First, remember that God is "the same yesterday, today, and forever" (Hebrews 13:8). He does not change; His love and sufficiency will never change. They are part of His character, proclaimed in His Word, and evident in the grace of His Son's death for you.

....

Father, forgive me for ever doubting Your love for me. May my faith in Your goodness and love never waver or diminish because of trials and adversity.

DR. STEVE DIGHTON, LENEXA BAPTIST CHURCH, LENEXA, KS

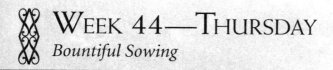

WEEK 44—THURSDAY
Bountiful Sowing

He who sows sparingly will also reap sparingly, and he who sows bountifully will also reap bountifully. So let each one give as he purposes in his heart, not grudgingly or of necessity; for God loves a cheerful giver. And God is able to make all grace abound toward you, that you, always having all sufficiency in all things, may have an abundance for every good work.

2 CORINTHIANS 9:6–8

Some of us have an easier time giving than others do. Some of us struggle to let go of the dollars God has entrusted to us, and others live with their eyes and their wallet wide open, looking around to see who they can help. Some people give joyfully, while others give dutifully and hope the joy will come. Wherever we fall on this continuum, the truth of 2 Corinthians 9:6–8 applies to us.

Today's passage teaches that the amount we receive back will be in proportion to what we give. In 2 Corinthians 8:1–3, Paul commended the Macedonian churches for their generosity as an example to the Corinthians. They gave not out of their abundance, but despite their poverty. And that is a point of application twenty-one centuries later: if you're waiting until you have an overflow of money to give to God, you will never give as you should. The person who doesn't tithe on one hundred dollars won't tithe on one million.

....

Father, Your Word tells me that You love generously, and I want to reflect Your generous love by giving generously of all You have entrusted to me. Forgive my stinginess and greed. Forgive my doubts about Your faithfulness. I know that as I give more freely, my faith in Your sufficiency will grow.

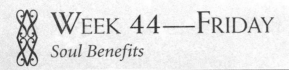

Week 44—Friday
Soul Benefits

Bless the LORD, O my soul, and forget not all His benefits: who forgives all your iniquities, who heals all your diseases, who redeems your life from destruction, who crowns you with lovingkindness and tender mercies.

PSALM 103:2–4

In over thirty years of pastoring, I have hired numerous employees. After I tell them the salary we're offering, they typically ask about the benefits: retirement, insurance, vacation, and so forth.

In today's psalm David is commanding his soul not to forget God's benefits. *Benefits* is *gemul* in Hebrew, and it means paying back what is deserved. In other words, since we belong to God's family, we are privileged to receive His benefits: forgiveness, healing, redemption, His steadfast love, and our satisfaction. When we, by faith, are given God's gift of salvation, we discover benefits galore, for God promises to us sufficiency in all things. Even in our darkest hours.

From a Roman prison, the apostle Paul wrote: "My God shall supply all your need according to His riches in glory by Christ Jesus" (Philippians 4:19). So the command this morning is remember! Remember God's steadfast love, His merciful and gracious hand, and His faithfulness. See if remembering those benefits doesn't result in contentment and joy.

....

Father, help me not forget Your benefits—Your constant presence, Your wisdom, Your limitless power, Your mercy and forgiveness and grace. You are my Healer and Redeemer, and You bless me with your lovingkindness.

DR. STEVE DIGHTON, LENEXA BAPTIST CHURCH, LENEXA, KS

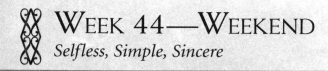
[The priests and Levites] said to [John], "Who are you, that we may give an answer to those who sent us? What do you say about yourself?" He said: "I am 'The voice of one crying in the wilderness: Make straight the way of the Lord,'" as the prophet Isaiah said."

JOHN 1:22–23

J ohn the Baptist has always been one of my favorite people in the Bible, and clearly his cousin Jesus thought the world of him too. Jesus said, "Among those born of women there has not risen one greater than John the Baptist" (Matthew 11:11). Enough said. Let's learn some of his qualities that we too might be more commendable by our Savior.

First, John was *selfless*. He clearly understood his mission and his role: "It is He who, coming after me, is preferred before me, whose sandal strap I am not worthy to loose" (John 1:27).

Second, John was *simple*. Consider this statement: "He [Jesus] must increase, but I must decrease" (John 3:30). More of Jesus and less of us is always a good goal. He was simple in his clothing: camel hair and a belt; his diet: locusts and wild honey; even his message: "Repent, for the kingdom of heaven is at hand!" (Matthew 3:2). The simplicity and the clear focus of John's life in the Judean desert beckon all of us to get the clutter and clamor out of our lives.

Finally John was *sincere*. His genuineness was part of the magnetism that drew people from throughout Galilee to beyond the Jordan. John's selflessness, simplicity, and sincerity are captivating Christlike qualities.

....

Father, help me to live so that one day I will hear You say, "Well done, good and faithful servant" (Matthew 25:21). May I live my life selflessly, with simplicity and sincerity. Amen.

WEEK 45—MONDAY
Spiritual Peanut Butter

You are in Christ Jesus, who became for us wisdom from God—and righteousness and sanctification and redemption.

1 CORINTHIANS 1:30

A poor man had wanted to go on a cruise all his life. As a youngster he had seen an advertisement for a luxury cruise, and ever since, he had dreamed of spending a week on a large ocean liner enjoying fresh sea air and relaxing in luxury. He saved money for years, carefully counting his pennies, often sacrificing personal needs so he could stretch his resources a little further.

Finally he had saved enough to purchase a ticket. He looked through brochures, picked one, and bought a ticket. He couldn't believe he was about to realize his childhood dream.

Knowing he couldn't afford the kind of elegant meals pictured in the brochure, he planned to take his own food for the week. Accustomed to moderation after years of frugal living—and with his entire savings going to pay for the cruise ticket—the man decided to take a loaf of bread and peanut butter. Yes, after the entire week of peanut butter and bread, he was sick of it. Only after the cruise did he realize that the delicious meals were included in the cost of the ticket. Like the man eating peanut butter instead of lobster, many of us don't realize what we receive when we accept Jesus Christ as our Savior and Lord. We receive the righteousness of Jesus Christ in exchange for our sin (2 Corinthians 5:21).

....

Lord God, show me where, figuratively speaking, I'm settling for peanut butter in my relationship with You—where, for instance, I could enjoy a richer prayer life, dig deeper into Your Word, live more keenly aware of Your Spirit, or be more willing to take a step of faith.

DR. BENNY TATE, ROCK SPRINGS CHURCH, MILNER, GA

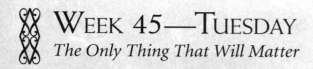

WEEK 45—TUESDAY
The Only Thing That Will Matter

I also count all things loss for the excellence of the knowledge of Christ Jesus my Lord, for whom I have suffered the loss of all things, and count them as rubbish, that I may gain Christ.

PHILIPPIANS 3:8

I never was the best in mathematics. I was the guy who said, "If you are right ninety percent of the time, who cares about the other five percent?" But Paul wasn't talking about arithmetic in Philippians 3. Twice in this verse and four times in the chapter, Paul was talking about counting in the sense of considering the value of something; in this case, the value of his credentials as an upstanding and highly respected Jew.

And what were the credentials that gave Paul such status in the Roman world? Paul was "a Hebrew of Hebrews" (Philippians 3:5), born of the strictest religious group, and committed to following the law blamelessly. But now none of that mattered because more than thirty years earlier, Paul had trusted in the righteousness of Jesus Christ, and that asset is the only one on his balance sheet. Everything else is rubbish.

One day every one of us will stand before the Lord Jesus Christ (2 Corinthians 5:10) and be judged for our actions, and I truly believe that what seemed so all-important here will not be important there. I also believe there will not be one person who will say, "I wish I had kept more or done more for myself." What we have done for Jesus is all that will matter.

. . . .

Lord, thank You for this big-picture perspective. Thank You for Paul's cautionary words. Help me look at my life and see what You see: I want to focus on what matters for Your eternal kingdom.

Week 45—Wednesday
The Winning Side

"No weapon formed against you shall prosper, and every tongue which rises against you in judgment you shall condemn. This is the heritage of the servants of the Lord, and their righteousness is from Me," says the Lord.

ISAIAH 54:17

When three bullies ganged up against him, the frail little boy bent over and drew a line in the sand. Looking the biggest bully in the eye, he said, "I dare you to step over this line." The bully did, and then he looked at the small boy and snarled, "Now what are you going to do about it?" The little boy replied, "I was just thinking, now we're on the same side."

Bullies may come against you, but always remember that you will be fine because the Lord is on your side.

Also, I've learned this about the Christian life: if God is blessing, the enemy is messing. The enemy will be coming at us with his weapons, his lies, his seeds of doubt, but, child of God, you have weapons:

The Word of God is quick, powerful, and "sharper than any two-edged sword" (Hebrews 4:12).

The Spirit of God is a weapon that Jeremiah, Daniel, Moses, and David did not have! The Spirit of God is inside you (Romans 8:9), and He "is greater than he who is in the world" (1 John 4:4).

Prayer releases God's power in a given situation: prayer means the difference between the best you can do and the best God can do.

....

Thank You, Almighty God, for the powerful and effective weapons I can use against the cosmic bully, Satan himself. I am blessed and grateful that You are on my side when the battle rages.

DR. BENNY TATE, ROCK SPRINGS CHURCH, MILNER, GA

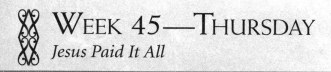
For if by the one man's offense death reigned through the one, much more those who receive abundance of grace and of the gift of righteousness will reign in life through the One, Jesus Christ.

ROMANS 5:17

God created Adam and Eve and placed them in a beautiful garden—and you know the story. Adam and Eve disobeyed God and sinned. When they did, the result was unbridgeable separation from God. Adam blamed the fall on the woman, the woman blamed it on the snake, and the snake didn't have a leg to stand on.

Nevertheless, because of that one decision, spiritual death was passed on to all of us. But that is *not* the end of the story. God saw our hopeless condition and extended His grace (Ephesians 2:8). We don't deserve salvation, and we can't earn it: grace is "**G**od's **R**iches **A**t **C**hrist's **E**xpense."

When you accept God's grace, you receive the gift of righteousness. And, yes, it is a gift. You can't do enough good works to earn it (Titus 3:5), yet many people today are trying hard to establish their own righteousness. But if we could do that, then Christ died in vain. Jesus paid our penalty for sin, and we can receive or reject that gift—but we can't earn it. Salvation is not about your performance, but His promise. It's not about your merit, but His mercy. It's not about your goodness, but His grace. Because of one man—Adam— sin did abound. But because of Jesus Christ, "grace abounded much more" (Romans 5:20).

....

Lord, I am amazed by Your grace. All the other religions of the world say "Do," but Christianity says "Done!" because, Jesus, You paid it all! I praise and thank You for Your mercy and grace, Your goodness and love!

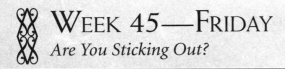

WEEK 45—FRIDAY
Are You Sticking Out?

Justice will dwell in the wilderness, and righteousness remain in the fruitful field. The work of righteousness will be peace, and the effect of righteousness, quietness and assurance forever.

ISAIAH 32:16–17

A young boy said to his mother, "Mom, if Jesus lives in me and is bigger than me, shouldn't He stick out?"

Yes, Jesus absolutely should stick out once we name Him our Savior and Lord. That's what Isaiah's picture means.

The wilderness of a life lived for self will become a fruitful field once we name Jesus as Lord (Isaiah 32:15). We will not only experience the righteousness of Christ, but we will also have the desire to live a life that is righteous (Titus 2:11–12). As Christians, we will never make a difference in this world until *we* are different. We are not called to blend in, but to stick out.

Not only should we stick out because Jesus' righteousness makes us desire righteousness, but also because His righteousness gives us peace. The finished work of Jesus Christ on the cross gives us peace with God, the peace of God, and peace with others. And that peace is a fruit of the Spirit of God in our lives.

When a young boy was flying a kite, it went so high that it was completely out of sight. The boy asked, "Dad, we can't see it. How do we know it's still up there?" His father responded, "Because you can feel the tug."

May you feel the tug of God's Spirit in your life today.

....

Thank You for the gift of Your Spirit, gracious God. Thank You that He enables me to live at peace with You, with others, and with myself. And thank You that He can help me stick out for You!

DR. BENNY TATE, ROCK SPRINGS CHURCH, MILNER, GA

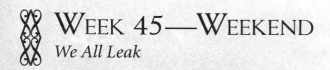

WEEK 45—WEEKEND
We All Leak

If Christ is in you, the body is dead because of sin, but the Spirit is life because of righteousness. But if the Spirit of Him who raised Jesus from the dead dwells in you, He who raised Christ from the dead will also give life to your mortal bodies through His Spirit who dwells in you.

ROMANS 8:10–11

D o you realize that Jesus said it was more important that the invisible Holy Spirit be on this earth than the visible Jesus (John 16:7)? One reason is that while Jesus was here, He could only be in one place at one time. But the Holy Spirit can be everywhere all of the time through believers.

Furthermore, the Christian life is impossible without the Holy Spirit. We have power over sin through the Holy Spirit (Romans 8:13). We worship in the Spirit (Philippians 3:3), we walk in the Spirit (Galatians 5:16) and we witness in the Spirit (Acts 1:8).

When we accepted Christ, we "were sealed with the Holy Spirit of promise" (Ephesians 1:13). A banking metaphor may help here. Think of the Spirit as a down payment that has been made and you will come back to get the item. God placed His Spirit in us as a down payment, and because we are His, God will welcome us into heaven one day.

In the meantime, we are to be filled with the Spirit (Ephesians 5:18), and a fresh presence of God's Spirit is vital. When someone asked D. L. Moody why he prayed for fresh fillings of the Spirit, he responded, "I leak!"

....

Lord, I leak! So please fill me afresh today with Your Spirit, that I may be used by You in whatever situations, interactions, and opportunities to love that this day holds!

WEEK 46—MONDAY
Praying with Confidence

"Ask, and it will be given to you; seek, and you will find; knock, and it will be opened to you. For everyone who asks receives, and he who seeks finds, and to him who knocks it will be opened."

MATTHEW 7:7–8

I'm a pastor, so people often ask me for counsel. I'm always grateful to help, but sometimes I want to say, "Have you asked the Lord about it?" Many times the reply is "Well, not yet." Seeking the Lord's wisdom is always the best place to start solving any problem. Why go to a pastor when you can go to your wise and powerful and good Savior? Notice that He says to *ask*, not *beg*. God is willing—and able—to meet your every need.

Ask! Seek! Knock! That's what Jesus wants us to do. And in response I want to ask—I always want to pray—like new believers pray. They haven't learned "Christianese" yet, so they do what Jesus says and just ask!

Our heavenly Father wants to meet our needs. He desires a relationship with us far more than we sometimes desire with Him. The Lord is ready to answer your prayers and touch you with His grace. Why don't you ask Him today for wisdom in your life? Ask your heavenly Father for whatever you need! God desires for you to walk with the confidence that He answers your prayers.

....

Dear God, I am humbled and grateful that You want to be in relationship with me. Teach me, I pray, to walk closely to You, to become very aware of Your presence with me always, and to pray to You with confidence in Your wisdom and love. Amen.

TIM ANDERSON, SENIOR PASTOR, CLEMENTS BAPTIST CHURCH, ATHENS, AL

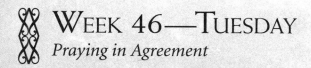

WEEK 46—TUESDAY
Praying in Agreement

"If two of you agree on earth concerning anything that they ask, it will be done for them by My Father in heaven. For where two or three are gathered together in My name, I am there in the midst of them."

MATTHEW 18:19–20

It has been said, "There is power in numbers." That has never been more profound than when it comes to prayer. If the fervent prayer of one righteous man avails much (James 5:16), then how much more effective will prayer be when two or three are gathered? Moses agreed, asking the people rhetorically, "How could one chase a thousand, and two put ten thousand to flight?" (Deuteronomy 32:30). That's a strange way to do math, but when two or more Christians gather to pray, they do find strength in the Lord.

The word *agree* means to "stand together" or to "harmonize." That's why hearing "Amens" in church is always welcoming. When one person is leading in prayer and the congregation hears something they agree with, their "Amen" is very encouraging. We are praying together; we are praying in harmony. And Jesus is honored when His people sound the same note.

Someone has said: "Prayer is God the Son, praying to God the Father, in the power of the Spirit—and the prayer room is in the believer's heart."

Do you have someone in whom you can confide and with whom you pray? If not, ask God to bring that person into your life. In the meantime listen to the Father say, "Amen."

....

Dear Lord, thank You for the assurance that You hear my prayers. You know when my heart-prayer is "I believe; help my unbelief." And You answer even when all I am able to offer is a mustard seed of faith.

WEEK 46—WEDNESDAY
Praying for God's Closeness

The LORD is near to all who call upon Him, to all who call upon Him in truth. He will fulfill the desire of those who fear Him; He also will hear their cry and save them.

PSALM 145:18–19

One of the most encouraging thoughts in the world is to know that God is close to me. God is no respecter of persons: He will come close to all who call upon His name. One of the great doctrines of the faith is the priesthood of believers (1 Peter 2:9). Many believe that God is remote and unapproachable, and we need to approach Him through a special person. Good news, you are that special person! You yourself can go "boldly to the throne of grace . . . obtain mercy and find grace to help in time of need" (Hebrews 4:16).

David added that we are to "call upon Him in truth," meaning we call upon God based on the truth about Him that we find in Scripture. One truth, for instance, is that God promises His presence with us when we commit to walking with Him in truth and obedience. We may not always feel His presence, but by faith we can be absolutely positive that He is near.

As a result of our salvation in Jesus Christ, we have direct access to God. If you feel that He is not as close to you as you would like, be sure you are walking in His truth: our obedience draws us closer to Him. If you aren't as close to the Lord as you used to be, guess who moved?

Jesus, thank You for being with me always, for the truth that nothing can separate me from Your love (Romans 8:35–39). Amen.

TIM ANDERSON, SENIOR PASTOR, CLEMENTS BAPTIST CHURCH, ATHENS, AL

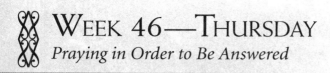

Week 46—Thursday
Praying in Order to Be Answered

"Call to Me, and I will answer you, and show you great and mighty things, which you do not know."

JEREMIAH 33:3

I find it strange that God was advising Jeremiah to "Call to Me." After all, Jeremiah was a prophet—and isn't that what prophets do? Preach and pray! Call to God!

Something must have happened to Jeremiah that drained all the energy out of him. Verse 1 supports that thought: "The word of the LORD came to Jeremiah a second time, while he was still shut up in the court of the prison." Jeremiah was in jail, and he had been there for quite a while. Why was the prophet in prison? Well, when people don't like the message, they shoot the messenger. Or, in this case, they put him into prison.

God promised not only to answer Jeremiah, but to show him "great and mighty things." Miraculous things! When the doctor says the womb is closed, God answers with a baby. When we think we have gone our last mile, God answers by giving us renewed energy and strength. When our hopes of a job have gradually faded over the past and very long twelve months, God answers with an employment opportunity. When cancer has spread throughout the body, God answers with peace or with healing. When your spouse is finished with the marriage, God answers with a renewed and softer heart.

What "great and mighty things" are you in need of today? Nothing is impossible with God!

....

Jesus, thank You for the many times You have answered my prayers by doing "great and mighty things." And thank You for giving me hope when all my hope was gone. Amen.

WEEK 46—FRIDAY
Praying in Secret

"When you pray, go into your room, and when you have shut your door, pray to your Father who is in the secret place; and your Father who sees in secret will reward you openly."

MATTHEW 6:6

One of the greatest moments of my day is early morning, because it is my personal devotional time with Jesus. I believe personal prayer and devotion to be the heart and soul of a believer's life. Vision for my life, family, and ministry all come from my time with God. There's nothing like an early morning cup of coffee, open Bible, pen, and an Oswald Chambers journal!

Never underestimate the power and value of prayer. After all, prayer is communion with the all-wise, all-powerful, all-loving God. No wonder the value of prayer is immeasurable in both the impact it has on our heart and on the people and situations we pray about.

Jesus said, "When you pray," alluding to the fact that there is no prescribed time to pray. The location and the time we pray aren't as important as our attitude: we approach God humbly, expectantly, listening for Him to speak. When Jesus said to "shut the door," He wants us to shut out everything else so that we can concentrate on God and not be distracted.

Jesus also said that He is aware of the time we spend with Him in a secret place, but He will reward us openly. We aren't told what type of reward we will receive, but God's acknowledgment of my spending time with Him is reward enough for me.

Do you have a personal prayer time? If not, consider starting this wonderful discipline today.

....

Dear Jesus, thank You for the privilege of prayer. Thank You for the preciousness of one-on-one time with You. Amen.

TIM ANDERSON, SENIOR PASTOR, CLEMENTS BAPTIST CHURCH, ATHENS, AL

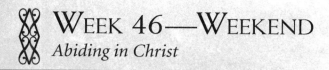

Week 46—Weekend
Abiding in Christ

"If you abide in Me, and My words abide in you, you will ask what you desire, and it shall be done for you. By this My Father is glorified, that you bear much fruit; so you will be My disciples."

JOHN 15:7–8

One of the greatest lessons I have learned in my Christian life is the abiding principle. *Abiding* means "keeping in fellowship with"—and that means reading the Word of God daily and confessing our sin regularly so that nothing will hinder our fellowship with Christ. Abiding in Christ includes worshipping, meditating, serving, and sacrificing. Once we experience these riches of a life committed to God, we will not be as easily tempted to go back to the former ways of life.

Furthermore, abiding in Christ always results in the fruit of strengthened faith, answered prayer, and a deeper love for God and others. We won't all bear the same amount of fruit, but we all bear some type of fruit. Remember that a living and abiding relationship with Christ is essential to producing fruit. And of course a good crop never comes up overnight.

Also, remember that fruit is never produced for oneself; fruit is for others, for their nourishment and refreshment. Of all the different fruit the Bible refers to, the fruit most evident in our lives should be love, joy, and peace. So may we be the type of disciple who feeds others by our words and deeds.

What kind of fruit is your life producing?

....

Lord, Your gracious invitation to fellowship has changed my life. As I abide in You—as I study Scripture, worship, and serve—may You bear fruit in my life that You can use to draw people to You—for their good and Your glory.

WEEK 47—MONDAY
Forgiveness Is Hard Work!

"If you forgive men their trespasses, your heavenly Father will also forgive you. But if you do not forgive men their trespasses, neither will your Father forgive your trespasses."

MATTHEW 6:14–15

A long time ago, someone injured me deeply with his words and his actions—and I *thought* I had forgiven him. Then, years later, I was standing at the back of an elevator when this man stepped on. When I saw him, all of the hurt, anger, and bitterness I believed I'd let go of came rushing back. This person still had no idea that he had ever hurt me, but I knew that I needed to forgive him in my heart. I prayed, "God, forgive me for not forgiving. Give me Your grace to forgive this man." As I prayed that prayer, I knew that this time I had truly forgiven.

Forgiving is one of the hardest things we ever have to do. Sometimes we resist forgiving because the wound we've suffered is all too real or painful or undeserved. At other times, as in my example above, we extend only surface-level forgiveness rather than dealing with the deep roots of our hurt.

Jesus taught that doing the hard work of forgiving others is essential to living in harmony with God. Refusing to forgive someone creates a barrier not only between you and that person, but also between you and the Lord. The greater that person's trespass is, the more you need God's grace to forgive. His grace, evident in His forgiving you, will empower you to forgive others.

Lord, forgiveness is hard work. Thank You that in my weakness I can know Your strength and—for my good and Your glory—be able to do this hard but vital work.

DR. STEPHEN RUMMAGE, BELL SHOALS BAPTIST CHURCH, BRANDON, FL

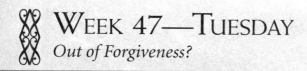

Week 47—Tuesday
Out of Forgiveness?

Peter came to Him and said, "Lord, how often shall my brother sin against me, and I forgive him? Up to seven times?" Jesus said to him, "I do not say to you, up to seven times, but up to seventy times seven."

MATTHEW 18:21–22

At 11:30 on a Thursday morning, my wife and I walked up to the counter of a fast-food chicken restaurant. Before we could place our order, the guy behind the counter said, "We're out of chicken." I pressed the issue just to be sure. *No original recipe? No extra-crispy? No rotisserie roasted? Not even any chicken nuggets?* He just looked at me and repeated, "We're out of chicken. We have mashed potatoes, French fries, corn on the cob, and slaw, but no chicken." We walked away hungry—and amused that a chicken restaurant would run out of chicken.

Less amusing and even more inconsistent are forgiven followers of Jesus who run out of forgiveness. How could we—whose sin God has mercifully and graciously forgiven—ever run short of forgiveness for others?

Peter brought Jesus a proposal that seemed big-hearted. The Jewish rabbis taught that we need only forgive a person three times for any offense. Peter doubled that number, added one for good measure, and then asked Jesus, "If someone sins against me, should I forgive him up to seven times?" Instead of commending Peter, Jesus increased the number exponentially: "Up to seventy times seven." Jesus couldn't have been clearer: He wants His followers to forgive without limits.

. . . .

Lord, sometimes I do feel like I'm out of forgiveness. Thank You that I can go to You and You'll enable me to forgive. And thank You that You never run out of forgiveness for me.

Week 47—Wednesday
Keep Moving Forward

"Do not remember the former things, nor consider the things of old. Behold, I will do a new thing, now it shall spring forth; shall you not know it? I will even make a road in the wilderness and rivers in the desert."

ISAIAH 43:18–19

Australia's coat of arms is a shield supported on one side by a red kangaroo and, on the other side, an emu. These unique animals were chosen not only because they are native to Australia, but because of the common belief that neither creature can easily move backward, making them great symbols of a nation moving forward. In fact, the earliest coats of arms bore the superscription "Advance Australia."

In the same way, God has made us to move forward, not backward—as the demise of Lot's wife dramatically illustrates. The command "Do not look behind you" had been given, but she looked backward at Sodom and Gomorrah and "became a pillar of salt" (Genesis 19:26). Like Lot's wife, we can become paralyzed when we only look back to the past, when we fail to see what God has for us in the future. There are always new things that He is doing, new visions and dreams He wants to place in our hearts, and new opportunities to serve Him.

....

Thank You, Lord, for the blessings of the past as well as the lessons You taught me in the past. As I reflect on Your goodness to me, may I with expectation keep my eyes looking forward to the new roads of blessing and new streams of grace You have for me.

DR. STEPHEN RUMMAGE, BELL SHOALS BAPTIST CHURCH, BRANDON, FL

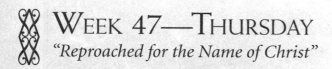

WEEK 47—THURSDAY
"Reproached for the Name of Christ"

If you are reproached for the name of Christ, blessed are you, for the Spirit of glory and of God rests upon you. On their part He is blasphemed, but on your part He is glorified.

1 PETER 4:14

Pastor Arnav serves a church in a remote village in northern India, where less than one half of one percent of the population follows Christ. His congregation regularly faces violent persecution because of their faith in Jesus. One afternoon, Arnav came home to find his wife viciously beaten by radical Hindus from his village. Her attackers went to the local magistrate and claimed that Arnav had assaulted his own wife.

Arnav spent months imprisoned while his wife and friends worked for him to be freed. Amazingly, once he was released, Arnav and his wife not only expressed forgiveness for the men who had brutalized her, but looked for ways to reach them with the gospel. Why? Because they count suffering for Jesus a blessing.

If we are following Jesus, people will mistreat us. We may hear snide remarks or insults, neighbors or classmates may snub us, we may be passed over for a promotion at work, or we might even be attacked physically. Whenever we suffer for our faith, it's easy to feel angry and become unforgiving. But remember this: Jesus died for those precious souls who, in their darkness, are ridiculing our faith or harassing us for following Him.

....

Lord Jesus, thank You for the reminders that those who persecute Christians are living in darkness and that You died on the cross for them. Please—by the power of Your Spirit—enable me to forgive those who persecute me for my faith in You.

Let all bitterness, wrath, anger, clamor, and evil speaking be put away from you, with all malice. And be kind to one another, tenderhearted, forgiving one another, even as God in Christ forgave you.

EPHESIANS 4:31–32

After years of struggling with her weight, Sarah spent ten months of serious exercise and dieting until she finally reached her goal. She felt better, loved the way she looked, and was thrilled to wear smaller sizes. As those ten months had passed, Sarah had been encouraged by the growing mound of old clothes in the corner of her closet. With joy, she had folded and stacked each dress, skirt, top, or pair of pants that had become too big.

Now Sarah faced a choice: What would she do with that stack of clothes that no longer fit? Deciding that keeping her old things would make it too easy to go back to her old weight, she boxed them up and gave them away.

Things like resentment, rage, harsh words, and mean-spiritedness may have been our normal wardrobe before we started following Jesus, but they no longer fit us. Instead of clothing ourselves with them or even keeping them close at hand, God calls us to get rid of those old sordid things. He wants us to wear the garments of His kindness, compassion, and forgiveness.

. . . .

Lord Jesus, please help me take an inventory of my closet of attitudes right now. Show me what I need to get rid of—and help me do exactly that. And clothe me, I pray, in Your kindness and love. I want to be able to treat others with the tenderheartedness, forgiveness, and grace You have treated me.

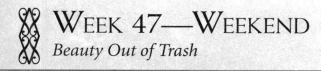
All of you be of one mind, . . . not returning evil for evil or reviling for reviling, but on the contrary blessing, knowing that you were called to this, that you may inherit a blessing.

1 PETER 3:8–9

The world sends us garbage. We send back music. That is the life philosophy of Favio Chavez, director and founder of an unusual orchestra in Cateura, Paraguay. A documentary called *Landfill Harmonic* tells the story of young musicians who play instruments lovingly crafted for them—out of trash—by people in their community.

Cateura is a slum built on a landfill that receives more than 1,500 tons of solid waste a day. Nearly three thousand families live there, staying alive by separating garbage for recycling, despite a dangerously polluted water supply. The smallest children are responsible for collecting and reselling the garbage.

Yet in the middle of this filth, young people are creating something beautiful. In the film, a young man nicknamed Bebi shows the camera his cello, fashioned from an oil can and old cooking tools. Then he draws the bow across the strings and gracefully plays Bach's Prelude to Cello Suite No. 1.

Let us learn from the young musicians of Cateura who turn trash into beauty. When the world throws evil and ugliness at us, God can enable us to give blessing and goodness in return. His grace gives us the power to forgive; to show love to those who hurt us; to turn trash into beauty.

··

Lord, You know the trash that fills my heart, and only You can make beauty—the beauty of grace and forgiveness—from that garbage. Help me cooperate with You as You enable me to forgive people who have harmed me, recently or deep in my past. Help me see ways to bless them and then do that good for them.

❁ WEEK 48—MONDAY
Talkers or Walkers?

If we say that we have fellowship with Him, and walk in darkness, we lie and do not practice the truth. But if we walk in the light as He is in the light, we have fellowship with one another, and the blood of Jesus Christ His Son cleanses us from all sin.

1 JOHN 1:6–7

When it comes to your relationship with Jesus, are you a talker or a walker?

Talkers like to keep their relationships shallow and superficial; they enjoy conversations and company as long as they don't have to make much of a commitment. They don't mind helping when it's convenient for them—or if they can save face, avoid feeling guilty about not helping, or be thought of as giving and caring rather than as selfish and cold. Talkers also tend to be quiet about their true feelings, either offering very little information or hiding behind an abundance of useless information.

Walkers are those who desire authentic relationships with people as the result of the authentic relationship they have with Jesus. Because these people walk in the light of God's love and grace, they enjoy transparency in their relationships, and they are able to care deeply and genuinely about others. Aware that the blood of Jesus allows them to have forgiveness of their sins, these individuals then freely forgive others. They also keep their relationships free from pettiness and pretense. Their deep abiding walk with Jesus impacts how they walk with others.

....

Lord Jesus, thank You for being a Friend who "loves at all times" (Proverbs 17:17). Help me forge authentic relationships that are free from pettiness and that reflect Your love to others. Let me be a good friend.

REV. BUCKY KENNEDY, FIRST BAPTIST CHURCH VIDALIA, VIDALIA, GA

WEEK 48—TUESDAY
The Scent and Sounds of Christlike Love

Walk in love, as Christ also has loved us and given Himself for us, an offering and a sacrifice to God for a sweet-smelling aroma. . . . [Speak] to one another in psalms and hymns and spiritual songs, singing and making melody in your heart to the Lord . . . For we are members of His body, of His flesh and of His bones.

EPHESIANS 5:2, 19, 30

*W*alk in love. These three words inspire, stirring us to love others with the love we have received from Jesus. But the apostle Paul didn't stop with inspiration. He moved on to instruction. And then to strengthen his instruction, Paul pointed us to the individual who can be an example for us: Christ Jesus is our model for what walking in love looks like.

Real love—Christlike love—makes sacrifices for the good of others and the glory of God. This kind of costly love has a sweetness to it that others find attractive and encouraging. This love not only smells good, but it sounds good as well. There is something uplifting about being around people who have a song in their heart and encouragement on their lips. You notice these rare individuals and appreciate them because they are so refreshing to be around.

Someone has said that becoming a believer is that last decision we make in isolation because then we are a member of the body of Christ. At that point what we say and do impacts others. The sacrifice you make for the benefit of one, for instance, will actually bless the body as a whole.

....

Lord, teach me to walk in love—staying close to You—so that Your presence will be a winsome aroma and a sweet song of joy to those around me.

WEEK 48—WEDNESDAY
Restraining to Serve

Now may the God of patience and comfort grant you to be like-minded toward one another, according to Christ Jesus, that you may with one mind and one mouth glorify the God and Father of our Lord Jesus Christ. Therefore receive one another, just as Christ also received us, to the glory of God.

ROMANS 15:5–7

As I read this, I can almost hear the apostle Paul saying, "All right, in order for you to be 'like-minded toward one another,' you're going to need patience. A lot of patience. The kind of patience only God can supply!" There is no other way that a body as diverse as the body of Christ can survive! The blessing of a supernatural patience given to us through the Person of Jesus Christ by the power of His Spirit is essential to a healthy body of believers.

A key element of that supernatural patience is restraint. Only with God reining me in will my involvement in the cause of Christ benefit others and glorify God. In other words, God-given patience enables me *not* to be me, so that I can more humbly and more selflessly join others in accomplishing the work of Christ. Without restraint, I would be less receptive to and less appreciative of what others have to offer as we serve God in this darkened world. God's patience restrains me and enables me to more wholeheartedly receive others so that we can accomplish together all that brings Christ glory.

Being part of the body of Christ is not about singing solo but about enjoying being a member of His choir.

....

Thank You, Lord God, for the special part in Your choir that You have chosen me to sing. May our song be harmonious and pleasing to Your ear.

REV. BUCKY KENNEDY, FIRST BAPTIST CHURCH VIDALIA, VIDALIA, GA

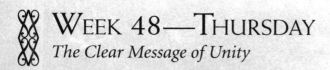

WEEK 48—THURSDAY
The Clear Message of Unity

I plead with you, brethren, by the name of our Lord Jesus Christ, that you all speak the same thing, and that there be no divisions among you, but that you be perfectly joined together in the same mind and in the same judgment.

1 CORINTHIANS 1:10

In an 1858 speech, Senate candidate Abraham Lincoln said this:

"A house divided against itself cannot stand." I believe this government cannot endure, permanently half slave and half free. I do not expect the Union to be dissolved—I do not expect the house to fall—but I do expect it will cease to be divided. It will become all one thing or all the other.[19]

Five years earlier a policy had been established: America would not practice slavery. But this policy was ignored by what would soon be known as the Confederacy of the Southern States. America was divided by slavery, and confusion and conflict resulted.

Well aware that division does cause confusion and conflicts, the apostle Paul begged for unity when he wrote to the church in Corinth. "Perfectly joined together in the same mind" sounds like an easier way to live and a more effective way to be God's light. When we are unified in the Person of Jesus Christ, we allow the world to see a clearer picture of Jesus and His message of hope and salvation. Without this unity, we lead people away from truth, away from hope, and away from Jesus.

. . . .

Lord God, please show me how I'm contributing to division, confusion, or conflict in Your body of believers. I ask Your forgiveness—I ask for Your transforming work in my life—so that You can use me as part of Your body to show the needy world the truth and hope of Jesus.

WEEK 48—FRIDAY
Uniquely Different and Specifically Placed

You are no longer strangers and foreigners, but fellow citizens with the saints and members of the household of God, having been built on the foundation of the apostles and prophets, Jesus Christ Himself being the chief cornerstone, in whom the whole building, being fitted together, grows into a holy temple in the Lord.

EPHESIANS 2:19–21

As a believer in Jesus Christ, I am blessed to be a citizen "with the saints and members of the household of God." Clearly, this word picture tells me that I am not alone. Furthermore, having fellow citizens tells me that I should be engaging with them and not isolating myself from them. This citizenship also affords me the privilege of fellowship: God never intended me to be the only brick in His house. As a matter of fact, He cast me to be fitted with other bricks—with other believers—in His household.

Also according to this text, the purpose of my existence—in part—is to encourage other citizens to holiness just as people before me have provided a foundation for my holiness, for the holiness of God's people as a body.

By God's grace and the working of His Spirit who dwells within us, every believer is growing into holiness in Christ, into a personalized holiness. I am uniquely different so that I can be specifically placed with others who are uniquely different and specifically placed so that we can jointly be a holy temple.

....

Thank You, Lord, for welcoming me into Your household and for enabling me to recognize the truth about Jesus proclaimed by the apostles and prophets. Use me, Lord, to encourage Your people to holiness even as I walk that path myself and as You grow us into a holy temple that honors and glorifies You.

REV. BUCKY KENNEDY, FIRST BAPTIST CHURCH VIDALIA, VIDALIA, GA

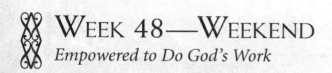

WEEK 48—WEEKEND
Empowered to Do God's Work

If there is any consolation in Christ, if any comfort of love, if any fellowship of the Spirit, if any affection and mercy, fulfill my joy by being like-minded, having the same love, being of one accord, of one mind.

PHILIPPIANS 2:1–2

L et's slow down and look more closely at the two parts of this beautiful yet long statement by the apostle Paul.

First is the *if* clause, which I'll summarize this way: "If you have experienced Christ's presence with you and among you in any way . . ."

After the *if* clause comes the instruction or charge: "then you need to live so that Jesus' presence with you is obvious." And Paul got specific: be like-minded, love one another, live in agreement and unity.

At Pentecost we saw God use 120 people, full of the Spirit, to introduce to the world the church of the risen Jesus (Acts 1:15). And we can learn from that: being filled with the Spirit enables us to do God's work in God's way. I'm so glad God didn't leave us to figure out *what* works but has instead equipped us with *who* works.

The *who* is the Holy Spirit—and every aspect of your life, every relationship in your life, would benefit in some way from a fresh outpouring of the Spirit of God. After all, by His Spirit within you, Jesus can use you to express His love for others.

....

Holy Spirit, here I am, yielding to You. Please use me to catch the attention of people living in darkness and to witness effectively for You. I ask You to fill me afresh moment by moment, day by day, and use me to share the healing, saving love of Jesus Christ with others.

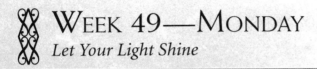

Week 49—Monday
Let Your Light Shine

"You are the light of the world. A city that is set on a hill cannot be hidden. Nor do they light a lamp and put it under a basket, but on a lampstand, and it gives light to all who are in the house."

Matthew 5:14–15

My wife has a collection of lighthouses, and on several trips we have visited lighthouses. My favorites are the Cape Henry Lighthouses in Virginia Beach, Virginia. (One dates back to 1792; the newer one was built in 1881.) As that light shines, it guides ships into Chesapeake Bay.

For sailors who have been at sea for far too long, a lighthouse signals they are almost home. For ships that are perilously off course, the light warns of danger. Lighthouses don't exist for those who are on the shore and already safe. Lighthouses exist for those who are not yet home, for those who are trying to navigate treacherous, stormy waters. Lighthouses offer a great picture of how we believers can be "the light of the world."

Jesus commanded us Christians to let our light shine. Some people you know are far from God and need the light of love and grace to help them get home. Others are in danger of being spiritually shipwrecked for all eternity. So let your light shine both in word and deed. The stakes of eternity are too high for us to hide our light under a basket.

....

Lord, I want the light of Your love to shine through me. Give me the courage to share Your gospel with those I encounter, to speak Your truth boldly with love. And, Lord Jesus, it would be a privilege and a joy to help someone come to know You as Lord and Savior. Amen.

DR. BOB MCCARTNEY, FIRST BAPTIST CHURCH, WICHITA FALLS, TX

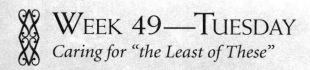

WEEK 49—TUESDAY
Caring for "the Least of These"

"Then the righteous will answer Him, saying, 'Lord, when did we see You hungry and feed You, or thirsty and give You drink?' . . . And the King will answer and say to them, 'Assuredly, I say to you, inasmuch as you did it to one of the least of these My brethren, you did it to Me.'"

MATTHEW 25:37, 40

It may be the greatest hidden humanitarian crisis of our time. I'm talking about the world's estimated 150 million orphans whom the media seldom, if ever, mentions and, tragically, whom even the church has largely ignored. Orphans have no voice, no political clout, and no resources. Orphans are certainly among those Jesus was talking about when He referred to "the least of these."

Most Christians would not hesitate to say that they care about orphans, widows, the homeless, and the strangers among us. But the Lord calls us to do more than care about the least of these; Jesus calls on us to care for them. To care *about* someone is an emotional response; to care *for* someone demands action.

Jesus' command here is an indictment of our selfishness, our comfort, and our materialism. We are called to serve willingly, love indiscriminately, and give freely of the resources He has entrusted to us. While the greatest needs of people are spiritual, we need to care for their physical and material needs as well.

....

Jesus, You don't call me merely to care about; *You call me to care* for. *So as You open my eyes to the very real poverty and pain in my world, please open my heart to be generous with Your blessings. And show me the specific action steps You'd have me take to care for "the least of these."*

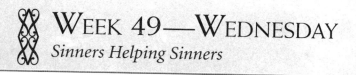

Week 49—Wednesday
Sinners Helping Sinners

If a man is overtaken in any trespass, you who are spiritual restore such a one in a spirit of gentleness, considering yourself lest you also be tempted. Bear one another's burdens, and so fulfill the law of Christ.

Galatians 6:1–2

It's tragic to hear about a high-profile Christian—a pastor, a congressman, a businessman—who stumbles and falls. The world delights in the moral failure of those who follow Christ. Satan smiles when his schemes wreck anyone's life, especially the life of a very public Christian figure. The media gloats when it has evidence of a Christian caught in sin. I suppose we should expect nothing less of the media and their followers, but God expects much more from His people. We must not respond to individuals caught in sin with the same gossip and ridicule that the world does.

In today's passage, Paul wrote about the responsibility of believers when a Christian fails: the one who sins is to repent, and we are to engage in the ministry of restoration. When a brother falls, we are to help him up, not kick him while he is down. Many Christians see others sin and allow their own hearts to grow judgmental and proud. That very human reaction prompted Paul to warn us: when we are restoring a brother or sister, we should guard our hearts because temptation will certainly come our way. Rather than criticizing, we are called to help the weak and wounded bear their burdens.

Lord, when I hear of a Christian caught in sin, let me see that person as You do. Holy Spirit, fill my heart with compassion. Let me speak humbly and with love only those words that edify and encourage.

DR. BOB MCCARTNEY, FIRST BAPTIST CHURCH, WICHITA FALLS, TX

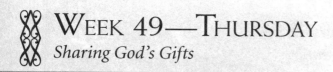

WEEK 49—THURSDAY
Sharing God's Gifts

By this we know love, because He laid down His life for us. And we also ought to lay down our lives for the brethren. But whoever has this world's goods, and sees his brother in need, and shuts up his heart from him, how does the love of God abide in him?

1 JOHN 3:16–17

If you are a parent, you probably remember your child's first word. My wife and I had a friendly competition to see if it would be "Mama" or "Dada." While I knew that Mom had the inside track, I thought I had a fighting chance since little girls have a special place in their hearts for Dad. Imagine our surprise when our little girl's first word was neither of those. She spoke her first intelligible word when another toddler came over to play. As the little guest picked up a toy, my sweet daughter immediately, forcefully, and quite clearly said, *"Mine!"*

Today's passage challenges us to set aside that childish attitude of "Mine." And we should replace this selfishness with a willingness to make sacrifices for others just as Jesus sacrificed His life for us.

John gave a concrete example of what he was talking about: if we have been blessed with material things, we should be willing to share out of our abundance with those in need. The question John posed in verse 17 is haunting: If we can't find it in our hearts to be generous, is the love of God even in our hearts?

....

Lord, help me remember that everything I have is a gift from You. Transform my heart so that I will cheerfully be generous with those in need.

"These words which I command you today shall be in your heart. You shall teach them diligently to your children, and shall talk of them when you sit in your house, when you walk by the way, when you lie down, and when you rise up."

DEUTERONOMY 6:6–7

When I grew up, my dad was a six-days-a-week, hardworking farmer. Providing for his family was never easy, and it left very little time for hobbies. But as busy as my dad was, he made time for one extra activity. He might be too busy to go hunting or fishing, but he was never too busy to coach my baseball team. And he taught us more than how to hit, catch, and throw. By his word and example, my dad taught us how to be Christian men.

Moses wrote today's passage in what appears to be a simpler time. Even though the pace may have been slower and the calendars less full, Moses emphasized the importance of using every possible moment to teach the next generation God's truth. Shaping a child's worldview takes more than an hour on Sunday. Parents, not the church, are primarily responsible for teaching God's truth to the next generation. The home is the best laboratory for learning biblical principles. Having a family devotional time is a great first step. Reading God's Word and praying for one another can do much to grow each person's faith. Beyond the formal devotional time, seize the teachable moment. When an athlete or a celebrity does something good or bad, simply ask, "What does God's Word say about that?"

Father, help me teach my children Your Word and lead them in Your paths. Give me the wisdom I need to raise children who love You.

DR. BOB MCCARTNEY, FIRST BAPTIST CHURCH, WICHITA FALLS, TX

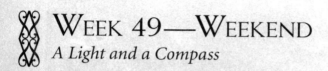

WEEK 49—WEEKEND
A Light and a Compass

"You shall lay up these words of mine in your heart and in your soul, and bind them as a sign on your hand, and they shall be as frontlets between your eyes. . . . And you shall write them on the doorposts of your house and on your gates."

DEUTERONOMY 11:18, 20

When I was a Boy Scout, I learned to use a compass. After we had a few lessons, our leader took some of us deep into the woods just after dark. We had two tools—a flashlight and a compass. Then he gave us several headings and distances—and left. Using the directions he'd given us, our flashlights, and our compasses, we were to find out way back to the campsite. I remember feeling like we were going the wrong way, but we ignored our feelings, followed the directions, and made it back safely.

The Word of God serves as both a light—revealing the safe path to walk as well as temptations that could easily trip us up—and a compass, pointing the way for us to go in a world darkened by sin. No wonder it is important to let God's Word saturate our hearts, our minds, our lives.

What are you doing to store God's Word in your heart and bind it on your hands and forehead? Where is scripture written in your home? What plan do you have for regularly studying, meditating on, and memorizing God's Word?

....

Lord, give me a hunger to know You more through Your Word. Help me to store Your Word in my heart that I may not sin against You but walk in Your ways.

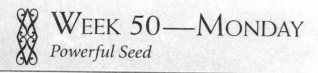

Week 50—Monday
Powerful Seed

Since you have purified your souls in obeying the truth through the Spirit in sincere love of the brethren, love one another fervently with a pure heart, having been born again, not of corruptible seed but incorruptible, through the word of God which lives and abides forever.

1 Peter 1:22–23

This passage calls us as believers to do some difficult things. "Love one another fervently" is not easy! It's hard enough to love others in the daily grind of life. In a culture of persecution and pain—the context of 1 Peter—it's even more difficult. Actually, it's impossible.

But what we could never do on our own, God's powerful Word does in us. The seed of the "incorruptible" and eternal Word of God—the seed of the gospel that first penetrated our heart—is the seed that gave us the new birth to salvation. Peter pointed to evidence of this new birth: we have purified our souls; we have been given a sincere love for others; we have a pure heart. All these come by the seed planted in us at salvation.

The seed of God's living truth, plus the transforming work of His Spirit within us, can produce all these things and more. We are able to have successful relationships, a clear conscience, and an eternal perspective on life in this fallen world. You and I can live for God—and we can "love one another fervently"—because of what God has placed in us: His Word and His Spirit. Rely on that today.

Lord, in whatever challenging situations today holds, I want to live according to Your Word and in the Spirit's power. I am depending on You to be a change-agent first in me and then through me. In Jesus' name, amen.

JOHN MEADOR, FIRST BAPTIST CHURCH, EULESS, TX

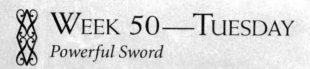

WEEK 50—TUESDAY
Powerful Sword

The word of God is living and powerful, and sharper than any two-edged sword, piercing even to the division of soul and spirit, and of joints and marrow, and is a discerner of the thoughts and intents of the heart.

HEBREWS 4:12

On my office wall, there is a display of swords I've collected over the years. These swords are a constant reminder of the supernatural spiritual power of God's Word, a power addressed in the Hebrews 4:12 description of Scripture.

God's Word is *living*. The Bible is not a lifeless collection of words; its message is powerful and eternally significant. The Greek word translated *alive* refers to the essence of life: God's Word gives life. And that *purpose* will continue to be fulfilled in the future just as it has in the past. God's Word speaks to you just as it spoke to Peter and Paul.

God's Word is *powerful*. The Greek word used here gives us our English word *energy*, and it is sometimes translated "active." God will actively use His Word to bring life-change. Scripture has the power to transform hearts and therefore lives! When you read Scripture, God will actively, powerfully produce the thought changes and heart changes that result in behavior changes.

The Word can function as a surgeon's scalpel, revealing the "intentions of the heart" (Jer. 17:10). As I read Scripture, I am convicted, but God reveals the solution, not just the problem. It might be pain, but it's life-saving measures.

....

God, today, use Your Word do the surgery in my spiritual life that needs to be done. Remove what needs to be removed, replace what must be replaced, so that I might live for You with all my heart. In Jesus' name, amen.

GOD IS FAITHFUL

WEEK 50—WEDNESDAY
Powerful Perspective

"So shall My word be that goes forth from My mouth; it shall not return to Me void, but it shall accomplish what I please, and it shall prosper in the thing for which I sent it."

ISAIAH 55:11

In Isaiah 55:11, God spoke through the prophet Isaiah and revealed the divine perspective on the written Word.

First, God said that His Word "goes forth from My mouth." God's Word is powerful because it is, literally, His Word. He spoke through the prophets, the epistles, and the Gospels: all of Scripture is directly from Him. When I was a young boy, my brother would relay instructions or a message from my father—and I always asked, "Did Dad say that?" If Dad didn't say it, it wasn't important. If he *did*, it was very important. God was telling us in Isaiah 55:11, "My Word is important!"

Second, God's Word will always accomplish its purpose, unlike seed that fails to sprout. The living Scripture will definitely bear fruit in God's perfect timing. Isaiah 55:10 compares God's Word to rain that comes down, waters the earth, and enables plants to bear fruit. Similarly, the Word of God will accomplish its purpose in your life.

When I'm discouraged or disillusioned, God will bring to mind a verse of Scripture that transforms my perspective, offers me hope, or reminds me of His love. Even if that verse was planted in my heart years earlier, the Holy Spirit brings it to the foreground exactly when I need it.

....

Lord, today, plant the seeds of Your truth deeply within me. I believe with my whole heart that You will use what I've read today to accomplish some great thing. In Jesus' name, amen.

JOHN MEADOR, FIRST BAPTIST CHURCH, EULESS, TX

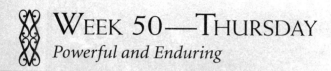
"Assuredly, I say to you, this generation will by no means pass away till all these things take place. Heaven and earth will pass away, but My words will by no means pass away."

MARK 13:30–31

Recently, a piece of pottery was discovered in an excavation in Jerusalem that dates back to the days of David. Nearly three thousand years old, this pottery shard contains the oldest known Hebrew inscription carved into it, but no one can decipher or understand those three-thousand-year-old words.

Human language comes and goes, but Jesus said that His words never pass away. In fact, His words will outlast heaven and earth. And this reality shouldn't surprise us.

After all, it was by God's *word* that the heavens and earth came into existence. The Word was in the beginning with God: "In the beginning was the Word, and the Word was with God, and the Word was God" (John 1:1). This powerful Word—Jesus Himself—was coexistent with God. The Word of God existed in eternity past.

Jesus said that His words will outlast heaven and earth (Mark 13:31), a statement that can only refer to eternity future. The word existed in eternity past, will exist in eternity future, and exists today—timeless, unchanging, and eternal. What a contrast to the words we fill our lives with and base our decisions on. It's truly amazing that the Bible you hold in your hands is eternally and supernaturally inspired by God.

. . . .

> *Dear Lord, I receive Your Word today as that which is breathed by You! No wonder Scripture is both personal and powerful. Enable me, I pray, to walk according to Your eternal Truth! In Jesus' name, amen.*

The word of the LORD is right, and all His work is done in truth. He loves righteousness and justice; the earth is full of the goodness of the LORD. By the word of the LORD the heavens were made, and all the host of them by the breath of His mouth.

PSALM 33:4–6

Psalm 33 is a powerful psalm of worship and praise that ties God's word of creation to His word of truth. Notice that the "word of the LORD" is described as "right," "truth," "righteousness," and "justice." Let's consider what connects creation and truth.

It's not simply that God's word aligns itself with truth and justice. It's that truth and justice are what they are because God spoke them into existence. According to the psalmist, in the same way that the word of the Lord made the heavens, God created truth, justice, and righteousness. And His creative word reflects who He is.

Before God spoke the world into existence, He existed as the true, righteous, and just God. Therefore, whatever He said "by the breath of His mouth" was always aligned with His character. Everything He created—all that He has brought into being—aligns itself with His eternal rule and order.

When God spoke, the elements of the world responded. When He spoke, the darkness was separated from the light, and the sea from the land. When God spoke, truth, justice, and righteousness became what they are—simply because God spoke them.

··

Lord, who am I to respond in any way other than awe, reverence, worship, and obedience to You who spoke all of creation into existence and who speaks to me today? As Creator God of the Universe, have Your way with me! In Jesus' name, amen.

JOHN MEADOR, FIRST BAPTIST CHURCH, EULESS, TX

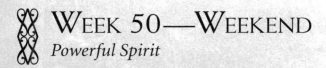

WEEK 50—WEEKEND
Powerful Spirit

No prophecy of Scripture is of any private interpretation, for prophecy never came by the will of man, but holy men of God spoke as they were moved by the Holy Spirit.

2 PETER 1:20–21

S cripture does not exist because several men decided to write an account of truth and circulate it. Neither is the Bible simply a collection of eyewitness accounts. And it's not merely a historical book. Any one of these would be a valuable book, but Scripture is far, far more than these.

"Holy men of God spoke as they were moved by the Holy Spirit," and the Greek for *moved* refers to something being lifted up and carried along by an outside force. As they wrote, the Spirit carried along those who penned the Scriptures just as the winds and waves of the sea lift and move a boat. On the Mount of Transfiguration, Peter, James, and John had been eyewitnesses, and they heard the voice of God. But when these men wrote what we now have as Scripture, they were "borne along" by God's Spirit.

Clearly, our God communicates! He writes. He speaks. He uses His finger to write on tablets of stone, His breath to speak through the mouths of the prophets, and the Holy Spirit to guide the thoughts of men in the giving of Scripture.

Since Scripture was written in the power of the Holy Spirit, may we read Scripture relying on the power of the Spirit.

....

Lord, I receive Your Word today. Do what You will with me. Change my life. Alter my direction. Take me on the journey with You. Anything, anytime, anywhere, I'm Yours. In Jesus' name, amen.

Week 51—Monday
God's Word, Our Inheritance

"Brethren, I commend you to God and to the word of His grace, which is able to build you up and give you an inheritance among all those who are sanctified."

ACTS 20:32

Why do we read Scripture at funerals and burials? Because the "word of His grace" reminds us of our inheritance. My word does not give you a spiritual, eternal inheritance; the words of your pastor or a TV preacher can't "give you an inheritance among those who are sanctified." We *depend* on the "word of [God's] grace"; we *hope* in the "word of [God's] grace."

Last words are important words—cherished and remembered. As I write this, I recall the last thing my mom said to our family before she passed. On her deathbed she said, "I want everyone to gather around the bed." When we did, then she said, "I want us to sing 'Rock of Ages.'" Through our tears we sang this precious hymn. Since then I have sung this song differently, for it now holds special meaning in my heart.

In our text, the apostle Paul met with the Ephesian church elders for the last time. These men whom he had affectionately loved and with whom he had ardently labored, listened intently as their spiritual father shared his final words. Of all he might have said, Paul chose to commend them to God and His Word! Why? Because God's Word offers *sweet* words of grace, *strengthening* words that "build you up," *secure* words that speak of our eternal inheritance, and *sanctifying* words of truth (John 17:17).

....

I thank You, Lord, for Your sweet Word that strengthens my faith, reminds me of my eternal security in You, and sanctifies me that You might use me in Your kingdom!

302   ALLAN TAYLOR, MINISTER OF EDUCATION, FIRST BAPTIST WOODSTOCK, WOODSTOCK, GA

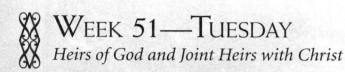

WEEK 51—TUESDAY
Heirs of God and Joint Heirs with Christ

The Spirit Himself bears witness with our spirit that we are children of God, and if children, then heirs—heirs of God and joint heirs with Christ, if indeed we suffer with Him, that we may also be glorified together.

ROMANS 8:16–17

It can be argued that Romans 8 is one of the greatest chapters in all the Word of God. It starts by telling us there is "no condemnation to those who are in Christ Jesus" (v. 1). It ends by telling us that nothing "shall be able to separate us from the love of God" (v. 39). In between, we read about the Holy Spirit's work in our lives.

Each night after I turn off the light and crawl into bed, I spend some time with my conscience and my God. No pretending, no faking. Just me and God to whom "all things are naked and open" (Hebrews 4:13). God already knows the truth about me. I might look good in church or around others, but there's no fooling God. At that moment I'm vulnerable before Him, so I can address the truth about me.

One of the great works of the Holy Spirit is to "bear witness with our spirit that we are children of God." Does God's Spirit bear witness in your spirit, the real you, that you are one of His children? If so, rejoice! If not, repent! Turn *from* your sin and turn *to* Jesus. He wants you to be His child, His heir and a joint heir with Christ.

....

No condemnation! Never any separation from Your love! Reassurance that I am Your child! Thank You that these are true, by Your grace, for me, a sinner. I can't fool You about my sin or, Father God, about my gratitude!

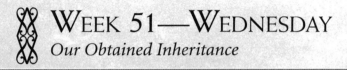

WEEK 51—WEDNESDAY
Our Obtained Inheritance

In Him also we have obtained an inheritance, being predestined according to the purpose of Him who works all things according to the counsel of His will, that we who first trusted in Christ should be to the praise of His glory.

EPHESIANS 1:11–12

Ephesians 1 reveals three wonderful things Jesus does for believers. He redeems, He reveals the mystery of His will, and He rewards. Here are six questions that address those rewards:

Who? Believers: "we who first trusted in Christ." The inheritance is predestined to any and to all who will trust in Christ.

What? An inheritance. Paul said it was our "hope which is laid up for you in heaven" (Colossians 1:5).

When? At the moment of salvation, we receive an inheritance. Although the full realization of it is still lies in the future, we have it now: "we *have* obtained." Our inheritance is already in the books!

Where? "In heavenly places" (Ephesians 1:3, 20; 2:6; 3:10). Our inheritance awaits in heaven.

How? By faith "we have *obtained* an inheritance." We did not—indeed, we could not—have *attained* an inheritance. Our inheritance is a matter of God's grace, not our merit.

Why? "To the praise of His glory." Believers exist to bring God glory. Living to glorify God will bring purpose and joy to your life.

....

Gracious Jesus, walking through life with You is blessing and reward enough! Thank You for the future reward—our heavenly inheritance!

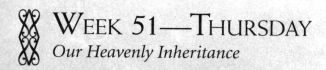

WEEK 51—THURSDAY
Our Heavenly Inheritance

Blessed be the God and Father of our Lord Jesus Christ, who according to His abundant mercy has begotten us again to a living hope through the resurrection of Jesus Christ from the dead, to an inheritance incorruptible and undefiled and that does not fade away, reserved in heaven for you.

1 PETER 1:3–4

In Luke 24 two disciples were walking from Jerusalem to Emmaus on the third day after the crucifixion of Jesus. The resurrected Christ came and walked with them, but they didn't recognize Him. As the two spoke of the events of the preceding three days, they explained to this "stranger" about Jesus: "But we were hoping that it was He who was going to redeem Israel" (v. 21). They spoke of their hope in the past tense: when Jesus died, their hopes of His redeeming Israel died. But that hope would soon be revived!

Then, some thirty years later, the apostle Peter wrote (v. 3) that we are "begotten . . . again," a second time. He was begotten the first time by the life of Jesus. He has been begotten a second time by Christ's bodily resurrection from the dead. But to what was Peter "begotten"? "To a living hope . . . to an inheritance" (vv. 3–4). From this point on the apostle would live with hope in the present and look toward his inheritance in heaven.

An inheritance is a parent's undeserved gift of love and grace. God, our heavenly Father, has reserved for us an inheritance in heaven where it cannot be corrupted or defiled in any way.

Paul is called the Apostle of Faith; John, the Apostle of Love; Peter, the Apostle of Hope—and rightfully so!

....

Lord, thank You for these spokesmen of faith, love, and hope who encourage me as I journey through life!

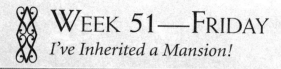

In My Father's house are many mansions; if it were not so, I would have told you. I go to prepare a place for you. And if I go and prepare a place for you, I will come again and receive you to Myself; that where I am, there you may be also.

JOHN 14:2–3

For most people, a house is the most expensive item they will ever own. We want to buy a nice house, and we continually work on it to make it better. It becomes our most treasured possession. When we die, we usually pass the house on to our children as part of their inheritance.

One day when Jesus was walking through Jericho, He looked up into a tree and there sat Zacchaeus. Jesus said to him, "Make haste and come down, for today I must stay at your house" (Luke 19:5). When Zacchaeus trusted Christ as his Savior, salvation came to his house (v. 9), and he immediately owned another house—in heaven!

Lazarus the beggar (Luke 16) begged for crumbs from the rich man's table, yet he too has a home in heaven!

Jesus, a carpenter by trade, has gone to prepare you a mansion in heaven. (If you think your subdivision is nice, wait until you see His!) But please understand that before Jesus can give you a home in heaven, you first have to give Him a home in your heart!

If you have done so, then one day you will inherit a mansion made for you in heaven.

....

Jesus, my Savior and Lord, thank You for wanting to make Your home in my heart. May I work diligently to stay on top of home maintenance and to make regular home improvements!

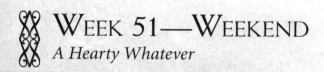

WEEK 51—WEEKEND
A Hearty Whatever

Whatever you do, do it heartily, as to the Lord and not to men, knowing that from the Lord you will receive the reward of the inheritance; for you serve the Lord Christ.

COLOSSIANS 3:23–24

We often see life in parts: there's home, there's work, there's church. We may even function in parts: we act one way at home, another at work, and yet another at church. God, however, sees life not in parts, but as a whole. It is therefore not acceptable, for instance, to be kind at church, but not at home or at work. We are to worship, work, play, vote, shop, eat, golf, and so forth in a manner consistent with our Christianity: "*whatever* you do, do it heartily, as to the Lord" (emphasis added).

Believers often ask if they can do certain things. "Can I drink a beer?" Response: "Can you do it heartily, as to the Lord?" "Can I miss church to golf, go fishing, or play in travel baseball?" Response: "Can you do it heartily, as to the Lord?" The ultimate question is "Where is your heart?" We are to "serve the Lord Christ" and not man, and when we live for Jesus, we "will receive the reward of the inheritance."

You see, God wants all of you and every aspect of your life. He wants your family life, your work life, your church life, even your recreational life. He wants to be Lord of *all*! So, wherever you are, be all there for the Lord!

··

Lord God, I want to love You with all my heart. I want to focus on "things above" as I live here on earth (Colossians 3:2). As I do that, may I—by Your grace—find myself doing whatever heartily, as unto You!

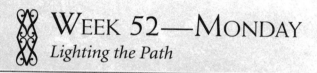

Week 52—Monday
Lighting the Path

Your word is a lamp to my feet and a light to my path. I have sworn and confirmed that I will keep Your righteous judgments.

Psalm 119:105–106

When it's described as a lamp and a light, it's easy to understand why the Bible is indispensable to the believer. The truth, the wisdom, and the encouragement found in the pages of God's Word enable us to not only avoid the world's snares and pitfalls but also to see more clearly where the Lord would have us walk.

The lamp the psalmist refers to shines enough light to show us the next step. In the psalmist's day, people carried little clay dishes containing oil, so the light illuminated only one step at a time. That metaphor definitely matches life: we don't see the whole route at one time, or faith wouldn't be necessary. But when in faith and obedience we take a step, the Lord shows us the next step.

The "light to my path" is not much more powerful than the psalmist's lamp. Shining a bit more light, we can at least see the direction we are heading. A light, no matter how bright, will not show us all the twists and turns ahead on the road, but it will give us a general sense of direction.

The Bible does not unfold the whole map of life before us. If it did, it could be terrifying! And if it did, we wouldn't be walking by faith.

....

Thank You, Lord, that Your Word is a lamp, giving me specific truths, and a light, providing general truths. Both enable me to know more clearly the path You want me to walk.

DR. JOHNNY HUNT, FIRST BAPTIST WOODSTOCK, WOODSTOCK, GA

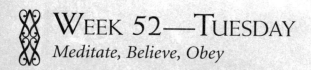

This Book of the Law shall not depart from your mouth, but you shall meditate in it day and night, that you may observe to do according to all that is written in it. For then you will make your way prosperous, and then you will have good success.

Joshua 1:8

Joshua was absolutely confident that strength and courage would come from *meditating* on God's Word, *believing* its promises, and *obeying* its commandments.

Personal devotion to Bible study is a must. No one can meditate on God's truth for you. It's up to you to to study the Scripture regularly; read it thoughtfully; linger over the verses or even the words that get your attention; make it the foundation for your daily life as well as your lifelong plans.

This meditating is, however, more than a mental exercise. Joshua was to meditate on God's Word so "that [he] may observe to do according to all that is written in it." That same instruction applies to us today. We need to appropriate the truths of Scripture and apply them to life. Essential to effective ministry is the understanding and application of Scripture.

As A. W. Tozer said in *Paths to Power*: "The Bible recognizes no faith that does not lead to obedience, nor does it recognize any obedience that does not spring from faith. . . . The trouble with many of us today is that we are trying to believe without intending to obey."[20]

And when we obey, Scripture says, "then you will make your way prosperous." You will complete your God-given task.

. . . .

The guideline is straightforward: know God's Word and do what it says. Please help me on both counts, Lord.

GOD IS FAITHFUL

WEEK 52—WEDNESDAY
Truth and Freedom

Jesus said to those Jews who believed Him, "If you abide in My word, you are My disciples indeed. And you shall know the truth, and the truth shall make you free."

JOHN 8:31–32

A disciple is a follower, and key to following Jesus is studying, knowing, and obeying the truths found in God's Word.

Discipleship begins with believing that Jesus is who He said He is—and believing that we are the sinners He says we are! But discipleship also means abiding or remaining in the Word. When He was tempted by Satan, Jesus responded to one test with "It is written, 'Man shall not live by bread alone, but by every word that proceeds from the mouth of God'" (Matthew 4:4). We need to realize that our spiritual health—the very health of our soul—is dependent on the truths of Scripture. We need to eat this bread regularly; we need to go to God's Word to receive the spiritual nourishment it alone offers.

Then, the listening to Jesus that we do as we study God's Word leads to being able to hear and recognize His voice. What we learn from Scripture and what we hear Jesus say lead to obeying Him. Persevering in obedience to Scripture is evidence of genuine faith. The acid test of life is remaining loyal to Jesus' teaching and consistent in our obedience.

When we study God's Word, we grow in spiritual knowledge. We come to understand better, for instance, the seriousness of sin and the price Jesus paid for our deliverance from sin. As we spend time reading Scripture, the Holy Spirit works to change our hearts, and His work enables us to gain freedom from sin.

....

Give me, I ask, a hearty—even an insatiable—appetite for Your Word, O Lord!

DR. JOHNNY HUNT, FIRST BAPTIST WOODSTOCK, WOODSTOCK, GA

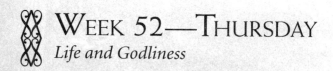

WEEK 52—THURSDAY
Life and Godliness

As His divine power has given to us all things that pertain to life and godliness, through the knowledge of Him who called us by glory and virtue, by which have been given to us exceedingly great and precious promises, that through these you may be partakers of the divine nature.

2 PETER 1:3–4

When God calls, He empowers.

God calls His children to life in Him and godliness—clearly a two-part goal that we can achieve on our own. A step ahead of us, God has provided "divine power" as the source of the believer's sufficiency and perseverance. Just as a healthy baby is born with all the physical equipment he needs for life and only needs to grow, so Christians have all that is needed for spiritual life and only need to grow. Christ provides the power for that growth; we need to receive it and use it.

We are also to receive God's Word, a vital tool that guides our efforts to a godly and God-glorifying life. By His Spirit, God does some of the transformational work inside us. But we are not passive in this process: by our choice, we take responsibility to live as He desires, as He outlines in His Word.

Then, through all that God has provided us so that we can be godly followers, we "may be partakers of the divine nature." Simply put, when we receive Jesus Christ as Savior and Lord, the Spirit of God uses the Word of God to impart the life and nature of God within us. Just as a baby shares the nature of its parents, a person born of God shares His divine nature.

....

Thank You, Father God, that my growth toward godliness is a partnership between You and me. Let's do this!

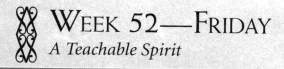

WEEK 52—FRIDAY
A Teachable Spirit

You are my hiding place; You shall preserve me from trouble; You shall surround me with songs of deliverance. I will instruct you and teach you in the way you should go; I will guide you with My eye.

PSALM 32:7–8

Following Jesus doesn't mean freedom from pain, danger, or loss. Throughout time God's people have never been—and never will be—exempt from trouble. We will, however, by God's grace, be preserved in it, not overwhelmed by it. David is a case in point: as he said in Psalm 32, he found in God relief and peace as his personal storm raged around him.

Satan will often use our troubles to worry us and try to weaken our faith in the goodness, power, or love of God. But God wants to use those trials—and He does use them—to strengthen us. In order to receive that grace, David exchanged hiding his sins for hiding himself in the Lord.

David still suffered from the consequences of his sins. But he did not suffer alone: God helped him through the hard times by providing His presence and His peace. The humbled and forgiven sinner is ready for instruction. Only those who are right with God can be taught by God.

God promised to "instruct," "teach," and "guide" David (and us) to speak of wisdom, knowledge, and obedience. We have to stay close to God to be blessed by His instructions, teaching, and guidance.

And that brings us to the last point. David was learning that forgiveness is good, but fellowship with God is better.

....

Forgiveness is good, Lord, and I thank You for that grace. I also thank You for the life-giving fellowship with You that is even better!

312   DR. JOHNNY HUNT, FIRST BAPTIST WOODSTOCK, WOODSTOCK, GA

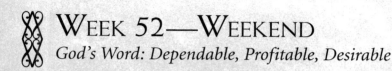

WEEK 52—WEEKEND
God's Word: Dependable, Profitable, Desirable

All Scripture is given by inspiration of God, and is profitable for doctrine, for reproof, for correction, for instruction in righteousness, that the man of God may be complete, thoroughly equipped for every good work.

2 TIMOTHY 3:16–17

In what would prove to be his last letter, Paul wrote to young Timothy, his "son in the faith" (1 Timothy 1:2), from a Roman jail. In these two verses, Paul summed up the importance of Scripture, showing why God's Word serves as a basis for all that the Christian church teaches.

> **The Bible is dependable** because it comes directly from God Himself. It is, in fact, inspired, "breathed out by God." More specifically, the Holy Spirit guided the Bible's writers, guaranteeing that what they wrote was accurate and trustworthy.
>
> **The Bible is profitable**: the information it contains is useful and beneficial for its readers in at least these four ways: doctrine addresses what *is* right; reproof addresses what *is not* right; correction, how to *get* right; and instruction, how to *stay* right.
>
> **The Bible is desirable** because its study means growth. Children of God grow in the Word of God, to the point of being "complete"—capable of doing everything God has called them to do—and "thoroughly equipped," able to meet all the demands of godly ministry and righteous living. Like a ship equipped for a voyage is a student of God's Word: all that will be required for the journey is placed onboard.

Gracious God, I praise You that You want to be known and in relationship with me. Thank You for the role Your written Word plays in that. Help me, I pray, become the student of Scripture You want me to be.

GOD IS FAITHFUL

CONTRIBUTORS

NOTES

WEEK 1

1. John Phillips, *Exploring Psalms, Volume One: An Expository Commentary* (Grand Rapids, MI: Kregel, 2002), 240.

2. Dietrich Bonhoeffer, *The Cost of Discipleship* (New York: Touchstone, 1995), 43.

3. Charles H. Spurgeon, quoted in Warren W. Wiersbe, *The Bible Exposition Commentary, vol. 1* (Wheaton, IL: Victor Books, 1996), 113.

4. Richard Owen Roberts, *Repentance: The First Word of the Gospel* (Wheaton, IL: Crossway, 2002), 184.

WEEK 2

5. "Footprints in the Sand," Mary Stevenson, copyright 1984 from original 1936 text, http://www.footprints-inthe-sand.com/index.php?page=Poem/Poem.php.

WEEK 10

6. Paul Lee Tan, *Encyclopedia of 7700 Illustrations: Signs of the Times* (Garland, TX: Bible Communications, Inc., 1996), 1255–1256.

7. Warren W. Wiersbe, *The Wiersbe Bible Commentary: The Complete New Testament in One Volume* (Colorado Springs, CO: David C. Cook, 2007), 281.

WEEK 13

8. Francis Schaeffer, *The Great Evangelical Disaster* (Wheaton, IL: Crossway Books, 1984).

WEEK 21

9. Jacqueline L. Salmon, "Most Americans Believe in Higher Power, Poll Finds," *The Washington Post*, June 24, 2008, accessed June 14, 2014, www.washingtonpost.com/wp-dyn/content/article/2008/06/23/AR2008062300813.html.

WEEK 22

10. Stephen F. Olford, *The Way of Holiness* (Wheaton, IL: Crossway Books, 1998), 82–83.

11. Mandi Steele, "Officials Try to Censor 'Religious' Speech," WorldNetDaily, June 11, 2002, accessed June 14, 2014, www.wnd.com/2002/06/14196/.

12. Charles H. Spurgeon, quoted in Johnnie Moore, *Honestly: Really Living What We Say We Believe* (Eugene, OR: Harvest House Publishers, 2011), 111.

WEEK 29

13. Dale Carnegie, *How to Win Friends and Influence People* (New York: Pocket Books, 1981), 105.

WEEK 35

14. Bill Hybels, *Courageous Leadership: Field-Tested Strategy for the 360° Leader* (Grand Rapids, MI: Zondervan, 2009), 23.

15. John Ortberg, *Soul Keeping: Caring for the Most Important Part of You* (Grand Rapids, MI: Zondervan, 2014), 171.

WEEK 36

16. A.W. Tozer, *The Knowledge of the Holy* (New York: HarperCollins, 1992), 127–128.

WEEK 43

17. Charles M. Sheldon, *In His Steps* (Grand Rapids, MI: Zondervan, 1967), 9.

WEEK 44

18. Baylus Benjamin McKinney, "Let Others See Jesus in You," *Baptist Hymnal* (Nashville: Convention Press, 1956), 348.

WEEK 48

19. "House Divided Speech," Abraham Lincoln Online, accessed May 18, 2014, http://www.abrahamlincolnonline.org/lincoln/speeches/house.htm.

WEEK 52

20. A.W. Tozer, *Paths to Power* (1911): 24–26, quoted in Tiffany Root and Kurt VandeGuchte, *For God So Loved the World . . . And Everyone In It* (Bloomington, IN: Westbow Press, 2011), 62.

SCRIPTURE INDEX

REVELATION